D1525320

Understanding, Dismantling, and Disrupting the Prison-to-School Pipeline

Understanding, Dismantling, and Disrupting the Prison-to-School Pipeline

Edited by Kenneth J. Fasching-Varner, Lori Latrice Martin, Roland W. Mitchell, Karen P. Bennett-Haron, and Arash Daneshzadeh

LEXINGTON BOOKS
Lanham • Boulder • New York • London

Published by Lexington Books
An imprint of The Rowman & Littlefield Publishing Group, Inc.
4501 Forbes Boulevard, Suite 200, Lanham, Maryland 20706
www.rowman.com

Unit A, Whitacre Mews, 26-34 Stannary Street, London SE11 4AB

British Library Cataloguing in Publication Information Available

Library of Congress Cataloging-in-Publication Data Available

ISBN 978-1-4985-3494-9 (cloth : alk. paper)
ISBN 978-1-4985-3495-6 (electronic)

♾️™ The paper used in this publication meets the minimum requirements of American National Standard for Information Sciences Permanence of Paper for Printed Library Materials, ANSI/NISO Z39.48-1992.

Printed in the United States of America

Contents

Foreword

Bettina L. Love

I write this foreword while sitting in an elementary school in Atlanta, GA, surrounded by the sounds of another school morning. Children laugh at the top of their lungs as they swing their book bags (or in the case of the smallest, drag them). Sneakers squeak against the hard floors as a group of students come to a screeching halt at the sight of their teachers. A teacher bends to place his hand on a child's shoulder and warmly asks him to stop running. The student apologizes with big brown eyes and a slight smile. Joyful chattering erupts all around me. It's 7:54 am, and the first bell of the day begins to ring. The hallways clear as students tuck themselves away in the classrooms.

I find a quiet spot to work. I reread a few chapters from this book and remind myself of the work of David Stovall, Bill Ayers, Monique Morris, Maisha T. Winn, Erica R. Meiners, Beth E. Richie, Michelle Fine, Anthony J. Nocella, Kimberlé Crenshaw, Priya Parmar, and Michelle Alexander. These scholars with laser sharp analyses have documented the well-calculated, premeditated, heartless, "spirit murdering" (Love, 2013, 2016) prison-industrial complex/nexus and educational reform-industry. These two industries are deliberately entangled to profit from America's systematic attack on Black and Brown bodies. Our youth's current condition—my current condition—rooted in White supremacy and human subjugation, never allows me to forget that I live and work in a carceral state, regardless of those children's smiles, dreams, natural gifts, and my best intentions.

Meiners (2010) writes, "The term carceral state alludes to how the logic of punishment shapes other governmental and institutional practices, even those not perceived as linked to prisons and policing" (p. 122). Meiners, like many other prolific scholars writing and working to eradicate prisons altogether, have argued that slavery, anti-immigration laws, and hyper patriarchy and heteronormativity are inextricably linked to our "prison nation [that] is not broken, but is functioning precisely as designed" (p. 123).

As I write, here, in a public charter school where my own children sit at their desks, and where I serve as the chair of the school board, my stomach drops at the realization that my life's work as a teacher-educator and public servant is deeply entangled in "the system." This school is filled with Black children who have yet to discover that their physical lives and African spirits of self-determination, awakened by educational practices that center their culture and present lives, are up for sale through market-based approaches posing as egalitarian school reform efforts. In moments like these, I turn to the incomparable Derrick Bell, as many authors do in this volume.

Defining the foundation of "racial realism," Bell (1992) writes, "The Realists argued that a worldview premised upon the public and private spheres is an attractive mirage that masks the reality of economic and political power" (p. 367). He states that racial realism brazenly acknowledges that Black people will *never* gain equality, and that our mind-set should be to avoid hopelessness and to "imagine and implement racial strategies that can bring fulfillment and even triumph" (p. 374). Bell reminds me that the strength to move an unmovable mountain is in the radical love and solidarity found through the work of critical resistance. I find sustenance in the intellectual work, direct action, and movement-building that produces language and strategies for everyday people to work toward collective liberation. I have no hope in "the system," but *all* the faith in Black and Brown people and allies/co-conspirators, who work endlessly toward creating a platform that will bear fruit for the humanity and dignity of Black people.

Therefore, this volume is not just timely and important, but each author passionately and with intellectual rigor contributes to the vision of racial realism. For academics, Bell's life and work should be an example of what is possible as we teach, resist, and create in peril. I lean on him when the world does not make sense, but his work reminds me that the injustice I am seeing and feeling in my everyday life has been ordered up like a lunch special at my favorite restaurant. The prison-industrial complex/nexus and educational reform-industry are predictable monsters. They feast on greed, and the authors in this book understand their appetites.

And so, it is with a heavy heart that I conclude this foreword, as I realize that many of the faces passing me by in the hallways of this very school will be stolen by America's massive tentacles of racial inequity and racial injustice. I write not to speak the hyperbolic language of an educational cynic, but to speak the *Truth*. In reading this book, if confronting these brazen words, and those of the authors that follow, brings discomfort, imagine doing so on a daily basis, since you drew your first breath, and know what it is to live as a child of color. As such, the authors in this volume center disrupting and dismantling the school-to-prison pipeline by critically examining the political economy of our social institutions in a neo-liberal world. This book therefore stands as not only as reinforcement that we, as a community, have a lot of work to do, but as another piece of valuable armor for our fight.

Bettina L. Love
   Atlanta, GA

Chapter One

Free-Market Super Predators and the Neo-liberal Engineering of Crisis

Examining Twenty-First-Century Educational and Penal Realism[1]

Kenneth J. Fasching-Varner, Lori L. Martin, Roland W. Mitchell, Karen P. Bennett-Haron, and Arash Daneshzadeh

We edit this book, and write this first chapter, with heavy hearts. We expect that readers may find themselves feeling angry, frustrated, and sad when thinking through realities of both the educational reform and the prison industrial complexes. We are motivated, as scholars, thinkers, and humans, to approach this work with the belief that continued discourse and action are needed to address the so-called school-to-prison pipeline, or what we call "death by education." To be certain, much attention has been paid to the school-to-prison pipeline (Archer, 2009; Christle, Jolivette, and Nelson, 2005; Cole and Heilig, 2011; Cooc, Currie-Rubin, and Kuttner, 2012; Darensbourg, Perez, and Blake, 2010; Feierman, Levick, and Mody, 2009; Fowler, 2011; Kim, Losen, and Hewitt, 2011; Skiba et al., 2003; Smith, 2009; Tuzzolo and Hewitt, 2006; Wald and Losen, 2003; Winn, 2011; Winn and Behizadeh, 2011). Several of the editors and authors of this volume contributed to a special issue of *Equity and Excellence in Education* dedicated to disrupting the school-to-prison pipeline with attention paid to the current landscape of academic dialogue on the nexus between schools and prisons. A significant body of research has also focused on the sanitized discourse of death by education framed as the "achievement gap" (Abdul-Adil and Farmer, 2006; Burris and Welner, 2005; Darling-Hammond, 2010; Fasching-Varner and Mitchell, 2013a; Ford, 2010; Gillborn, 2008; Gregory, Skiba, and Noguera, 2010; Gutiérrez, 2008; Irizarry, 2011a, 2011b; Irvine, 1990; Ladson-Billings, 2006; Lee, 2002; Lipman, 2011; Milner, 2010; Noguera, 2001; Noguera and Wing, 2006), with a complementary and long-standing discourse surrounding the alleged crisis of educational failure (Apple, 1992; Berliner and Biddle, 1995; Glasser, 1997; Lipman, 2011; McDermott, 1974; Ravitch, 1987; Taubman, 2007; Trueba, 1988; Varenne and McDermott, 1998). This book generally, and this chapter specifically, offers no solutions to the "crisis." Our fundamental premise, in fact, is that no crisis exists, because each institution—the educational system and the criminal justice system—functions per their design and the demands of the neoliberal, free-market, capitalist society that demands those systemic failures as a mechanism of maintenance. Racial and ethnic disparities are better understood not as dysfunctions of these important and foundational social institutions but rather as expected outcomes of these social institutions. (Un)surprisingly, current and historic educational reforms have resulted in significant variation of incarceration rates for Black and Latino populations compared to their white peers and equally disproportionate outcomes in achievement between white and non-white student populations.

If there is no "crisis," then how do we conceptualize the linkages between education and the criminal justice system? And, what's more, how do we account for the enduring racial divide in the American educational and justice systems specifically, as well as in the broader society more generally? We offer, as a belief, that one only need look to the economy in order to understand the nexus between so-called school failure and the rise of profit through incarceration. There is big business and economic gains to be had through the inflation of the both the prison-industrial (Kirkham, 2012) and educational reform-industrial (Fasching-Varner and Mitchell, 2013a) complexes. Those economic imperatives are centered in a materialist thirst produced by the desert of the free market. We offer that reform discourse within and about those systems is largely subterfuge, associated with decades of reform that to date has rendered no significant gains in educational outcomes for populations of color. In a classic illustration of neoliberalism, the political economy of the market fuels mounting incursions by the private sector into both schools and prisons, as well as in the most intimate facets of our lives, providing ever-expanding markets for new revenue. Simply stated, without school failure there is no opportunity for an educational reform-industrial complex, and without people to punish there is no need for the prison-industrial complex. Both complexes are inherently married to survival of free-market neo(liberal)-capitalism. Both school reform and the prison industry are currently multi-billion-dollar industries (Gaes, Camp, Nelson, and Saylor, 2004).

We were approached by the editors of Lexington Books for an edited volume that brought together current contemporary thinking about the school-to-prison pipeline (and we offer that it is really best understood in reverse as a prison-to-school pipeline). We accepted the challenge of bringing together a variety of voices to the conversation and have organized the inclusion of both senior and emerging scholars throughout this volume. Three groups of senior colleagues offer lengthier chapters, whereas new and emerging scholars offer shorter analytical essays. We are sensitive to the need for a plurality of voices to take center stage in this text. As editors we also offer this first chapter (a modified version of an article we published in *Equity and Excellence in Education*) to 1) help frame the issue at hand, 2) to extend the relatively new concept of educational and penal realism (Fasching-Varner, Mitchell, Martin, and Bennett-Haron, 2014) further into the literature base, and 3) to share our sense of pragmatic urgency about the topic at hand.

This piece also represents our continued attempt at diving into the rabbit hole(s) of contradictions associated with life and death in our United "Carceral" States of America (Meiners, 2010). Ayers, in personal conversations and in more academic forums, has often suggested that engaging contradictions is the best hope to reframe the conversation. By working against privileged interests we "dive into the contradictions head-first" and hope "to engage that thorny and contested space" where realism and honesty might help us to chart the next steps (Ayers, 2014). We suggest the need for a recognition that policies by which we educate and police/punish not only are inextricably linked but also that their "joined-at-the-hip" relationship is part of an economic imperative of free-market capitalism. Even as we put the finishing touches on this volume, police have systematically assassinated, hunted, shot at, and otherwise terrorized many within communities of color—most recently and notable in Baton Rouge, Louisiana, and Minneapolis, Minnesota, though the seemingly weekly assault has in many ways become so out of control to even attempt documenting every instance. Engaging in realism affords a glimpse into the work of freeing ourselves from the illusion that change is likely to occur without stopping our efforts to change it—the contradiction of realism. Once free of the intentionally nebulous illusion of change, we can begin working within the contradictions, not to back away from action but instead to draw our work together in a collective and organized way. What we hope happens with this chapter specifically, and the volume generally, is to let readers wrestle with contradictions to inform their work moving forward in, around, and against the school-to-prison pipeline.

A discourse about the relationship between race, failure, and poverty has swirled around the U.S. educational system since the onset of compulsory schooling (Mitchell, 2010). As educators we join the collective voice of critical scholars who have documented the way that the patrician class primarily responsible for establishing the U.S. public school system never intended for poor/working-class children to receive the same quality of education or access to wealth as the ruling class (Cleaver, 2005; Fordham, 1996; Siddle-Walker, 2001; Watkins, 2001). Despite pervasive meritocratic narratives heralding the importance of greater discipline and personal responsibility for children of color (as referenced by *Forbes* magazine contributor Gene Marks's now-infamous 2011 open letter "If I were a Poor Black Kid"), for the most part the idea of education providing a silver bullet for systemic social ills and economic stratification has simply not been realized (Samuels, 2004). Similar conversations take place concerning prisons, suggesting "the rhetoric of color-blind racism" curiously intertwined with personal responsibility "would have us believe that this situation is the unfortunate result of disproportionate Black and Latino participation in crime" (Brewer and Heitzeg, 2008, p. 629). It is consequently important to note that "the role of criminal justice in policing, prosecuting, imprisoning, and executing people of color has deep historical roots" that are well documented (Brewer and Heitzeg, 2008, p. 630).

In both the case of educational institutions and prisons, the idea of crisis is pivotal in moving the arguments along from all points within the sociopolitical spectrum from far right to far left. We loudly and firmly reject the discourse of crisis. Following earlier arguments in our own work, we suggest that the systems in place that organize both prisons and schools are far from broken, but rather they are well-oiled machines furthering the economic imperatives of the free market. We argue that by bolstering the economy, the systems which organize schools and prisons clearly and openly benefit those with significant wealth and access. School failure and expanding prisons, consequently represent remarkably stable and predictable market opportunities for largely white and male populations, while being extremely oppressive to working-class communities of color caught in the collective grindhouse—a perfect environment needed to incubate the growth of the market (Fasching-Varner and Mitchell, 2013a, 2013b).

At professional conferences we see colleagues from around the world milling over problems like those we discuss here, ironically in convention centers and hotel ballrooms that depend on cheap labor. We watch as colleagues gathered in major cities across the country practically trip over the homeless, the poor, or populations of color to have these conversations while not being particularly engaged with the communities being addressed in the work. We too, in absolute clarity, have struggles with these real problems ourselves, both the educational inequities and our participation as actors within the free market. But, those struggles aside, we believe that we have to engage the contradiction that our obsession with all things consumer-driven and particularly service-based, contributes to the need to have segregated populations for whom the educational system intentionally must fail. Our ability as a society to obtain cheap goods and services is premised economically on employees not making living wages, outsourcing manufacturing work to countries outside of the United States willing to pay even lesser wages, and segregating the population through primary, secondary, and tertiary schooling (Shajahan, 2013). In essence, we play a real-life version of *Game of Thrones*, whose consequences represent very real access and segregation based on the economic system's need to sort to maintain its equilibrium.

We begin in this piece by overviewing the complexities of the mass incarceration of populations of color, particularly Black and Latino populations, along with the economic considerations in place. From that departure point we extend the concept of racial realism brought to us from Critical Race Theory (CRT) to continue advancing our concept of *educational and penal realism* (Fasching-Varner et al., 2014). Educational and penal realism take what we present here about prisons, along with what has been widely discussed in terms of educational inequity, to highlight some key tenets that might help turn the field away from idealism and/or a false hope for change. Away from false idealism we might work more practically and pragmatically within the contradictions of our schooling and penal complexes.

PEOPLE OF COLOR AND THE U.S. PRISON POPULATION

Over 2 million individuals are incarcerated in the United States (Sentencing Project, 2012). Between 1925 and 1972, the prison population increased by more than 200 percent; since that time, the number of prisoners grew over 700 percent. By 2008, the total number of people incarcerated in the United States reached a record high. One in 100 adults in the United States were incarcerated in 2010 (Pew Charitable Trust, 2010). The U.S. incarceration rate is the highest in world (Sentencing Project, 2012).

Upon further examination of the prison population, we find that most prisoners are male. In fact, over 93 percent of incarcerated people are male. Although Blacks make up about 13 percent of the U.S. population, nearly 40 percent of people in state or federal prisons were Black in 2012. "Black males have a 32% chance of serving time in prison at some point in their lives; Hispanic males have a 17% chance; white males have a 6% chance" (Sentencing Project, 2012). According to the Sentencing Project, the rate of incarceration for Black women was 2.5 times higher than the rate for white women. The incarceration rate for white males was 681 per 100,000; 89,200 per 100,000 for Black males; and 39,200 per 100,000 Latino males (Austin et al., 2007).

Scholars have identified a number of causes contributing to the mass incarceration of individuals in the United States, including the mass incarceration of people of color. Prison populations have grown "not because of growing crime rates, but because of changes in sentencing polic[ies] that resulted in dramatic increases in the proportion of felony convictions resulting in prison sentences and in the length-of-stay in prison that those sentences required" (Austin et al., 2007, p. 1). Steiker (2012) comes to the sobering conclusion that, "the incarceration rate for black Americans relative to white Americans is higher than it was before the Civil Rights Movement" (Steiker, 2012, p. 1). Some 20 percent of Black males between the ages of 25 and 44 have experienced imprisonment at some point in their lives (Austin et al., 2007). The incarceration rate of Black males is, as Austin et al. (2007) described it, "a national tragedy."

EFFECTS OF MASS INCARCERATION
ON THE BLACK POPULATION

Mass incarceration impacts society in many ways, and at many levels (Thomas, 2013). It impacts the individual behind bars as well as the family and community of that person (Geller, 2013). The growth in the Black male prison population exacerbates a host of persistent social problems in the Black community. The mass incarceration of Black males impacts families, particularly children. More than half of prisoners in state and federal prisons are parents with minor children (Sentencing Project, 2012). From 1991 through 2007, the number of fathers and mothers in prisons has increased significantly (76 percent and 120 percent respectively. "Black children are 7.5 times more likely, and Hispanic children are 2.6 times more likely, than are white children to have a parent in prison" (Sentencing Project, 2012). Most of these parents were physically present in the lives of their children prior to incarceration. Once incarcerated, parents were often in prisons located more than 100 miles from their most recent address.

The Sentencing Project reported that ex-offenders also face a number of challenges providing for their children. Parental rights may be terminated when a child is in foster care for 15 of the past 22 months, in accordance with the Adoption and Safe Families Act of 1997. Under the Welfare Reform Act of 1996, people convicted of felony drug crimes can no longer receive Temporary Assistance for Needed Families. A history of incarceration also limits housing options. Public housing authorities can deny access to individuals convicted of a drug-related crime or a violent crime based on the Violent Crime Control and Law Enforcement Act of 1994. Mass incarceration is "undermining . . . institutions of social control such as families and communities" (Lynch and Sabol, 2004, p. 268). One's potential for future access to the benefits of the free market, post-conviction, are extremely limited, which conveniently eliminates any competitive threat, real or perceived, these folks might make to those with wealth and access.

MASS INCARCERATION AND THE PRODUCTION AND REPRODUCTION OF RACIAL WEALTH INEQUALITY

The Pew Charitable Trust (2010) examined the impact of mass incarceration on economic mobility, revealing dire consequences for all parties involved. The findings showed, as an example, that serving time reduced wages for men by about 11 percent. "Incarceration depresses the total earnings of white males by 2 percent . . . Hispanic males by 6 percent, and . . . black males by 9 percent" (Pew Charitable Trust, 2010, p. 4). The findings also reveal that "former inmates experience less upward economic mobility than those who are never incarcerated" (Pew Charitable Trust, 2010, p. 4). Moreover, "family income averaged over the years a father is incarcerated is 22% lower than family income was the year before a father is incarcerated. Even in the year after the father is released, family income remains 15% lower than it was the year before incarceration" (Pew Charitable Trust, 2010, p. 4).

Given that parental income and parental educational attainment are strong predictors of children's socioeconomic status, these findings are cause for alarm (Pew Charitable Trust, 2010). Perhaps even more alarming was the absence of indicators of asset ownership in the Pew Charitable Trust (2010) study, and others. Income and assets are not one and the same. Researchers have consistently shown that traditional measures of socioeconomic status (e.g., income, education, occupational prestige) do not paint an adequate picture of the true nature of the overall economic well-being of an individual, household, or community (Martin, 2013). Oliver and Shapiro (1995) reminded us that many are income rich and asset poor. Individuals or households with relatively high levels of income may carry heavy debt loads and possess relatively few assets, leaving them at risk during harsh economic times.

There exists overwhelming evidence of the existence of wealth inequality and asset poverty, especially racial wealth inequality and Black asset poverty. Yet little, if any, attention is devoted to the impact of mass incarceration on the types and levels of assets owned by ex-offenders, their families, and their communities, particularly important as many are locked up and locked out of the wealth-accumulation process given that most inmates are eventually released back into society. Many return home, still in debt to society, relying on the goodwill of already strapped family members and friends (Martin, 2012) for survival—and so the cycles repeat.

The racial wealth gap and the over-representation of Blacks among the asset poor can only get worse as Blacks, especially Black males, continue to be incarcerated in such great numbers, and for longer periods. One need only look at recent data on differences in the types and levels of assets owned for Blacks versus Whites. Data from the U.S. Census Bureau showed differences in the median value of assets for Black and white households. In 2011, the overall net assets were $110,500 for Whites and only $6,314 for Blacks. Excluding equity in home ownership, the median net worth for white households was $33,408 in 2011, compared to $2,124 for Black households. Racial differences were observed on other asset holdings, including regular checking accounts, stocks and mutual fund shares, equity in business or profession, rental property, and 401k and thrift savings plans (U.S. Census Bureau, 2013a).

On average, in 2011 white households had more than three times the amount Black households had in regular checking accounts: $800 for white households compared to $242 for Black households. While Whites reported an average of $24,000 in stocks and mutual fund shares, Blacks reported only $4,750. Households led by Whites reported $10,000 in equity in business or profession, and Black households reported one fifth of that amount, or $2,000. For white households with rental property, the value of said property averaged $180,000; the value of rental property for Black households was $150,000. The median value of 401k and thrift savings plans was $35,000 for white households and less than half of that for Black households. The median value of 401k and thrift savings across racial groups plans was only $12,000 (U.S. Census Bureau, 2013a).

About one third of white households reported having a regular checking account in 2011, compared to about one quarter of Black households. Although almost 25 percent of white households had stocks and mutual fund shares in 2011, less than 7 percent of Blacks possessed these assets. Similar patterns were observed with respect to business ownership, rental property, and 401k and thrift savings plans. Over 15 percent of Whites owned a business compared to 6.4 percent of Black households. About 6 percent of Whites had rental property in 2011, but less than 3 percent of Blacks had rental property. Almost half of white households possessed a 401k and/or thrift savings plan compared to about 32 percent of Black households (U.S. Census Bureau, 2013b).

"Wealth isn't just money in the bank, it's insurance against tough times, tuition to get a better education and a better job, savings to retire on, and a springboard in the middle class. In short, wealth translates into opportunity," stated McKernan et al. (2013, p. 1). Those who are locked up are locked out of the wealth-accumulation process and are faced with very limited opportunities, both for themselves and for their families and communities.

Changes to mandatory sentences for drug offenses are expected to alleviate some of the pain of prison. President Obama recently visited prisons (the first sitting president to engage in this act), and has worked steadily at commuting the sentences of individuals sentenced under some of the nation's harshest and most racially discriminatory laws. One of the individuals, a student at Southern University in Baton Rouge, Louisiana, was Clarence Aaron, who had no previous criminal record. Aaron introduced his cousin and some friends from Mobile to a classmate in Louisiana. They wanted to make a cocaine deal. Aaron was paid $1,500. Arrested in a cocaine conspiracy, he received life without parole. The others, all with long criminal records, were arrested first and testified against Aaron. His cousin got probation. The so-called kingpin received twelve years. Aaron became the poster boy in the fight against mandatory federal drug sentences, conspiracy laws, and a federal justice system that encouraged testifying against others in plea deals.

The war on drugs, which Alexander (2010) claimed started before the actual drug epidemic, is being replaced by strategies allegedly aimed at curbing violent crimes and breaking up gang activities. The seemingly colorblind tactics involve the profiling of Blacks, especially Black males in poor communities. The tactics involve racially profiling poor Black males as potential perpetrators of violence and poor Black neighborhoods as danger zones. Stop-and-frisk in New York and civil gang injunctions in California are two examples. The direct, as well as the collateral, damage caused by these tactics is far reaching. Stop-and-frisk and civil gang injunctions do the work in the colorblind era that discriminatory policies such as redlining did in the Jim Crow era. They mark the Black body and Black space as hazardous and inferior, therefore unworthy of assimilation.

THE ECONOMIC BENEFITS OF A GROWING INMATE POPULATION

While understanding the financial impact prison has on those incarcerated, it is equally important, if we are to understand that there is no crisis in place for "the system," to also understand the economic benefits of incarceration. That is to say that while the prison culture has negative social and financial impacts on the individuals being "punished," it has great rewards for those in the prison business. Engels (1843), in his famous piece *Outlines of a Critique of Political Economy,* asserted, "The struggle of capital against capital, of labour against labour, of land against land, drives production to a feverpitch at which production turns all natural and rational relations upsidedown" (p. 1). While it appears unnatural and irrational to want to incarcerate individuals, doing so in ways that disproportionately impact populations considered by the dominant factions of society to be those without value, eliminates said segment of the population from accessing the wealth of the dominant group. Such an approach also creates an industry (infrastructure, employment, and market) in keeping those "undesirables" away from wealth and access. In essence, those in prison do not simply help maintain the balance of wealth and power, they actually serve to create larger differences between "haves" and "have nots." Not only do the imprisoned remain poor, but their families (as shown earlier) remain poor, helping those with power and privilege to gain more. As Engels (1843) asserted, "with the fusion of the interests now opposed to each other there disappears the contradiction between excess population here and excess wealth there" (p. 5). Neutralizing and isolating a segment of the population, and creating an industry whose sole purpose is to neutralize and isolate, works in tandem to reproduce inequities that allow both wealth and poverty to grow in disproportion.

Chang and Thompkins (2002) asserted, "the dominant classes use imprisonment as a means of political, economic, and social control" (p. 47). One end of that social control is seeking to create economic market balance. That is, the state adjusts incarceration practices to match the economic equilibrium within the society. In times of low unemployment, less imprisonment occurs, but "when unemployment is high, the state imprisons greater numbers to absorb surplus labor and suppress social unrest associated with economic deprivation" (Chang and Thompkins, 2002). Chang and Thompkins (2002) also suggested, "increases in the unemployment rate, poverty, income inequality, racial conflict, and political conservatism contribute to an increase in the incarceration rate, independent of the crime rate" (p. 47).

A major shift in economic trends of modern times traces back to the Reagan administration's military-like assault on the economy in which the privileged became more privileged and the masses were fed the lie that money would trickle down as a result of protecting and privileging the wealthy—*Reaganomics*. The early 1980s mark a decisive turn, which has only accelerated as time passes, toward leveraging crime, punishment, and incarceration as a nouveau industry—a mechanism for wealth to replicate and for those not deemed worthy to produce more than they consume. Many benefit from our industrial approach to incarceration, including "construction companies, architects, and the suppliers of high-tech surveillance equipment and other materials [who] earn profits when a new prison is built . . . [creating] the transformation of prisoners into profits" (Sudbury, 2004, p. 12). As Samara (2000) suggested, the 1980s and 1990s saw a widespread and swift expansion of prison construction. The 21st century has seen that expansion of prisons notably shift toward privatization. Private prisons turn profit by lowering labor costs, which Chang and Thompkins (2002) have noted are responsible for upwards of 60 percent of prison budgets. Lowering labor costs means accessing a labor force just slightly beyond those imprisoned, who are willing to work for low wages, often in rural communities plagued by the elimination of manufacturing industries (Chang and Thompkins, 2002; Hallett, 2002; Samara, 2000; Sudbury, 2004). Our industrialized approach to punishment "has become a key economic development strategy for rural towns devastated by the economic restructuring brought about by globalization" (Sudbury, 2004, p. 13). Consequently, rural communities in need of economic stimulation are willing to provide cheaper labor costs for private prisons, expanding the profit margins for the corporations that run these prisons. The landscape, then, is rural communities engaged in battles to make the most attractive offer for private prisons to invest. According to Samara (2000), "much like Third World nations competing to attract foreign investment, rural communities fighting each other for prisons risk engaging in a race to the bottom and becoming dependent on their community's new employer and the crime that supports it" (p. 42). The business of prisons is big, and to put the picture into better perspective, "the United States spends more than $146 billion dollars on the criminal justice system, including police, the judiciary and court systems, and corrections. More than $50 billion of this is spent directly on corrections" (Brewer and Heitzeg, 2008, p. 637). Put differently, if the judiciary, police, and criminal justice system were a country, it would be 57 out of 200 in top GDP and would rank higher than the lowest 67 countries combined (World Factbook, 2014).

Once built, there is a need to fill the private prisons with "residents" ensured to stay for long periods of time and, hopefully, once let out, recidivate to return. The goal in these prisons, according to Samara (2000), is not rehabilitation or correction but, in fact, failure:

> If the prison-industrial complex is successful, it will be the cause of its own demise. If it fails . . . this failure will be used to expand the industry. From the point of view of the prison business, then, failure is much more likely to lead to success. (p. 43)

Additionally, the private prison industry, according to Dolovich (2005), exerts considerable force, through lobbying, on legislators both for expansion and in sentencing guidelines. According to Sarabi and Bender (2000), through donations and hyper-lobbying think tanks, legislation is created that favors incarceration; the market has significant influence on our approaches to punishment. According to Sudbury (2004), the sphere of influence extends to prison guard unions, politicians, and the media, who use fear of crime and the criminalization of minority peoples as ways to advocate their own financial interests. Dolovich highlighted that "any time criminal justice policy is influenced by parties hoping to further their own financial interests through increased incarceration . . . is cause for concern" (p. 533). To provide a clear and succinct analysis of what is in place with respect to the prison-industrial complex, it is important to understand that

> This complex now includes more than 3,300 jails, more than 1,500 state prisons, and 100 federal prisons in the United States. Nearly 300 of these are private prisons. More than 30 of these institutions are super-maximum facil-

ities, not including the super-maximum units located in most other prisons. (Brewer and Heitzeg, 2008, p. 637)

While the academic conversation has consistently called the pipeline "school-to-prison," including the framing of many chapters in this book, the economic and market forces driving the prison-industrial complex urge us, as editors and authors ourselves, to consider reframing the pipeline as one working from "prison-to-school." We do not believe that incarceration occurs simply because crime is committed or because of cracks in the schooling system. We believe that the impact of prisons opens our vision to seeing that prisons demand a clientele, particularly given the relative economic instability over the last thirty-five years. This economic state requires prisons, as previously mentioned, to regulate unemployment and to create financial separation between races, ethnicities, and socioeconomic groups. Prisons, increasingly privatized, do not simply meet society's demand for a space to enact punishment; they create an entire enterprise and a well-lobbied one, whose base function rallies around having a population to punish. Without that population ready for punishment, the economic equilibrium is threatened as more people have a need for employment that would otherwise be locked up, and the prison profiteers lose serious wealth potential, a reality that the free market will not allow to come to fruition. Schools, consequently, are used as a social landscape, particularly within urban centers, to prepare the next generation of future inmates.

EDUCATIONAL AND PENAL REALISM

Racial realism is a concept developed by legal scholar Derrick Bell addressing the permanence of race. Bell's (1992) own articulation of racial realism asserted that

> Black people will never gain full equality in this country. Even those herculean efforts we hail as successful will produce no more than temporary "peaks of progress," short-lived victories that slide into irrelevance as racial patterns adapt in ways that maintain white dominance. This is a hard-to-accept fact that all history verifies. We must acknowledge it and move on to adopt policies based on what I call: "Racial Realism." This mind-set or philosophy requires us to acknowledge the permanence of our subordinate status. That acknowledgement enables us to avoid despair, and frees us to imagine and implement racial strategies that can bring fulfillment and even triumph. (pp. 373–374)

According to Powell (1991), "the core message of *Racial Realism* is that the racial domination and subjugation of Blacks in America is immutable . . . a permanent fixture in our society" (pp. 533–534). The logic of Bell's racial realism suggests that "systemic racism confers a permanent minority status to

Blacks that is ignored in contemporary treatments of race," where ideological dreams and articulations of equality permeate the discourse but rarely manifest in reality (Curry, 2008, p. 40). Bell (1992) asserted, "it is time we concede that a commitment to racial equality merely perpetuates our disempowerment . . . we need a mechanism to make life bearable in a society where Blacks are a permanent, subordinate class" (p. 377).

Bell (1992) encouraged us, particularly those who are genuinely committed to change, to

> simultaneously acknowledge that our actions are not likely to lead to transcendent change and, despite our best efforts, may be of more help to the system we despise than to the victims of that system we are trying to help. (p. 378)

Ladson-Billings (2006) suggests that many of the programs, approaches, and reform efforts realized are akin to paying interest on a debt whose principle is never addressed. For those looking to be profiteers from educational reform, there are significant economic gains to be had from that interest—that is, so long as the principle debt remains, the services of educational reformers will be necessary, and the "interest" paid toward the education debt materializes in real money for those in educational reform, regardless of whether or not reform actually occurs. The parallel phenomenon is true of our correction system in terms of the profit and growth potential being better served by never addressing the principle of the debts levied against those most vulnerable in our society.

Racial realism is not content with accepting the permanence of racism in and of itself but accepting that the solutions to racism will never come from approaches within the oppressors' playbook. Racial realism, then, might best be understood as an activist project whose baseline assumptions acknowledge the permanence of racism and racists within the U.S. landscape while calling on action outside of the oppressors' playbook.

So we end this chapter with what might be some beginning working tenets of educational and penal realism that will help those committed to change to renegotiate the ways in which they approach reform, while calling for and shedding a more direct light on those committed to profit in the name of change. In the spirit of racial realism, we articulate the following seven tenets to suggest what might be the contours of educational and penal realism.

1. There is no crisis in schools or prisons—each institution is functioning per their design and the demands of the society.

Curry (2008) suggested that "the common home remedy of denial" by those with ideological commitments to making change from within the system distract us from what is at hand. The increase in noise and clutter through the articulation of educational and correctional crisis has led to certain denials about what is happening both with corrections and with education. When the glasses of denial are removed, we see an educational system that has produced no sustained or substantive gains in achievement or access for children of color. Further, with respect to correctional institutions, there have been significant changes affecting populations of color over the past twenty years, but, as discussed earlier, those changes have further disenfranchised populations of color. The first tenet of realizing educational and penal realism is to question why have there been no gains for populations of color in schooling, yet significant and disproportionate punishment for people of color through the criminal justice system? The most direct answer is that both education (schools, universities, etc.) and the criminal justice system (police, courts, jails, prisons, etc.) are "the system," or at least strong component representatives of the system." The free market economically drives the system within the United States, a market that requires stratified economic classes and a population of disposable (see tenet five) citizens who serve two corners of the market—the educational reform and the prison-industrial complexes. Consequently, schools are doing their jobs, and were populations of color or poor populations to make significant gains, those gains would not be praised but instead would be immediately counterbalanced to maintain stasis.

2. Neither schools nor prisons will ever represent, serve, or address the interests of the most marginalized and underrepresented of society but they will do so for those from dominant and overrepresented factions of society.

As the framers of the constitution and founding fathers of the country intended, schools are designed, in principle, to ensure that a select group of the population (white, Christian, middle to upper class, and heterosexual) will have access. Over time, and with most distance from their creation, schools have had to open their doors to everyone, though they do not represent, serve, or address the interests of everyone. To combat the influx of the "undesirable" in schooling, the nation first created separate schooling options, under the yoke of Jim Crow segregation to ensure that white interests where taken care of, allowing for some select people of color to gain access, and likewise to ensure that the masses of people of color remained isolated from access. When it was realized that there was a larger financial interest, the white (not the right) thing to do, schools desegregated and created new mechanisms (magnets, schools-within-schools, suburban schools, honors programs, AP, increased private and selective admissions schools) to allow for physical integration while maintaining their core operating practice of benefiting Whites and keeping people of color sorted out from access. In more modern times, the rise of charters, expensive legislation, and standards movements with no teeth to bring about change (No Child Left Behind, Race to the Top, Common Core State Standards, and College Readiness Assessment) allow for schools to remain open to the entire public while serving only the limited interests of those dominant groups and the few token minorities allowed through. In recent times, even the Supreme Court has reversed its own stance in *Brown v. Board* in the *Parents Involved in Community Schools v. Seattle School District N.1* case when there was a realization that people of color may actually benefit from a schooling approach aimed at equity. The realist perspective, suggested Curry (2008),

> points to the need of a continuing struggle and a deep-seated dissatisfaction with both the illusory progress given under the liberalist integration fantasy, and the realities of anti-Black racism, black poverty, and Blacks' vulnerability to white interests" as seen in schools. (p. 43)

Similarly, the criminal justice system selectively chooses which things they will prosecute: the sentencing guidelines for crimes that disproportionally affect populations of color, and the conditions of imprisonment that intensely isolate individuals from their home communities while creating market interests that serve largely white communities, creating a prison profit margin for dominant groups. To tenet one's end—these schooling and prison practices are intentional.

3. Economic imperatives are the central driving force in decisions to sort and separate the marginalized from the oppressors both in education and correction.

The economy is the driving force behind the maintenance of oppression through schools and prisons. Not only is there money to be made through educational reform and penal institutions, but schools and prisons allow the society to select who will have access to the economy and at what levels. Decisions about housing, employment, access to goods and services, as well as the free flow of knowledge and information have bookends in schools and prisons. While the approach has shifted post-civil rights in some surface-level ways, "what is not new is the racist and classist economic and political agenda that is foundational" (Brewer and Heitzeg, 2008, p. 630). The free market thrives by having a segment of the population it can remove, through prisons, from access to the employment market; the setup for that eventuality begins as early as kindergarten. We agree strongly when Brewer and Heitzeg (2008) state,

> The prison industrial complex is an expression and re-articulation of the political economy of late capitalism. The intense concentration and privatization of wealth in a few hands continues unchecked in this country. Indeed, the unparalleled growth of corporate power is at the heart of the economic inequality African Americans and all working people are confronting. (p. 636)

Sudbury (2004) articulated that "companies such as Lehman Brothers [are] turning prisons into a commodity on the stock market and investors into jailors," (p. 12), and we suggest both to Sudbury and Brewer and Heitzeg's points that educational reformers and many urban educational settings provide a pedagogical pathway to prison that is intentional and that works in tandem with the prison-industrial complex. For the two educator authors of this article, this reality is all too apparent as we visit local schools in Louisiana (the largest police and prison state in the world), where kindergartners are walked on lines with their hands behind their backs in silence, expected to eat lunch in silence, and treated to a borage of crime-and-punishment pedagogical approaches engaged with a panoptic gaze, similar to the supermax prisons of our state (Foucault, 1977). Noguera (2003) stated, "schools sort children . . . and place them on trajectories that influence the economic roles and occupations they will assume as adults" (p. 344). In urban settings, "Disciplinary practices in schools often bear a striking similarity to the strategies used to punish adults in society. Typically, schools rely on some form of exclusion or ostracism to control the behavior of students" (Noguera, 2003, p. 342). Gregory, Skiba, and Noguera (2010) highlighted that the "use of school exclusion as a discipline practice may contribute to the well-documented racial gaps in academic achievement" (p. 59). Brewer and Heitzeg (2008), while addressing the prison-industrial complex, addressed the relationship to the educational reform industrial complex as well by succinctly addressing this tenet, stating,

> the prison industrial complex is a self-perpetuating machine where the vast profits (e.g., cheap labor, private and public supply and construction contracts, job creation, continued media profits from exaggerated crime reporting, and crime/punishment as entertainment) and perceived political benefits (e.g., reduced unemployment rates, "get tough on crime" and public safety rhetoric, funding increases for police, and criminal justice system agencies and professionals) lead to policies that are additionally designed to ensure an endless supply of "clients" for the criminal justice system (e.g., enhanced police presence in poor neighborhoods and communities of color; racial profiling; decreased funding for public education combined with zero-tolerance policies and increased rates of expulsion for students of color; increased rates of adult certification for juvenile offenders; mandatory minimum and three-strikes sentencing; draconian conditions of incarceration and a reduction of prison services that contribute to the likelihood of recidivism; collateral consequences—such as felony disenfranchisement, prohibitions on welfare receipt, public housing, gun ownership, voting and political participation, and employment—that nearly guarantee continued participation in crime and return to the prison industrial complex following initial release). (p. 637)

Consequently, for many urban students the training they receive in schools involves preparing them to be the future prisoners, and this training is as important to the "welfare" of the free market as is training the future presidents, scientists, and businesspeople. The separation and sorting of classes and peoples is reified through schools and recycled through prisons.

4. All actors in the system, whether well intentioned or not, both contribute to and benefit from educational and correctional oppression—desires to serve in activist roles have limits, through convergence with personal economic interests.

Even those with genuine interest in change operate within the landscape of educational and correctional racism and classism. Academics to activists and beyond are all players within the free market, creating a contradiction that is not often discussed: the interests in fighting "the system" are tempered by the fact that those actors are themselves "the system" and operate within the rabbit hole of the free market. Consequently, interests matter, and the level of activism one exhibits is often linked to the convergence such activism has with their interests—that is to say, when our interests are threatened by our participation or action, those interests cease to converge and our participation in change ends; the free market is willing to "take" from those who do not comply with the imperatives of the market. As educators (and particularly the member of our team who works directly with pre-service teachers), we can attest to the significant number of well-intended, middle-class, white females who make up the bulk of the U.S. teaching force. They often enter the profession well prepared in their subject matter but clueless about how to work in communities of color or to work within the realities we discuss in this piece. These understandings are vital for communicating their subject matter knowledge to their students. And despite the fact that we regularly hear pre-service teachers state that they went into teaching because "I love kids," the fact is that lacking a measured purpose for entering the profession and, more importantly, meaningful understanding/critical consciousness about their positionality (Fasching-Varner, 2012) in that system, we see many well-intended teachers co-opted into being cogs in a system that produces/supports the type of race/class-based stratification in society we have discussed, to the financial benefit of those with power.

5. Because personal and private interests allow for human sacrifice, populations of color and those of poor socioeconomic standing will continue to be offered up in service of the historically and contemporarily over-represented particularly through schooling and corrections efforts.

One of the first economic principles we learn as a child is that fiscally, 100 percent of wealth and assets is the maximum that can be worked with. If a society had 100 people, and one person possessed 80 percent of the wealth and assets within that society, the others would be left with only 20 percent to be distributed among the other 99 people, and those assets would not likely be distributed evenly. Those other 99 people could not equally possess 80 percent; 100 percent is the maximum that can be distributed. The economic system of the free market, consequently, needs ultimate winners, relative winners, relative losers, and ultimate losers to function. This reality "requires that we accept the fact that not all students will succeed and that some students must be deemed expendable so that others can be saved" (Noguera, 2003, p. 346). Prisons provide a convenience in that they generate income for those who are already resourced while eliminating the competition from those incarcerated. K–12 schools as preparation for future participation in society serve as a thirteen-year lesson in creating winners and losers and helping tertiary institutions of education pluck out a selective group to be in the relative and ultimate winner categories. Obviously, there are exceptions (Bill Gates with no tertiary education is an ultimate winner, and Bernie Madoff with tertiary education became an ultimate loser), but the rule of the economy systematically plays out to ensure that members of society have access to their portion of the 100 percent of wealth that is available to them, and most often that level is bound. Because "public schools in the hyperghetto have . . . deteriorated to the point where they operate in the manner of institutions of confinement whose primary mission is not to educate but to ensure custody and control," the link between an education that has sacrificial students and a prison waiting to receive sacrificed citizens is an important nexus (Noguera, 2003, p. 349). Schools and prisons are key institutions in regulating who has access to how much of that wealth—and their relationship is hyper-connected at all points.

6. Equality is a ruse aimed at distracting the populace. Even if equality were achievable, the term suggests that the dominant group is still the valued group furthering assimilationist principles geared toward the privileged.

Equality means achieving likeness—but likeness with what? In the case of civil and human rights, the principle of equality suggests that those marginalized in the system ought to "work" toward likeness with those for whom the system is working. This stance is problematic, as it further bolsters the relative position of those in power and puts the onus for change on those already oppressed, suggesting to them that the goal is to be like your oppressor. Such an approach "replaces the existence of a people with the caricatures of that people embraced by the imagination of whites" (Curry, 2008, p. 42). Schools, typically staffed by white females (Fasching-Varner, 2013a), work to create winners out of those most willing to sell out their race and for boys their gender to model white female lower-middle-class beliefs (Fordham, 1996, 1988; Fordham and Ogbu, 1986; Young, 2007, 2010). Equality is not only insulting, but it is assaultive unless the equality is to have those from dominant groups receive the same and equal access that those of color currently receive and hold the difference in trust to rebuild a new reality—not only is that solution not likely, it works against the free market, which, as we have already articulated, will always win. Consequently, given the previously discussed tenet of disposability, schools and prisons do not seek equality; they seek equal replication of the society (with its asymmetrical favoritism toward the privileged), and both institutions are agents of replication. Curry (2008) stated, and we agree, "equality only serves as an imaginative allure—

a fantasy, and this is the reality that must be conceptually disengaged" (p. 42).

7. Equity, consequently, is the only potential course of action that could counterbalance the racist underpinnings of both educational and correctional structures.

Equity is significantly different from equality. The principal of equity allows the creation of solutions that intentionally treat people differently to remedy past treatment. As a society, we do not simply get to walk away from hundreds of years of oppression quietly and imagine a space where we all get to be equal. That ideological stance ignores realities that equity does not ignore. Equity, fiercely and unapologetically, works to divert and invest resources in disproportion to counteract what had already been in place, and its goal is, with time, to work toward equality. Equality without equity is fantasy, as it asks us to ignore the intentional abuses and mistreatment of people who created the unbalance to begin with. The hypothetical "take from the rich and give to the poor" solution articulated above might work toward equity; that is, no new society created in the image of all of its people could be imagined until those with power and privilege experience oppression and marginalization for such a time that they understood, through a lived experience, the feelings of those who have received the losing end of the oppressor-oppressed paradigm.

Similarly, oppressed and marginalized people would need to experience the power and benefits of privilege, not simply watching those qualities from a distance, before the bargain and negotiation of a new society could be structured. We realize that such a stance is not realistic within the current system, and that imagining it does little good, but confronting oppression day by day and step by step in an unapologetic way may help us work toward that equitable end, and in the short term at least annoy and bother those with power through the threat of this solution. Bell (1992) reminded us that confrontation with our oppressors is not our sole reason for engaging—continued struggle can bring about unexpected benefits and gains that in themselves justify continued endeavor. The fight in itself has meaning and should give us hope for the future (p. 378).

CONCLUSION

In conclusion, it is our aim that this piece, as well as the others in this special issue, provide the space to wrestle with key issues and contradictions about what we have characterized as a manufactured crisis. Further, we hope that readers are compelled to begin the no doubt laborious, but still critical, work of simultaneously disjoining and reconfiguring the political economy of schooling, incarceration, and the free-market system in the United States. In

Zami a New Spelling of my Name (1982), Lorde insightfully cautioned that one of the primary ways that oppression maintains its influence is by trapping both the oppressed and oppressor in a prison of political apathy once they conceptualize the totality and systemic nature of their position in the system. The concept of educational and penal realism is our offering, to disrupt the illusion at the root of the apathy that Lorde laments. At its core, educational and penal realism potentially opens the prison gates and surfaces the absurdity of the manufactured crisis and its resulting hollow answers. Consequently, the seven working tenets of educational and penal realism offer individual and systemic entry points to initiate the vitally needed "recruitment of educators who will question the tendency to punish through exclusion and humiliation, and who see themselves as advocates of children and not as wardens and prison guards" (Noguera, 2003, p. 350). And in a basic sense, the fact that the role of teacher/warden and student/inmate are synonymous highlights the significance of the conversation put forth in this volume. As we promised in the beginning, it will not be fun to read this book; there is no happy ending, but the work must be done.

NOTE

1. Significant portions of this chapter appeared in Fasching-Varner, K. J., Mitchell, R. W., Martin, L. L., and Bennett-Haron, K. P. (2014). Beyond school-to-prison pipeline and toward an educational and penal realism. *Equity and Excellence in Education*, 47(4), 410–429; and are used with express permission of the Taylor & Francis Group.

Chapter Two

Too Much, Too Little,
but Never Too Late

*Countering the Extremes in Gifted and Special Education
for Black and Hispanic Students*

Donna Y. Ford, Gilman W. Whiting,
Ramon B. Goings, and Sheree N. Alexander

The educational experiences of Black and Hispanic students are complex, riddled with extremes, contradictions, and inequities that have great impact. At one extreme, these two groups of students are miseducated by being denied access to gifted education and other classes and programs that prime the higher education pipeline. At the other extreme, these students are miseducated by being over-represented in special education, particularly high-incidence areas that are plagued with subjectivity and limit access to higher education while also increasing access to the prison pipeline—suspensions, expulsions, and dropping out. These extremes and injustices are most noticeable and inequitable for Black and Hispanic males.

In this chapter, we take on these thorny and contentious educational issues. Our goal is to prime the higher education pipeline and disrupt the prison pipeline. We kvetch about the issues and offer recommendations for change. This discussion begins with gifted education inequities, followed by special education inequities. The chapter ends with attention to the Scholar Identity Model as a fundamental prevention and intervention program.

UNDER-REPRESENTATION OF BLACK AND HISPANIC
STUDENTS IN GIFTED EDUCATION

Discourse on the poor and abysmal participation of Black and Hispanic students in gifted education is often relegated to second class status if not virtually ignored and trivialized in the educational field. More to the point, the inequities in gifted education tend to be swept under the proverbial rug and subsequently ignored in the omnibus achievement gap scholarship. Lack of access to gifted education classes and programs contributes to under-achievement and achievement gaps, with Black and Hispanic students being most at risk for denied access (Ford 2010).

The data speak volumes. Black students make up 19 percent of public schools nationally but represent only 10 percent of gifted education students. Hispanic students represent 25 percent of schools but only 16 percent of gifted programs (see http://ocrdata.ed.gov). The discrepancies are drastic, resulting in a total of 500,000 Black and Hispanic students being mis-educated nationally (Ford, 2013). If one agrees, as the co-authors do, that education is one of the greatest equalizers (see Horace Mann, 1848), then there is grave reason for alarm.

A number of explanations shed light on why these two groups have been denied access for several decades. To be clear, segregation in gifted education has a long history, spanning more than six decades, as outlined by Ford (2013a). Few, if any, of our nearly 4,000 schools have equitable numbers and percentages of Black and Hispanic students in gifted education. This denied access feeds the national racial achievement gap (Ford, 2010) and disrupts the higher education pipeline. Under-challenged students not only disengage but also act out due to boredom, which contributes to office referrals, and possible suspension and/or expulsion.

The most impactful barriers to gifted education access are educators, followed by instruments, and then policies and procedures. Subjective views of teachers and other educators (counselors, school psychologists, administrators) profoundly hinder their referrals and letters of support for these gifted students of color. Ford, Grantham, and Whiting (2008) analyzed all studies on teacher referrals of gifted students and found that, in all studies, teachers under-referred Black students; in half of the studies, Hispanic were under-referred. Deficit thinking grounded in negative and entrenched stereotypes must not be negated. Educators have a great deal of power, and their views matter, sometimes to the detriment of racial progress and equity.

The problems with testing are thorny and contentious, accompanied by a long history (Gould, 1996). But sufficient data indicate that intelligence tests remain unfair and biased against these students of color while advantaging White students. Other issues fail to prime the higher education pipeline. For example, ample data indicate that access to gifted education increases access to Advanced Placement (AP); access to AP increases access to not just higher education but enrollment at elite colleges and universities. The College Board has determined racial equity goals for all states—virtually all states are inequitable, mainly for Black students. They urge educators to ensure equity in AP access, offering at least three recommendations: (1) eliminate barriers that restrict access to AP for students from ethnic, racial, and socioeconomic groups that have been traditionally underserved; (2) make every effort to ensure their AP classes reflect the diversity of their student population; and (3) provide all students with access to academically challenging coursework *before* they enroll in AP classes (https://professionals.collegeboard.org).

The cycle and/or pipeline is clear—access to gifted education results in more fruitful careers, all of which are a form of social capital. Policies and procedures, such as what tests are adopted, when students are assessed, cutoff scores, and use of national versus local and building norms, further fuels the broken gifted education pipeline and massive achievement and opportunities gaps. With this brief overview of gifted and AP education, we now turn to the other extreme—special education over-representation.

OVER-REPRESENTATION OF BLACK AND HISPANIC STUDENTS IN SPECIAL EDUCATION

The reauthorization of the Individuals with Disabilities Education Act (IDEA) 2004 reinforced the necessity of legislation requiring states to ensure services for students with disabilities (U.S. Department of Education, 2007). This reauthorization required states to collect and disaggregate data to illustrate the prevalence and demographics of students specifically being identified with special education needs. Part of this change was also grounded in the need to hold educators accountable to being just in identification and services, which includes decreasing and ideally eliminating over-representation. Despite this attention and legislation, special education classrooms continue to have a majority of Black and Hispanic students, mainly males, at discriminatory and inequitable rates and percentages.

Scholars (Ford, 2012, 2013b; Goings, 2015) and organizations (e.g., Schott Foundation; Harvard Poverty Law Center) have discussed in great detail the indefensible and unjust over-representation of Black and Hispanic students in special education classrooms. For instance, Sullivan and Bal (2013) posited that Black students are two to three times more likely to be diagnosed as emotionally disturbed or having a cognitive impairment than their White counterparts. To make matters worse, according to the US Department of Education Office of Civil Rights (OCR, 2014), when students are placed in special education classrooms, "more than one out of four boys of color with disabilities (served by IDEA)—and nearly one in five girls of color with disabilities—receives an out-of-school suspension" (p. 1). These figures are catastrophic because for students who need the individualized attention of teachers the most, they are the most likely to be removed from classroom instruction time. It is equally egregious because far too many Black students, mostly males, are being mis-educated by being misplaced in special education classes and programs with diagnoses, medication, and interventions they do not need.

Researchers, policy makers, and practitioners have grappled with the causes of the over-representation of Black and Hispanic students in special education. For some, the issues start with who is standing in front of children each day—the teacher. Unfortunately, as our schools continue to serve a majority Black and Hispanic student population, the teacher workforce does not reflect this diversity. Teachers of color constitute 17 percent of the teacher workforce (National Center of Educational Statistics [NCES], 2013), with 7 percent being Black and 7 percent being Hispanic. As a result of the under-representation of teachers of color, scholars have explained that there is a cultural mismatch between teachers and students in our schools (Grissom and Redding, 2016; Ladson-Billings, 2006, 2009). Moreover, this cultural mismatch and related clashes results in students (mostly Black and Hispanic) being misplaced into special education classrooms.

Ford (2012) argued that educators often take a colorblind approach to teaching where they do not acknowledge their students' cultures and fail to make them a central component of their teaching style and curricular offerings. The lack of cultural integration into teaching is most apparent with the educational experiences of African American students generally, and males specifically (Goings, Smith, Harris, Wilson, and Lancaster, 2015). Given that teachers have the opportunity each day to make an impact on the academic trajectory of their students, Gay (2002, 2010) argued that part of an educator's pedagogical skill set is their ability to recognize students' cultural foundation. Extending Gay's argument further, we argue that without acknowledging students' culture, we will continue to see Black and Hispanic students being moved into special education classrooms and unfortunately, as we discuss in the next section, being placed into special education unjustly prepares children (who need the most support) for entrance into the unjust race-based school-to-prison pipeline.

CONNECTING THE DOTS: OVER-REPRESENTATION OF BLACK AND HISPANIC STUDENTS IN SPED AND THE SCHOOL-TO-PRISON PIPELINE

In 2015, the slamming of an African American female high school student at Spring Valley High School in South Carolina by a school police officer reignited a national conversation about the role of law enforcement in our nation's schools (http://www.nytimes.com). This conversation was reignited as many political pundits and concerned educational stakeholders advocated for the use of school resource officers (SROs) after the shootings at Sandy Hook Elementary School in Newtown, Connecticut. These events also sparked a resurgence of dialogue about the ways in which schools contribute to students becoming trapped in the school-to-prison pipeline.

Using Morris's (2012) definition, the school-to prison-pipeline "refers to the collection of policies, practices, conditions, and prevailing consciousness that facilitate both the criminalization within educational environments and the processes by which this criminalization results in the incarceration of youth and young adults" (p. 2). When examining this unjust and race-based pipeline, national suspension data shows that Black students, who represent 16 percent of students in public schools, are 32 percent to 42 percent of students suspended or expelled and Black boys and girls have the highest percentage of out of school suspensions (OCR, 2014). Table 2.1 provides national suspension trends for students disaggregated by race/ethnicity.

Table 2.1. **Rates of Suspension and Expulsion by Race/Ethnicity**

	Black/ African American	Hispanic/ Latino of Any Race	White	Two or More Races	Asian	American Indian/ Alaska Native	Native Hawaiian/ Other Pacific Islander
Enrollment	16%	24%	51%	2%	5%	0.5%	0.5%
In School suspension	32%	22%	40%	3%	1%	0.2%	0.2%
Out-of-school suspension	33%	23%	36%	3%	2%	2%	0.4%
Expulsion	34%	22%	36%	3%	1%	3%	0.3%

Data retrieved from U.S. Department of Education Office for Civil Rights Data. Snapshot: School Discipline (2014).

While using the term "pipeline" provides a visual and mental image where youth who are in are schools are arrested for various violations and then become involved in the criminal justice system, it is important to look at the data to analyze *who* is entering this broken and often dead-end pipeline. For students in special education classrooms, the data provide a connection between the special education classroom and being involved in the criminal justice system for Black and Hispanic students. For example, students with disabilities are over two times more likely to be suspended from school when compared to students without a disability (OCR, 2014). Along with being suspended, students receiving special education services represent approximately 25 percent of students who receive law enforcement arrests or referrals, but only constitute 12 percent of the student population. Thus, the use of 'pipeline' in this context as a conduit is justified. The proverbial and real pipeline is not just leaky but broken and corrupt.

In popular discourse about the school-to-prison pipeline, pundits typically focus on middle and high school as the target areas to prevent students with disabilities from being involved with the criminal justice system. However, OCR (2014) reports that school discipline begins as early as preschool, and Black students who constitute 18 percent of preschool enrollment represent 42 percent of preschoolers who are suspended at least once. The pipeline is primed from birth.

The school-to-prison pipeline is very much a reality for many Black and Hispanic students in our schools and nation. Regrettably, Black and Hispanic students with and without disabilities are more likely to have some encounter with law enforcement in their schools. For many of these students, the subjective nature of behavior referrals from their teachers has led to many Black and Hispanic students being unnecessarily recommended for special education evaluation and services. Then once these students enter special education classrooms it is still highly likely that their behaviors will be met with not only educational consequences (e.g., loss of time in school), but legal consequences as well. In this chapter, we seek not only to highlight the problems, but provide solutions to solve this pressing issue.

School-to-Prison Pipeline

While there is a grave over-representation of Black and Hispanic students in special education, and an equally egregious under-representation of Black and Hispanic students in gifted programs and AP classes (Ford, 2013), Black and Hispanic students are also disproportionately disciplined, suspended, and expelled from school when compared with White students (e.g., Losen, 2013). This combination presents as a miserable cocktail that slings the plight of poor, Hispanic, and Black students back into the pre-Civil Rights era. The most lethal escorts from school to prison are the "zero-tolerance" disciplinary policies.

Wilson (2014) described how the causal link between educational the interconnected exclusion and criminalization of youth is a byproduct of "zero-tolerance" policies that have been widely criticized and discredited, yet the practices are still widespread. School failure and exclusion predict poor life outcomes and are implicated in the mass incarceration of boys and young men of color. Still, these are not insoluble problems as educators and policy makers are discovering effective strategies to engage instead of exclude these students.

A U.S. Department of Education Office for Civil Rights survey reveals that since the 1970s there has been a persistent and pervasive over-representation of minorities in certain special education eligibility categories. The greatest over-representation occurs for Black students, and is even greater for Black males. In the 1980s, Black students represented only 16 percent of the total school population, while representing 38 percent of children in classes for the intellectually disabled. Almost four decades later, little has changed—Black children constitute 17 percent of total school enrollment and 33 percent of enrollment in classes for the intellectually disabled. The progress is slow and dismal. Explanations for the past, current, and growing disparity in the identification of Black students in certain special education disability categories are complex.

In the pre-Civil Rights era, unequal educational opportunity was an uncontested reality and Blacks were seen as intellectually inferior and less than human (Ford, 2013). The ideology of Black intellectual inferiority, in the South and in some communities in other parts of the country, has been explicit. An entire complex of social relations, the exercise of power, and distribution of economic resources, goods, and services were organized in support of this ideological position. What Whites and those in leadership roles and positions of power thought of Blacks was expressed in visible practices and dictated whether, and to what kind of schools, African Americans had access (Perry, Steele, and Hilliard, 2003). The effects of inequality, inequity, and segregation based upon the ideology of Black intellectual inferiority continue to negatively affect the school experiences of many Black and Hispanic students.

More than five decades later, despite the powerful impact of the 1954 *Brown vs. Board of Education* ruling, the more things change, the more they stay the same. The root of this educational dilemma stems from centuries of educational deprivation for Blacks brought to America through slavery, making African Americans part of racial caste group (Ogbu, 1978, 1997; Osborne, 1999), in addition to the extraneous forces and the entrenched bulwark of White racism and male superiority that pervade this society. As a result, they are forced to the lowest rungs of the social, political, and economic hierarchy, existence for Blacks is deliberately and openly controlled.

While the current phenomena of Black students lagging in performance can be attributed to societal factors that many minority students encounter such as poverty, negative stereotypes, disparity in schools, and lack of culturally competent instruction, the great inequities that continue to exist between the schooling experiences of White middle-class students and those of poor African American and Latino students are a logical and predictable result of a racialized society in which discussions of race and racism continue to be muted and marginalized (Dixon and Rousseau, 2006). From the beginning, American constructions of race and class have determined who had and has access to education, and to a large degree those constructions still shape how we think about who can benefit from it (Tatum, 2007). It has become clear that while many or most educators espouse that "All children can learn," and the law states that every child is entitled to a Free Appropriate Public Education (U.S. Dept. of Education, 2010), the individual needs of Black children, inclusive of many variables, generally remain ignored with the answer being referral to special education or exclusion via suspension and/or expulsion, as well as denial of access to gifted education and AP classes.

According to Perry et al. (2003), the ideology of African American intellectual inferiority is increasingly robust, in terms of its impact on students, even more so than it was in the pre-Civil Rights era. Then, although schools were segregated, Perry and colleagues contend that the school community was counterhegemonic in that it acknowledged the nature and extent of the ideological and material oppression of African Americans as students, and intentionally organized itself to counter the effects of this oppression. Today, more but not enough, institutions acknowledge and counter the reproduction of the ideology of Black inferiority and its potential impact on African American and Hispanic students.

Teachers' perceptions and low academic expectations, in addition to biased testing, high-stakes assessments, and the ways in which the inequities of power and privilege exist in classrooms to create complex barriers for Black youth that challenge students' psychosocial identity and well-being (Swanson, Cunningham, and Spencer, 2003). These hegemonic practices that are ramified throughout society, as well as local communities outside of school, are also alive and well inside classrooms, permeating and framing the school experiences of Black students.

African American children go to K-12 schools in the post-Civil Rights era with little acknowledgment by teachers, administrators, and parents that they are being battered at every turn by the ideology of African American inferiority (Perry et al., 2003; Steele, 2012; Valencia, 2010). While some scholars contend that African American students have received equal and greater educational opportunities as a result of *Brown vs. Board of Education* (1954), others claim that trade-offs, such as the demotion of Black principals, the paucity of Black and Hispanic teachers, the closing of formerly Black schools, the busing of Black students out of their neighborhoods, and the quality of the education received by African American students in integrated settings have been detrimental to them (Barton and Coley, 2009; Karpinski, 2006; Kozol, 2005; Lyons and Chestley, 2004). Most, if not all of the historically Black schools that African American children attended were intentionally organized in opposition to the ideology of Black intellectual inferiority (Perry et al., 2003; Tillman, 2008).

SCHOOL EXPERIENCES AND ACHIEVEMENT

There is considerable evidence that the racial/ethnic and socioeconomic backgrounds of students have a bearing on how students are perceived and treated by the adults who work with them within schools (Brookover and Erickson, 1969; Landsman and Lewis, 2011; Morrow and Torres, 1995). In contrast to the increased diversity of students, the population of teachers is homogeneous; that is to say, with each passing year, there are fewer teachers of color to represent the diverse group of students in today's schools (Condition of Education, 2015). Only about 15 percent of teachers come from racially or ethnically diverse groups. Compounding these data is the reality that college graduates entering the teaching force are not sufficiently prepared to teach ethnically diverse students (Ford, 2011; Gay, 2010). Many novice and veteran teachers lack the cultural awareness and, thus, competence, necessary to reach the diverse population of P-12 students, which results in further perpetuating the hegemonic culture that exists throughout American school.

STRATEGIES TO REDUCE OVER-REPRESENTATION

"Any educational or training system that ignores the history or perspective of its learners or does not attempt to adjust its teaching practices to benefit all its learners is contributing to inequality of opportunity" (Wlodkowski and Ginsberg, 1995, as cited by Brown, 2004, p. 26). In many schools across the United States, the teaching population does not reflect the student population, racially, ethnically and culturally. This can cause and has contributed to a disconnect between teachers, students and families, ultimately depriving students of a quality or rigorous education. Thus, educators leaving teacher preparation programs need to be prepared to implement methodology and techniques that are not just pedagogically sound but also culturally responsive. In essence, there needs to be both a more diverse population of teachers and a teaching population that reflects more accurately the population of the student body (Banks, 2000, 2013; Gay, 2010).

Teaching that is not culturally responsive contributes to this trend. The structure and culture of schools play a major role in reinforcing and maintaining racial categories and the stereotypes associated with them. As schools sort children by perceived measures of their ability, and as they single out certain children for discipline, implicit and explicit messages about racial and gender identities are conveyed (Byrd and Chavous, 2011; Noguera, 2003). Explanations of the achievement gap relating to how schools are organized have concentrated on curriculum issues, teaching strategies, school achievement climate, and expectations. How schools structure students' opportunities to learn influences academic achievement. If students do not believe that their teachers care about them and are actively concerned about their academic performance, the likelihood that they will succeed is greatly reduced and compromised.

Culturally responsive teaching involves responsive management, a caring attitude, establishing assertiveness and authority, and congruent communication processes while demanding effort (Brown, 2004; Ford, 2013). Culturally responsive management focuses on many teaching components and essential research-based pedagogical processes as well as the ability to respond appropriately to the emotional, social, cultural, academic, and cognitive needs of students. This is a complex process that involves interpersonal and pedagogical awareness and application in both realms.

Decades ago, Siddle-Walker (1996) noted that the attributes of Black teachers have a cultural history. In segregated schools, Black teachers typically emphasized the importance of education for political and economic success. The teachers were also united in their approach to developing students' awareness of the role of education in their lives. Black teachers have fulfilled many roles in the lives of Black students (Ladson-Billings, 2009). The same holds true for Hispanic teachers and educators. Research conducted by Meier, Stewart, and England (1989) has also shown that the higher the percentage of Black teachers in schools, the lower the numbers of Black students placed in special education, or subjected to expulsion or suspension. Relatedly, with more Black teachers there is an increased number of Black students referred for gifted education (e.g., Ford, Grantham, and Harris, 1997; Grissom and Redding, 2016).

As Togut (2011) sharply posits, in almost sixty years since the United States Supreme Court decision of *Brown v. Board of Education*, public schools have experienced a different kind of discrimination—an undeniable over-representation of Black students in special education classes and programs and pervasive racial disparity in school discipline. This invidious discrimination not only segregates such "minorities" from their White peers, it also segregates them into classes for students with disabilities. Does the unjustified identification and placement of Black students into classes for students with disabilities and racial inequity of school discipline constitute the twenty-first century's rebirth of "separate but equal" facilities for children of color? Simply put, the answer is yes. Black children are adultified, criminalized, and vilified not only in the media, but in places that are designed to guide educate and protect them—schools. One of the main culprits feeding the school-to-prison pipeline is "zero tolerance," which, according to Wilson (2014), fuels the school-to-prison pipeline and is a major causal link between educational exclusion and the criminalization of such youth.

In the late 1980s, as Reagan was waging a war on drugs, violent drug-related crimes soared in urban areas creating fear which led to jurisdictions raising the penalties for juvenile offenders. Alexander (2012) discusses in detail how schools funnel students from school to prison. The initial push into this pipeline begins with exclusionary discipline, where teachers exclude students from their classrooms in order to punish them for an infraction, which is often subjective. These infractions usually range from being uncooperative to being openly defiant, disrespectful, or disruptive. The teacher sends the student out, which most often is a Black male, under the guise of "saving" the rest of the class. Many teachers utilize exclusionary discipline and believe that the isolation will result in a changed behavior on the part of students. However, educators take little to no responsibility for their own actions as adults and as professionals.

This thought directly contradicts the notion of replacing an undesired behavior with a desired one. Educators who frequently and systematically remove students from their classrooms either fear losing control of the classroom, which is less about having control and more about ensuring students are engaged with, can relate to, and find meaning in what is being taught. It is troubling that the topic of exclusionary school discipline is ignored or dismissed since it is both the most unresolved problem in our schools and the precursor to related unresolved social and academic issues in our country, particularly the school-to-prison pipeline (Pane and Rocco, 2014).

Year after year, many of the Black girls who were repeatedly excluded from academic classes and assigned to the SAC seemed to merely "serve their time" in anger, return to class angry and find themselves back in the SAC on a consistent basis, still angry. The revolving door is evident. According to discipline referrals, Black females were written up for repeated offenses of gross disrespect toward school employees, lateness, incitement or intent to fight, and misconduct (Alexander, 2009). Very often, the girls would seek this teacher out to discuss their frustrations with the school, their teachers, and their peers. Frequently, the girls would begin the conversation with, "I hate this school!" Hearing these sentiments repeatedly from the girls made it clear that their school experiences to some degree were not positive and something had to be done.

Strategies that can be implemented immediately to slow and eventually eradicate the school-to-prison pipeline include: Teacher Inquiry, Reflective Practice, Restorative Practice, and Professional Learning Communities (PLCs) (Clandinin and Connelly, 2000; Duncan-Andrade, 2005; Ferriter and Graham, 2009; Meyer and Evans, 2010, 2012). A truly democratic classroom is a place where students and teachers feel responsible for contributing toward a common goal of critical (transformative) pedagogy—acting and reflecting on the world in order to change it (Wink, 2005).

Teacher inquiry as defined by Clarke and Erickson (2004) is insider research that critically examines teaching and student development. Both further assert that teaching as a profession evolves from the insider's research promoting reflective practice. Reflective practice ultimately helps teachers examine their own classroom practices and the impact of these practices on student learning. Facilitating Teacher Inquiry groups consists of involving teachers in inquiry that will have meaning for them within their context, their classroom, and informing them of a problem that exists.

Mental Models

According to Senge (1990), our "mental models" determine not only how we make sense of the world, but how we take action (p. 175). Senge concurs with Argyris's (1990) view that although people do not always behave congruently with their espoused theories, they do behave congruently with their theories-in-use. In any classrooms across the country there is a disparity between teachers' espoused theories and their theories in use. In addressing our mental models, Senge (1990), points out that two people with different mental models can observe the same event and describe it differently because they have looked at different details. He quotes Albert Einstein—"Our theories determine what we measure." Despite various programs geared toward building student achievement, implementing a free and reduced breakfast and lunch program, and volunteering for the mentor-mentee program, until teachers in classrooms across our country change the way and what they think about their Black and Hispanic students and seriously consider the position they sit in as racialized, gendered, and socially classed beings, programs that are implemented without their changed thought patterns will remain ineffective. Without immediate action, Black and Hispanic students will continue to be excluded and farmed from *our* schools to *their* prisons.

THE SCHOLAR IDENTITY MODEL: DISRUPTING THE PIPELINE

The ongoing buzz word "pipeline" is being researched across the K-20 education spectrum. Despite lack of progress, recommendations and programs to fix the leaky and broken pipeline are plentiful. Many have merit in their own right, but some are too generic to have the impact needed, especially when it comes to Black males. More specifically, recommendations most often focus on how educators and parents/families can support and advocate for their children. Frequently missing is how students must unfortunately, advocate for themselves. This is where Gilman Whiting's Scholar Identity Model (SIM) comes into play. Students must believe in themselves, they must believe that achievement is possible, they must want to be scholars. In essence, however unfortunate, Kozol (1991) in *Savage Inequalities* talks of a class of first graders chanting at the beginning of the day a quote that has been credited to William H. Johnsen: "If it's meant to be, it's up to me."

The meaning says take responsibility, take charge, and stop waiting for someone else to do the job. This quote was actually intended for adults dealing with (Cabot) investing. As Kozol (1991) stated, it sounded great, almost chanting-like, but to ask young inner-city poor Black children to assume the responsibility for their education and future is tantamount to cruel and unusual treatment. And in no predominantly White school would this sort of "pull yourself up by your bootstraps" behavior be accepted. Whiting Scholar Identity Model addresses this by involving all stakeholders to share in the psycho-social development of all children entrusted. The SIM's nine constructs are described next, and more details have been summarized by Whiting (2006a, 2006b, 2009a, 2009b, 2014).

Self-Efficacy (SE)

Self-efficacy is the foundation and core of SIM. According to Bandura (1977, 1994), self-efficacy is defined as people's beliefs about their capabilities to produce designated levels of performance that exercise influence over events that affect their lives. Self-efficacy beliefs determine how people feel, think, motivate themselves, and behave. Such beliefs produce these diverse effects through four major processes. They include cognitive, motivational, affective, and selection processes. Self-efficacy (SE) is the foundational construct for the SIM from which all the other constructs are developed and flow. Self-efficacy is the belief in one's self to accomplish a given task with the full knowledge and comprehension of the requirements for completion. In the development of the SIM and the populations engaged, SE is central to academic achievement and attainment (Zimmerman, Bandura, and Martinez-Pons, 1992). The SIM is also concerned with the intersections of race, gender, culture, and socioeconomic status with SE.

During the implementation of our Scholar Identity Institute (SII), which is a program working with adolescents in various settings, we found an increased level of academic SE across the board. These students demonstrated an increased self-confidence, self-control, and resiliency. They began to believe they could succeed at problem solving when fully comprehending a task (e.g., when using the scale of SE, it was noted that when faced with a task of cognitive ability, the students did not feel what Steele and Aronson [1995] refer to as a stereotype threat). As the summer's SII progressed, the Black student participants' levels of SE became stronger. In words and deeds, they were more than whistling Vivaldi (Steele, 2012); they pushed back against negative stereotypes about Black students. They exceeded with regularity the requirements and sought out new ways to challenge themselves. Initially, many of the students would wing it when they did not know an answer; many would also blame extenuating circumstances (especially racism) for their missteps. Issues relating to masculinity and stereotype threat initially interfered with asking for assistance—to ask for help was to be "weak" and not "masculine" in their eyes and limited experiences. However, after one summer's work, when faced with an unfamiliar or difficult obstacle, the Black male students asked for assistance. Once all the students understood the importance of their SE, they were ready for future orientation, to envision life beyond their present circumstances. Advocates who are interested is closing the pipeline must be well versed in scholarship on self-efficacy in their efforts to guide and support all students, but particularly those whom Bell (1992a) referred to as faces at the bottom of the well.

Future Orientation (FO)

The construct future orientation is concerned with the relationship between conscious goals, intentions, and task performance. According to Locke (1968), (a) hard goals produce a higher level of performance (output) than easy goals, (b) specific hard goals produce a higher level of output than a goal of do your best, and (c) behavioral intentions regulate choice behavior. Locke and the SIM also view goals and intentions as mediators of the effects of incentives on task performance, and recognize that an individual's conscious ideas regulate his or her actions. Much of the goal setting is identified with the task at-hand. For example, if one interrogates a student entering college, the student's focus or field of vision into the future is usually one semester and oftentimes one class or the next exam at a time, whereas fifth and sixth graders could only envision that week and usually just the day or what the afternoon held. Based on the age of the individual, realistic goal setting will vary; goal setting is a learned and practiced skill, as students mature they are able to plan further into the future. When working with junior high (eleven to fourteen years old) and high school students (fifteen to eighteen years old) who are from low-income and minority groups, knowledge of and plans for setting goals for postsecondary educational studies or careers cannot be emphasized enough. And with those in college, conversations about postgraduate work and employment preparation should begin in the first year. The thought process is a trained process; the more frequently one envisions goals, the more preparation goes into making them a reality. Motivation theories indicate that people who have aspirations tend to stay focused and prepare for success (Deci and Ryan, 1985, 2002; Dweck, 2006; Dweck and Elliott, 1988; Grantham, 2003). They think about the present and the future, particularly regarding how one's current behaviors and decisions influence future achievements. Diverse students with future targets are not overly concerned about immediate gratification and short-term passing interests and ephemeral goals. These students set realistic goals; likewise, they recognize the importance of a high grade-point average, excellent school attendance, and participation in challenging courses as helpmates to reaching their dreams. They also not only have a plan, but a plan B and a plan C. Because very few of these young eighteen- to twenty-one-year-olds know fully what they want or are actually capable of achieving, having productive alternative scenarios is encouraged. Successful advocates of closing or lessening the opportunity to keep the pipeline open know the vital importance of future orientation (goal setting) to achieving goals and dreams and they must ensure that diverse students also know this.

Willing to Make Sacrifices (W2MS)

To accomplish academic goals, choices have to be made concerning time, effort, and resources. Sociologist Merton (1948) noted the importance of the familiar phrase "self-fulfilling prophecy," which is the process whereby a person or group that has a strongly held value, belief, or an expectation, true or false, affects the outcome of a situation. Many adults have learned through experiences of trials and tribulations that sacrifices are necessary for reaching short-, medium-, and long-term goals. Black students who possess or are working toward a scholar identity also understand that sacrifice may be necessary to attain various goals. They believe and understand, and are more likely to relinquish some aspects of a social life (e.g., particular friends, parties, too many social organizations, popularity, and so forth), other distractions (e.g., Internet surfing and social networking sites), gaming, and television (including hours of watching sports and entertainment) to reach those desired goals. They will plan or limit social time, allocating the bulk of their time and effort toward becoming more productive scholars. Black students who are willing to make sacrifices, understand that success comes with pain (no pain, no gain); to be successful or accomplished, they must give up things they value. And this can be painful. Anyone working to address the vital points of W2MS must understand the oftentimes difficulty of making the hard choice and be there to guide and counsel Black students through these challenges and tribulations.

Internal Locus of Control (ILOC)

A student receives (in his or her estimation) a poor grade on an exam. Many of us have been there; what we attribute that grade to makes all the difference in future endeavors. Was it bad luck? Fate? Were we incapable, or did we not muster enough effort? (Weiner, 1980). Knowing which of these categories (luck, fate, ability, and effort) the student chooses to associate with or attribute to their success or failure is at the core of locus of control. The students who have a strong internal locus of control are optimistic, even when faced with poor results; these students believe they can do well because they (a) have experienced success in the face of challenges, (b) planned for the difficult (time-consuming) work, (c) made the time to study and prepare for the examination, and (d) are willing, when uncertain and vulnerable, to ask for help. Thus, when they receive a less than positive result, they don't blame the test, the assignment, or a teacher with malevolent intentions. These students take responsibility and live with the results. And most importantly, they challenge themselves to do better next time. Adults recognizing a student's aversion to taking responsibility for their actions must engage and re-direct them and provide avenues of opportunity to take that responsibility. Advocates can help these students to engage and increase their internal locus of control by helping them understand the importance of effort and the work ethic in success. They can guide diverse students in being more accountable for their achievements, while keeping in mind and not discounting school and social injustices.

Self-Awareness (SA)

The teacher says, "Young man, please pull your pants up." The young man complies, but thinks, "This is the style and everyone thinks I am cool and look great." As soon as he is out of the teacher's view, and until called on the infraction again, he continues his sagging (wearing pants well-below his waist). Self-awareness is an honest appraisal and understanding of one's perceived and real strengths and limitations. It is not only how you see yourself, but also how you are viewed by others and how you contribute to that view. Self-awareness is bound up with effort, etiquette, sincerity, character, and self-control (G. Pesare, personal communication, April 15, 1991). Students who have a realistic grasp on those areas in need of work are willing to consider and process new (and disagreeable) information, ideas, and societal expectations toward their self-improvement (e.g., they seek a tutor in classes where they are not doing well, they study longer and more often, and they realize that certain attire triggers negative assumptions). And finally, they take immediate and sustained actions to make appropriate transitions based on their situation. While the current youth culture of sagging is often associated with a troubled and negative place or space (American prisons), it has become part of a contemporary vogue similar to women smoking in the Roaring Twenties, the Fonzie style of the 1950s, or the long hair of hippies in the 1960s. And as with other periods in time, these various fads are seen as troubling to the status quo. In this era, though, and particularly for Black male students, the stakes appear much higher: criminalization, incarceration, and even murder (e.g., Trayvon Martin). Therefore, as a part of self-awareness, young Black and Hispanic men must be able to code switch as they make the transition into adulthood. Those truly concerned with the pipeline can help all students make decisions that increase, counter, and/or improve the images and messages others have of them. When having discussions with students about seeing oneself as others do (not "selling-out," or "acting-white") these very real, and necessary conversations can help students be more self-reflective, which increases their self-awareness so that they make wise(r) choices in school and life.

Achievement > Affiliation (A>A)

The need for achievement and the need for affiliation are found in varying degrees in all students. Neither is inherently wrong. The need-for achievement student is achievement motivated and therefore seeks attainment of realistic but challenging goals and academic advancement. The student has a strong desire for feedback as it relates to achievement and progress, and a need for a sense of accomplishment. The need-for-affiliation student is affiliation motivated and has a need for friendly relationships and seeks interaction with other people. The affiliation driver produces motivation and the need to be liked and held in popular regard (McClelland, 1978).

When the goal of academic success is foremost, but the student assigns the need for affiliation greater importance and yet still expects to receive high academic marks, discontinuity arises. Harvard economist Fryer (2006) found that Black and Hispanic students often opt for more friends and forego higher grade-point averages. A student with a strong scholar identity knows this and makes the sacrifice of having friends who are not motivated toward similar academic goals. For these diverse students, the need for achievement is stronger than the need for affiliation; thus, the number of friends they have or their popularity does not determine their identity. While they may be social and desire meaningful friendships, they are not troubled about being popular for the sake of popularity. Black and Hispanic students with a strong need for achievement understand that high academic achievement will take them far in life. Conflicts about a student turning his back on his community, culture, or race in pursuit of academic goals may exist. The scholar identity student possesses an unassuming confidence, preferably drawn from having family and friends who respect and support him and do not impede his progress. If you are sincerely interested in moving just one student away from suction at the opening of pipeline, you are needed to guide diverse students in ensuring that they know how to prioritize assignments and tasks with friendships.

Academic Self-Confidence (AS-C)

A teacher wields unimaginable power and influence. A child's academic self-confidence is developed through a series of successful encounters not just at home but also at school. Teachers' expectations drive student achievement; therefore, developing a strong sense of academic self-confidence in young Black and Hispanic students must be understood as an imperative—pushing without coddling. Unfortunately, seemingly inconsequential microaggressions (Sue, Capodilupo, and Holder, 2008) set the standard for how students view themselves. When questioned about how they did so well on an assignment, these students may refuse to complete further work. Students who believe they are strong students feel comfortable and confident in academic settings, learning and playing with ideas. Most importantly, they do not feel inferior in school, and they do not feel the need to negate, deny, or minimize their academic abilities and skills. These students have a strong work ethic—they spend time doing schoolwork, they study, and they require little prodding from parents and teachers. An often under-used cog in the teacher tool kit is the role of the teacher as a facilitator, a guide, and a as confident person, one who will allow himself or herself to see and not be threatened by an outgoing student with verve. Verve is the propensity for energetic, intense, highly stylized body language, and is an essential component of a learning style of expression for African American children (Boykin, 1994.)

This does not mean allowing Black and Hispanic students to be the class clown or disruptive in class, but it does mean understanding and having the savvy to use such behavior as a teachable moment. Here we are referring to the ability to understand the underlying battles taking place in all classrooms every day, with students pushing against authority merely as a stage of development. For most male students (as with female students), the onset of puberty marks a point where students, even when faced with the fact that they are wrong, once they commit to leaning into an idea, thought, or position, they are unable or unwilling to back down. It is at this point when the adult drawn into this battle of wills must appear to concede ground, turn (only momentarily), and give way in the direction the student is pushing. It is then and only then that the student can relax enough to hear the adult. While listening and learning from the student, we begin to turn them in the direction we wanted them to go all along. The turn may be subtle, or it may be a hairpin turn, but we must be willing to hear and see it when they cannot.

Ultimately, students with a high academic self-concept understand that in order to be successful, effort is just as important, or more important, than ability. In essence, a student does not care what we (the adult) know until he knows we (the adult) care. We can and must guide Black and Hispanic students in their journey to be confident in academic settings.

Race Consciousness (Formerly Racial Identity and Pride) (RC)

Even before the inauguration of America's first African American president (Barack Obama), keyboards across the nation could be heard tapping away about the so-called Obama effect. Writers across the nation heralded the arrival of a new post-racial society. It was as if the 2008 election of President Barack Obama marked the end of race and racism. That notion has been beaten back (Bonilla-Silva, 2006; Hughley and Jost, 2011; Kaplan, 2011; Metzler, 2008; Sharpley-Whiting, 2009; Touré and Dyson, 2012; Wise, 2010). In too many ways, society has and continues to remind Black and Hispanic students of their place and race. The average Black teen acts in line with (and sometimes against) stereotypical racialized scenarios daily. In any case, self esteem and self-concept, racial identity, and pride affect students' achievement and motivation (Cross and Vandiver, 2001). Teachers, and others in positions of authority in teaching and learning capacities, must receive continued professional development regarding the persistent significance of race, identity, and racism. For diverse students, race and a scholar identity have high salience; racially conscious students are comfortable in their skin and simultaneously aware of the limitations from without that are placed on the skin they're in. They push back against the boundaries on their racially gendered identity. They seek greater self-understanding as racialized beings. They attempt to grapple with the historical and social implications and constructions of their raced and gendered identities, but they are also highly cognizant of the importance of adapting to racially heterogeneous and homogeneous (if they are the only diverse student therein) environments, of being bicultural or multicultural (Cross and Vandiver, 2001). Just as important, they do not equate achievement with acting White or selling out (Ferguson, 2001; Ford, 2010; Fordham, 1988; Fryer, 2006; Whiting, 2006, 2009). These young students refuse to be constrained by social injustices based on gender, socioeconomic status, and race or ethnicity. Far too many classroom teachers have not received training to address the social and emotional needs and identities of their students, including but not limited to self-esteem and self-concept. When working with any student of a minority group, particularly Black students, teachers cannot be colorblind. They must be grounded and versed in race conscientiousness.

Masculinity (M)

Masculinity is often a difficult concept to pin down. Broadly, masculinity is recognized as possessing the qualities or characteristics of manliness or of being a man. There are nonetheless myriad ways of being a man and expressing manliness, even though as a culture the United States tends to accept hegemonic masculinity—tough, hard, domineering, and dominating—as normative. Contemporary representations of and ideas about American Black masculinity tend to lean toward the negative—hypersexual, thug, gangster, violent, abusive, less intelligent athlete, and absent father. Out of whole cloth and against the grain of mainstream culture, Black men, women, and boys have attempted to craft an oppositional narrative of Black masculinity that at times conforms with hegemonic American masculinity, confirms the worst stereotypes of American Black masculinity, or upends the former narratives. The role of the SIM in schools is crucial to combatting retrogressive notions about Black masculinity as well as exploring how performances of normative masculinity are at odds with academic success. Studies like Kozol's *Savage Inequalities: Children in America's Schools* (1991) and *The Shame of the Nation: The Restoration of Apartheid Schooling in America* (2005) reveal how counselors, teachers, administrators, and peer pressure can exacerbate negative identities and undermine a scholar identity. Using ethnographic accounts, Ferguson (2001) also presents in *Bad Boys: Public Schools in the Making of Black Masculinity* the structural rituals that lead to the hardening of young Black boys during their school years that oftentimes contribute to feelings of uselessness and desperation.

But here the SIM counters that Black male students with a scholar identity do not equate hard work, the pursuit of high academic ranking, intelligence, and studiousness with being unmanly. Moreover, they do not equate success with selling out or acting White. Rather, being a scholar is taught and celebrated as an integral part of a self-possessed masculinity. Such students do not feel the need to belittle and resist learning opportunities. In fact, students with a scholar identity feel empowered as young men in that they are able to access knowledge that will add to their future goals and expectations. Like the American teacher's race and gender distribution, the demographics of counselors also skew European American (White)—which has the potential to lead to cultural clashes. Teachers working at majority minority schools or those who are unschooled with cultural differences often have lower expectations due to race, gender, and class. This is where it becomes imperative for the teachers to be proactive, to reach out to learn more about all the students and not see Black and Hispanic as broken.

SUMMARY AND CONCLUSION

The prison pipeline in education takes its toll on students who are not just culturally different but those who are also gifted and have special education needs. For many, the pipeline is clear or clearer when special education is the focus. Over-representation is undeniably a problem. However, the ramifications of denied access to gifted education is all but ignored and discounted in the leaky and broken pipeline that can ultimately result in prison. This is a tragic waste of human potential. It is by no means cliché to state that a mind is a terrible thing to waste (United Negro College Fund). In fact, if we do not make changes, we can only blame ourselves. It is our hope that this chapter opens up a conversation on how to support our Black and Hispanic students through a strengths-based perspective. Our students have much to offer, it is past time to establish environments that let these students meet their highest potential.

Chapter Three

Pipeline in Crisis

*A Call to Sociological and Criminological Studies
Scholars to Dismantle the School-to-Prison Pipeline*

Melinda Jackson, Tifanie Pulley, and Dari Green

An enormous amount of attention has been paid to the school-to-prison pipeline over the past ten to fifteen years. Given the harsh disciplinary policies employed in mostly urban elementary and secondary schools across the United States, students of color are funneled directly from the school into the criminal justice system. Students of color are suspended and expelled at rates three times higher than their White peers. This unprecedented development of the school-to-prison pipeline has taken place with little public debate and scholarly analysis on how to dismantle it, which is quite troubling. As sociological and criminological scholars, we are particularly attentive to the problems that contribute to the school-to-prison pipeline in the United States. The silences that exist are triggered by the consistent denial of the enduring racial divide in the American educational and justice systems and by the absence of institutional and scholarly support for prison scholarship and education. This chapter seeks to dismantle these silences by demanding public dialogue, teaching, and sociological and criminological research about the school-to-prison pipeline model. We are interested in mapping this pressing issue by documenting and exposing the school-to-prison pipeline and other harsh disciplinary policies that are endorsed by urban schools and establishing research, action, and education agendas for future scholarly works. Therefore, we are calling upon our colleagues to reexamine the policies that reinforce the school-to-prison pipeline and become active agents in continuing to dismantle the practices that criminalize America's youth. The idea that school procedures could be, at least in part, accountable for directing students into the criminal justice system is disturbing; any policies or movements to break this pipeline are extremely important. As such, we offer both a comprehensive action plan and strategies for pursuing new practices of scholarship, pedagogy, and social action. By using a meta-analysis approach, we hope to launch nothing less than a revolution, shaping how sociological and criminological scholars perceive their relationship to the school-to-prison pipeline, the miseducation of Black youth, and the persistent racial economic inequality in US society as a whole. America's schools were not created to function as a gateway that feeds at-risk children to prisons. The presence of a school-to-prison pipeline in America symbolically represents an unnecessary evil with irreversible implications if not properly addressed.

MAPPING THE SCHOOL-TO-PRISON PIPELINE (HISTORICAL OVERVIEW)

To begin mapping the school-to-prison pipeline one must first consider the history of the symbiotic relationship between the criminal justice and education system. Since the early 1970s the United States has quadrupled its prison population with the incarceration rate being five to ten times that of many other democratic countries. More than half of the state prisoners that make up the population are incarcerated for nonviolent crimes, causing a devastating effect on American families and communities (Martin, 2011; Smith and Roberts, 2004). With over 2.2 million prisoners, over two million American children have lost a parent to the criminal justice system.

Consequently, these same children may often experience similar trouble themselves in the school system. While there have been a number of policies proposed to help transform the education system and thus society, the reality has been a reflection and reinforcement of society by and large, rather than the proposed transformation. This is not a surprising fact due to the historical model of the school system itself, In the 1920s; for example, schools were organized in a stratified manner. Lower-class youth prepared for factory jobs, while their counterparts were groomed to occupy more prestigious occupations. Despite the fact that since the 1970s many of the factory jobs are no longer available in most inner-city neighborhoods in America, the same model prevails. As a result, children in the inner city, which tend to be predominantly children of color, often find themselves being fed into a prison system instead.

The schools that they attend often support this pipeline by modeling schools in a similar fashion to that of the prison system—having students enter through metal detectors, have armed police guards do bodily searches and hallway sweeps. Many of the schools that embrace this so-called pipeline have inadequate resources, a lack of qualified teachers, and overcrowded

classrooms. With the lack of resources the students experience a higher likelihood of disengagement and dropout enforced by zero-tolerance policies.
With a disproportionate number of men of color labeled "special educa-
tions," schools are able to bypass protections of due process and route students from school to the jailhouse.

THE INTERSECTIONS OF RACE, CLASS, AND
GENDER IN THE SCHOOL-TO-PRISON PIPELINE

The school-to-prison pipeline presents the intersection of a K-12 educational
system that produces and reproduces many of our nation's most preposterous
practices regarding racial discrimination. The risk of being entered into the
school-to-prison pipeline is not by any chance, random. For example, for the
same misconduct, students of color are suspended, expelled, and receive
more corporal punishment than their non-minority peers. These disparities
are so embedded that the school-to-prison pipeline operates as an apparatus
of racial inequality that fuels racism in America. At what point did America's
education system become the gateway for its prison system? Answering this
question is quite thorny, as we consider marginalized populations. Within the
school-to-prison pipeline, for example, are the intersections of race, class,
and gender, in terms of the disproportionate rates of suspensions, arrests, and
referrals to law enforcement for black children and other students of color
(U.S. Department of Education Office for Civil Rights—School Discipline
Data, 2014). Black students are three times as likely to be expelled or suspended as whites. Suspension patterns begin as early as preschool, with
Black children only representing 18 percent of the enrollment, they more
than double their enrollment percentage with 48 percent receiving more than
one out-of-school suspension (U.S. Department of Education Office for Civil
Rights—School Discipline Data, 2014). By contrast, white students constitute 43 percent of preschool enrollment with a more than one out-of-school
suspension rate of 26 percent. A critical conversation is required as we consider the ways in which access to education is becoming more and more
problematized with the various transformative approaches to both public and
private education.

Furthermore, research data appears to indicate no significant difference
by race when considering the percentage of Black students referred to law
enforcement is 27 percent and of whites is 41 percent, or 39 percent of
students subjected to a school-related arrest are white and 31 percent are
Black, however, the enrollment for Black students is only 16 percent as
opposed to 51 percent whites (U.S. Department of Education Office for Civil
Rights—School Discipline Data, 2014).

It is impossible to ignore the similarities between the Education Reform Industry (ERI) and the Prison Industrial Complex (PIC). For example, although Black students lag behind in school enrollment, they reach parity and surpass harsh disciplinary outcomes in comparison to whites. At the nexus of an overconcentration of minority communities that populate America's prisons is the emerging school-to-prison pipeline. Driven by its bottom line, the Education Reform Industry (ERI) problematizes access to education as more and more public schools are closing and private/charter schools are erected in their place (Russakoff, 2015). America's most under-served and under-resourced are caught in between a hybrid model of education reform and zero tolerance (Martin, Fasching-Varner, Quinn, and Jackson, 2014; Fasching-Varner, Mitchell, Martin, and Bennett-Haron, 2014). Our education system should not resemble our prison system at any level, which arguably reveals a troubling educational trajectory. America's school-to-prison pipeline is not the legacy we should employ for our future K-12 education system. In other words, as one of the primary agents of socialization in America and abroad, education pedagogically transcends race, class, and gender categories. Business models are not the quintessential tool when America's most economically deprived are hanging in the balance. Profitability and pathology are the prescriptive for a 'pipeline in crisis.'

Three Strategies for Dismantling the Pipeline in Crisis: A Meta-Analysis to Dismantling the Prison-to-School Pipeline

Having presented a map of some of the crisis of the school-to-prison pipeline, we now take a meta-analysis approach with hopes to launch nothing less than a revolution in sociological and criminological scholarship and a new movement of social action. We provide three strategies for pursuing new practices of research, pedagogy, and social action: (1) Acknowledge the Devil: The Pipeline in Crisis, (2) Keep Fighting: Teaching and Practicing Equality, and (3) Expand on Successful Educational Tactics Offered Both Inside and Outside of Schools.

Acknowledge the Devil: The Pipeline in Crisis

The devil in this context represents the true evil of the school-to-prison pipeline that will eventually diminish a race of people's true citizenship if this cycle continues. Researchers have consistently recognized how poor students of color are funneled directly from the school into the courtrooms and then into cages (Wilson, 2014). The denial of adequate educational support sets up our nation's most at-risk youth for failure. A lack of effective teachers and school leaders, overcrowded classrooms, and insufficient funding, for example, increase students' disengagement and their possibility of dropping out.

The fight by communities of color to attain freedom, equality, and justice is as old as this nation (Bell, 1992). There must always be a subordinate group in order for the dominant group, or those with power, to benefit. Consequently, the dominant group continues to oppress large segments of the Black population (Martin, Fasching-Varner, Quinn, and Jackson, 2014). Through prisons, the power of dominant groups is maintained and sustained as they receive huge proceeds from private corporations and gain politically for "tough on crime" policies, which starts by tracking students out of educational institutions, mainly through "zero tolerance" techniques (Heitzeg, 2009). These policies and practices, however, are greater than politics; there are over two million American citizens, primarily Black men, who are highly susceptible to exploitable labor, which many corporations profit from. To stay running, jails and prison cells are packed with defenseless, oftentimes young, poor, men of color. Men of color are not only excluded from employment, housing, voting, and educational opportunity once labeled felons, but are exploited for very low wages in a system fueled by capitalism. This vicious cycle continues to build prisons for profit that fail to rehabilitate inmates and provide cheap labor to corporations, just as they have been doing throughout most of American history (Alexander, 2012). Consequently, the more prisons that are built, the more people they need to lock up in cages.

The school-to-prison pipeline is a system that works by punishing and imprisoning oppressed and disadvantaged groups. Instead of investing in education, policy makers have chosen instead to fund incarceration—indeed for corporate profit and political gain, but at ridiculous social costs (Heitzeg, 2009). While underprivileged schools struggle to provide adequate resources for students, politicians spend over $50,000 yearly to send that same child to prison (Kozol, 2005). Different policies and practices would probably be in place if the students at risk were wealthy or white, but they are not (Heitzeg, 2009). Those that are able to benefit from this system politically or economically from incarceration being accepted as a catch-all solution to social problems are also unlikely to propose alternative solutions. When rehabilitation is not at the forefront, recidivism is highly likely.

Despite the importance of public education, the system is counterproductive. For instance, the lack of resources coupled with poverty, racial isolation, and unsafe and poorly equipped facilities actually creates perverse incentives that push the neediest students out of their schools. School funding continues to decline, while funding for heightened security measures continues to increase. The behavior that previously resulted in a visit to the principal's office is now grounds for a visit in prison (Heitzeg, 2009), which is similar to those practices we supposedly left behind. The school-to-prison pipeline is feeding into the prison-industrial complex.

The prison system has progressively come to be influenced by private companies and businesses that supply goods to governmental prison agencies. Both the school-to-prison pipeline and prison-industrial complex are based on this flawed belief that increasing the prison system will effectively solve systemic problems related to poverty and education. Prisons are often seen in a positive light due to the fact that they create jobs and give skills to inmates; however, these things are motivated by capitalism, not necessarily as a means to reduce crime or rehabilitate inmates. What is seen as a solution has actually disturbed many families, diminished funds for education, and created, many times unwarranted, fear of crime in American society. Similar to the prison-industrial complex, the school-to-prison pipeline has become an outrageous creature that must constantly be fed while intimidating the well-being of equality in America.

Due to these special interests and increased spending on imprisonment, the United States has become addicted to incarceration. The United States has a higher incarceration rate than any other country and sadly, this rate continues to increase. We must understand that the ultimate goal behind prisons is not to rehabilitate its prisoners but rather exploit them for cheap labor. This practice then creates a mechanism we term as "prisoner's-labor-for profit." The lure of big money is mortifying the nation's criminal-justice system and as a result has caused prisons to become the most expensive form of punishment. Critical to this argument is the extraction of Black and Brown bodies framed as conventional offenders and targets for harsh treatment and unequal sentencing as they are a perceived threat to civil society (Alexander, 2012). The racial realism that our community of color must obtain is simply an understanding and acknowledgment of racism as it is and our subordinate position within it. As Curry (2008) states, and we support, "equality only serves as an imaginative allure—a fantasy, and this is the reality that must be conceptually disengaged" (p. 42). Ultimately, the crisis of the school-to-prison pipeline can only be truly dismantled by first acknowledging the racist and classist underpinning purpose of those in power.

Keep Fighting: Teaching, Practicing, and Extending the Conversation

By acknowledging the devil, as our slave ancestors did, we must continue to fight for equality without stopping our efforts to change it, even if it's at the bottom of the scale (Bell, 1992). To fight a system put in place by capitalism, educators need to participate in professional dialogue about the policies of the "pipeline in crisis" to understand what works and what does not. Dismantling the school-to-prison pipeline involves personal as well as system change. Putting the needs of students of color first is primary. This requires new ways of teaching, practicing, and responding to disruptive behavior so these issues become learning opportunities—both for students and staff (Wilson, 2014). Pedagogical practices that have a proven track record, which involve the proverbial notion "each one, teach one" is still needed in the communities that are labeled as the least likely to succeed. Our children are teachable, but accountability is a collective effort that involves students, staff, and policy makers. The greatest divide is found in the space between top-down models and bottom-up. Oftentimes, the top-down model rejects the subjective experiences of the bottom-up and relegates the marginalized to an underachieving status. Social stratification implicates that such ideologies weaken the ability for education to transcend if students, particularly students of color, are conceived as insubordinate and willfully defiant. Research indicates that the outcomes associated with chronic suspension and expulsions are poor and do very little to enhance student's academic standing. Behavior is only one component of understanding the multi-layered identity of the children consequently subjected to unequal discipline policies across racial categories (U.S. Department of Education Office for Civil Rights—School Discipline, 2014; Martin, Fasching-Varner, Quinn, and Jackson, 2014; Fasching-Varner, Mitchell, Martin, and Bennett-Haron, 2014). In an effort to reverse this cycle, schools are being challenged to change their discipline policies despite racial inequality due to the cancerous effects. By teaching, practicing, and extending the conversation, as sociology and criminology educators, we can help teach students of color how to identify and evaluate the issues that exist in a society designed to benefit those in power.

Build on Successful Educational Tactics Offered both Inside and Outside of Schools

A final way to address the challenges of the school-to-prison pipeline is based on a bottom-up approach, by concentrating on a child-by-child, teacher-by-teacher, and school-by-school method. Since racism continues to shift, change and oftentimes develop into unrecognizable practices (Alexander, 2012); we suggest two ways this method can be applied in schools of color. First, we suggest that by developing personal and professional knowledge about what works for each child individually, educators can reverse the damaging flow of poverty that deprives the poorest children of their true potential. This enables teachers and educators to engage in each student need and develop effective classroom management practices and teaching skills to tackle those individual needs (Wilson, 2014). Second, existing research has revealed that teachers can prevent students of color from entering this "pipeline in crisis" by forming relationships of mutual trust, building a warm learning space, and applying positive behavioral methods that will prevent the way behavioral problems are solved. These elements are essential, given that many of these kids come from the most economically disadvantaged families, which typically have the greatest learning needs. All in all, eliminating zero-tolerance practices from the educator's toolbox will involve serious staff participation and an acknowledgment of the negative influences of a racialized society that functions to limit educational and social opportunities for people of color (Wilson, 2014; Hayes, Juarez, and Escoffery-Runnels, 2014).

CONCLUDING THOUGHTS: HOW HISTORY DEMANDS ACTION

Racial and class discrimination are greatly entangled in the school-to prison pipeline. From 1973 to 2006, African American students who were suspended went from two to more than three times as likely to be suspended and expelled in comparison to their white counterparts (Witt 2007). This chapter offers three strategies for dismantling and moving forward to readdress the school-to-prison pipeline that exists within U.S. dominant White society. First, we argue that if systemic change is to happen we have to first acknowledge and understand the crisis that exists. The reality is that a disproportionate amount of Black youth comes from families in poverty, attends under-resourced schools, and is incarcerated at rates higher than their white counterparts. This provides some of the best evidence of the continuing significance of race (Martin et al., 2014).

Second, we suggest that as sociological and criminological scholars, we must know how to free ourselves from the delusion that change is likely to happen without discontinuing our efforts to dismantle it—the contradiction of realism. It is vital that we keep fighting, teaching, and practicing equality while extending the conversation within a society where race does matter. The permanence of racism in the United States has not ended but simply transformed into unrecognizable practices that fit seamlessly into the fabric of the American consciousness (Alexander, 2012). Teaching students of color about the nature of their social position will allow them to be mindful of the ways capitalists continue to oppress large segments of the Black population that people of color are faced with in virtually every social institution (Martin et al., 2014). Teaching and helping students of color acknowledge their inferior position would allow students to think, plan, and react within a society tailored to benefiting those in power. By applying this pedagogy and continued social action, our final suggestion is to build on successful educational tactics offered both inside and outside of schools.

This chapter seeks to provide a space for discussing these issues by providing three strategies that may be useful in dismantling one or several parts of this pipeline. Together as scholars, educators, advocates, and policy makers we can help others teach, identify, and evaluate the pipeline in crisis, which is affecting the life chances of students of color. The youth who are suffering greatly from these practices are highly likely to be those who need the most support, including students from low-income families, students of color, youth in foster care and students with disabilities. Unfortunately, it is important to understand that the system in place is operating in the way that it has always intended (Fasching-Varner et al., 2014). Rather than rely on race, politicians put policies in place that not only label students of color as criminals but also encourage them to lose faith, making them more likely to be incarcerated (Alexander, 2012). Therefore, it takes "a village" devoted in the educational system to teach and give students the educational opportunities that will allow them to understand their true potential in a society where race will always matter. "As the school to prison pipeline exists in a larger context, so too must efforts to dismantle it" (Heitzeg, 2009).

Chapter Four

"I got in trouble, but I really didn't get caught"

The Discursive Construction of 'Throwaway Youth'

Tracey M. Pyscher and Brian D. Lozenski

> In working niggers, we always calculate that they will not labor at all except to avoid punishment, and they will never do more than just enough to save themselves from being punished, and no amount of punishment will prevent their working carelessly or indifferently. It always seems on the plantations as if they took pains to break all the tools and spoil all the cattle that they possibly can, even when they know they'll be directly punished for it (Bauer and Bauer, 1942).

The above quote was the remark of someone described as "a well-informed capitalist and slaveholder" in Bauer and Bauer's (1942) documenting of the day-to-day resistant acts of enslaved Africans in the United States. We are, obviously, not foolish enough to compare antebellum plantations to modern classrooms, which would be disrespectful to enslaved Africans, their descendants, and others who exist in schools today. What caught our attention about the above quote was the logic of punishment, which is still pervasive in many schools with regard to certain groups of youth. There exist a great number of young people in U.S. schools that only do schoolwork to avoid punishment, either at the hands of the school officials or their guardians. This chapter focuses on the great number of youth who defy authority in the direct knowledge that they will receive punishment, yet threat or reality of punishment does not deter them. School personnel at all levels have put a great deal of time and energy into imagining, designing, and implementing protocols of punishment ranging from classroom detentions, to suspensions, to physical abuse (e.g., paddling, handcuffing), to psychological abuse (e.g., isolation,

53

threats). Even "tools of learning and assessment" such as homework and grades are often used to enact punishment. It is well documented that these punishments are meted out disproportionately and their severity has disparate consequences for youth based on factors such as race, ethnicity, class, gender, sexual identity, and ability constructs. Our purpose in this writing is to illuminate how youth who are socially and culturally located within matrices of racialized and domestic violence (i.e., youth with histories of domestic violence or HDV youth) at the hands of schools and caretakers navigate the constructs of punishment in what constitutes the school-to-prison-pipeline. We argue that the pipeline, while ultimately resulting in a material experience of physical detention, begins with the discursive construction of a "bad kid," a "problem child," and in many ways a "throwaway youth" (Pyscher and Lozenski, 2014).

Sabotage, "break[ing] all the tools," the slowing down of work, seeming disinterest in the task at hand—these are tried and true methods of resistance used by those who are despised and exploited; those who are looked upon as discardable and are labeled the dregs—burdens to society (Bauman, 2009; Scott, 1990). In places where social hierarchy goes unquestioned, and people are measured by their ability to produce, which is twistedly conflated with their proclivity to consume, those who do not produce (and thus consume) are not useful, and thus must be punished. In earlier writing (Pyscher and Lozenski, 2014), we argued that schools, like other commodity-based systems, have a desire to produce a certain type of output, namely, youth who are acculturated to the neoliberal logics of commodification and prepared to take their place in the social hierarchy as deemed appropriate by the very education systems that shaped them. Historically, schools have been highly effective sorting technologies, churning out workers, managers, and industry leaders, as documented by myriad social reproduction theorists (Anyon, 1997; Bowles and Gintis, 1976; Giroux, 2001, Willis, 1977). Yet, in any commodity-based system there are products, or outputs, that are defective. Drawing from Bauman's (2009) theorization of industries of waste disposal, we argued that educational subindustries are created to deal with youth as defective outputs. These subindustries are marked by segregated, self-contained spaces (e.g., EBD classrooms, In-School-Suspension rooms) where youth are warehoused until they can be efficiently "thrown away" into the unseen world of mass incarceration.

We simply can't throw kids away anymore. Thus, they must first be rationalized as discardable. This rationalization is done through the technology of labeling. Whether they are labeled "at-risk," "EBD," or simply "a bad kid," these are the first instances of the discursive matrix that manifests as the school-to-prison pipeline. Our analysis explores how youth who have experienced both domestic violence and racialized (both historical and current) acts of violence navigate these technologies and, yet, uncover their own forms of resistive agency (Scott, 1990). We draw from Scott's (1990) theorization that marginalized resistance resides between the tension-filled relationships of hidden and public transcripts, which offer a complicated view of the interplay between normative and hegemonic powers, and how high and low forms of youth resistance play out in school settings.

We highlighted the historical violences of schools against youth of African descent and Native American youth, which we juxtaposed to HDV youth. We reject commonly held notions that youth and communities that possess cultural knowledges built through social violence are somehow "broken." In fact we identify that belief as something that reifies paternalistic relationships between communities of color, HDV youth, and oppressive school systems. Rather, we understand these experiences of lived and generational racialized violence as sociocultural locations through which youth see and know the world. We argued that these youths are most apt to be labeled "throwaway youth," and consequently, are in the best position to hold firm critiques of schooling structures and develop resistive practices for self-preservation that have either been passed down through generations or acquired as a part of their *habitus* as protection from lived experiences of violence through low and high forms of resistance (Bourdieu, 1997; Pyscher, 2015a, 2015b; Pyscher and Lozenski, 2014). Our contention is that these performances of low and high resistances serve as barometers measuring moments of social violation between youth and educators in the atmosphere of schools.

How do we understand the resistive acts of youth who "break the tools" and smile in the faces of those who seek to punish them? Our analysis of how labeling acts as a technology of the school-to-prison pipeline becomes apparent in the tracing of the experiences of a young, black, HDV woman and her grandmother as they struggle to navigate an unforgiving schooling environment. What emerges through this analysis is that the school-to-prison pipeline is not necessarily an escalating series of consequences for youth who break the rules, or are targeted disproportionately, but also an overlaying matrix of discourses: "troubled," "bad kid," "disordered," "broken"—that position youth to be subject to what Foucault (1977) describes as a panopticon, where school and prison constitute one another. It is in this discursive intersection that we locate "Mac," the focal youth in this analysis.

NECESSARY ACTS OF RESISTIVE AMBIVALENCE: MAC'S RUPTURES OF HIDDEN AND PUBLIC TRANSCRIPTS

"I thought, if these people just knew what these kids went through, they didn't know. Just give them a chance . . . they couldn't actually see Mac for what she was."
—Makita (Mac's grandmother)

Mac, a female eighth-grade student and an HDV youth participant in Pyscher's (2015a) larger study, identified as African American, HDV, and queer. Mac carried herself in a gregarious manner, often interacting with friends and school staff with humor and a sense of vitality. Mac openly, with a sense of pride, shared her childhood histories of domestic violence. Her violent childhood experiences can be described as extreme and sustained. Mac was shuffled between her mother, grandmother, and the foster care system between birth and third grade. From pre-kindergarten to first grade, she described her mother's frequent drug use and incarceration, along with daily sexual abuse at the hands of her grandmother's boyfriend for a number of years. At the age of seven, she and her sister were placed in foster care with an older adult woman in whose care Mac's experiences of domestic violence continued through physical abuse and neglect. Two years after her foster care placement, her grandmother, "Makita," managed to get custody, once again, of Mac and her sister. They relocated from a southern state to a northern Midwestern state to "restart their lives." Based on many visits to their family's subsidized apartment, it was evident that the family lived in abject poverty. In response, Pyscher organized multiple efforts to find social services, clothing, towels, cooking ware, and furniture for the family.

Mac and Makita talked extensively of socially violating experiences both had with educators in elementary school. These experiences made it necessary for an HDV youth like Mac to perform acts of low and high resistance (Scott, 1990) as she navigated violating interactions with educators. Douglas (1966) suggests that the relationships between the marginalized (the dirty) and the dominant (the pure) are under constant tension and restraint, where "everything we do is significant, nothing is without its conscious symbolic load. Moreover, nothing is lost on the audience" (p. 124). During interviews in Pyscher's larger study (2015a), Mac and Makita showed this relational navigation is central to their marginalized experiences in their interactions with Mac's elementary educators. The theme of resistive ambivalence, or the rupture between hidden and public transcripts, became a central analytic in understanding how normative and hegemonic forces collide in discursive school processes and intersections of throwaway youth (Pyscher, 2015a, 2015b; Pyscher and Lozenski, 2014; Scott, 1990).

We choose to highlight Mac's stories because her descriptions of navigating socially violating school interactions embodied necessary and sustained performances of low resistance (i.e., hidden transcripts) and high forms of resistance (i.e., resistive ambivalence). Mac's stories about her first- through fifth-grade experiences unearth a range of oppressive conditions, including frequent disciplinary actions as a way to control her body movements, removal from classes, suspensions, and being paddled as punishment. For children and youth like Mac, these are the cogs that constitute the generative force driving the mechanisms of school-to-prison pipeline. This constant

vigilance and surveillance on the part of school staff created normative hegemonic conditions to which Mac responded in kind.

"I got in trouble, but I really didn't get caught."

The following stories, told by Mac and Makita, highlight a variety of resistive responses Mac employed to counteract violating interactions in school.
For Mac, in her earliest elementary grades, acts of low resistance included
strategic stalling where she would move into and out of spaces slowly while
also refusing to perform pretenses like raising her hand in the classroom
when clearly the teacher knew her name. As a cultural necessity for physical
or psychic protection, HDV youth like Mac learn to read and resist socially
violating interactions in complicated ways (hidden transcripts). When racialized, poor, and HDV youth like Mac clash with normative hegemonic interactions like these (public transcripts), often perpetuated by educators, ruptures or resistive ambivalence become a necessity.

In the following interview excerpts, Mac discusses her low and high
forms of resistance taken from her earliest formal school experiences while
Makita frames these similar experiences of social violation from a caregiver
perspective. The following dialogue between Mac and Pyscher captured stories of sustained low and high forms of resistance with powerful clarity.

(P = Pyscher; M = Mac)

P: How did you do in school?

M: Well, kindergarten, it was kind of good, kind of bad. My years . . . My
school years have been bad. Kindergarten, then I did a lot in kindergarten.

P: What do you mean? OK, when you were in elementary school did you
get in trouble?

M: Yes.

P: Why did you get in trouble? Tell me about that.

M: When I was in kindergarten, I got in trouble one time or several, I
didn't know why. I was whooped at school. For the first time I got
paddled in kindergarten. Well in first grade because I was walking
around. I took my socks off. I was a bad kid. Uhm . . . I took my shoes off
and then I started running around the rug at reading time, but my teacher
earlier didn't say nothing so I thought it was OK. But then my principal
came in. She was like, "Call her mom please." Then she told my grandma
that I was . . . No, she told my grandma that I was being bad or whatev-

er . . . Or my foster . . . you know, Miss Loretta. That's her name. So her . . . that she was gonna give me a whooping so she had to paddle me and stuff like that.

P: Wow, the school paddled you?

M: Mm-hm.

P: With what?

M: A paddle!

P: How many times did they paddle you?

M: Two.

P: . . . Did you get in trouble again?

M: Mm-mm. (smiling). I been good ever since then (laughing). I try not to get in trouble (sarcastic voice).

P: Since the paddle?

M: 'Cause it hurted (grinning and smiling).

P: Keep it real (smiling back). So how about in other grades? How did you do in other grades?

M: *I got in trouble, but I really didn't get caught.*

P: Ah! (laughing). Tell me about that! What do you mean?

M: Uhm, I, like, I would take a long time . . . I was *stalling* back in the years.

P: . . . Stalling? What does that look like? What does that mean?

M: Stalling like taking a long time.

P: Yeah, but tell me what it looks like.

M: OK so, I, like . . . we have these cubbies and stuff like that. And we supposed to put our stuff away and then I took too long because I didn't want to do the lesson or whatever. And so I just took a long time and I got in trouble.

As a common occurrence, resistive acts like stalling, or what Mac refers to as "getting into trouble, but not really getting caught," permeate Mac's memories of school. The double meaning in Mac's response highlights the agentic aspects of resistance through her hidden transcripts or low forms of resistance. Mac maintains her own desires and narratives while educators are led to believe the resistant act is the problem. This sleight of hand exposes the superficial ways in which teachers and administrators often deal with HDV youth and youth from racialized violence, avoiding the real issues underlying the resistant acts, namely, experiences of social violation.

Fast-forwarding to Mac's fifth-grade experiences, similar examples of her resistive acts emerge. Makita retold these stories. During Mac's fourth- and fifth-grade years, Makita, who served as Mac's primary caregiver, struggled on a daily basis with Mac's elementary school's administrative disciplinary responses to Mac's "troubling" behavioral issues with school staff. The school would report Mac's problematic behavior through daily phone calls that created deep anxiety for Makita. Importantly, Makita did not place her frustrations on Mac and her "disciplinary" problems, but rather she pointed the responsibility directly at the school's administration, questioning why the school was so intent on controlling even the simplest of Mac's actions.

In the following interview excerpt with Makita, it is evident that Mac's resistive actions in response to what felt like social violation continued throughout her elementary school years.

(M = Makita; P = Pyscher).

P: Can you describe what you think most influenced Mac's experience in school and outside of school?

M: She has her church activities. But her basketball, her love for basketball cause she wants one day be big celebrity basketball player and at school, Mac became a different person.

P: What school was that? . . .

M: UA school [a pseudonym] and it's kind of like a school for troubled people. And she was not troubled, but she was there at that school. They would ask her questions she wouldn't have the answers, she wouldn't . . . Very miserable. She was, I didn't know she was so miserable. She go to school, but and she'd make good grades, but it was just not something she wanted to do.

P: How was it so different?

M: Because everything, if she took a deep breath, somebody'd call me. If she went down the hall and stayed too long, somebody . . . I couldn't go to the grocery store. I couldn't go nowhere. I couldn't do anything. I had to work.

P: What would they say to you when they called about Mac's behavior?

M: "Grandmother, Miss B., Mac is sitting outside of the class. She was asked to go back to class, but she continued to sit there." And I'd say, "Well, do you want me to come up?" "No, we want you to know." Then they'd call me another day, "Mac's not eating her lunch; she threw it in the garbage and I just want you to know." Mac did this and Mac did that and they said Mac was bounced back on the doors and just everything. I could not go, I kid you not, I couldn't go anywhere. I couldn't go to the grocery store. I couldn't go nowhere. When I went in, when I came back and looked at the caller i.d. and see if I had a call from them. It just got worse. It just got worse.

P: Did she get suspended?

M: Mm-mm. They would talk to me, but you know, they [administration] would say, "Grandma, I feel so bad for you cause here we gotta tell you about Mac today, and I feel so sad for you." And everything, you know. It was just the little things. God, if I'm gonna be upset about something, let me be upset about something major, not just something minor. So you know.

P: Why do you think that they were doing that? So they were almost like just wanting to watch her . . .

M: I think they were so used to focus on children with behavior problems, they couldn't actually see Mac for what she was.

Again, it was clear that this was the typical, almost daily experience for Mac and Makita as they both navigated these tension-filled interactions with school staff. Pyscher asked directly how Mac talked to her about these daily occurrences once she returned home from school. Makita's response was telling, for it drew out how Mac refused to perform social pretense that she culturally read as violating when interacting with school staff.

P: It sounds like she was in trouble like every day.

M: Yes, just about. Just about.

P: And what would Mac say about it? When she would get home?

M: She would get home and she would just be defeated and I would just say, "Why? Why did you not answer the teacher? Why did you not raise your hand? Why did you not answer to the roll?!" [Mac response] "But Mama, she saw me sittin' there." That is no answer. OK, so then they called me to tell me, "She not participating in roll. She won't raise her hand in roll." I talked to her and we practiced and I said, "You know these answers, raise your hand." Then she's taking too much control. She's not letting other children answer, but she answering and not giving the rest of them the chance to answer.

P: They called you about that?

M: Mm-hm. And then they'd call me about when it's time for her evaluation, I got told then.

P: What do you mean for her evaluation?

M: You know, when it's time for parent-teacher conferences.

P: Oh, yeah. Hm. Do you remember anything else Mac would tell you why she just would be . . . would you call it a resistance? Is that fair? Was she kind of resisting them?

M: She just, she didn't want to be there and she didn't want, she didn't speak out and say, "I don't want to be here." She went every day because it's a routine. You go to school.

P: Right. Yeah, Mac has talked to me in a similar way you're talking about it. Is that she would just, when they would write her up a referral for her behavior, she would take it and let it drop and watch them. Cause she said, "They didn't care about me."

M: It was, I don't know. She just, I'm telling you, if you had known her then, you would not think this is the same Mac.

HDV youth, like Mac, navigate and perform their historical and HDV identities in response to what we read as violating and violent conditions in school experiences, and yet, they are labeled, at best, "troubled" children and youth. What meaning might be held if educators started to consider what Mac's refusal to raise her hand was illuminating or what her slowed and stalled walk represented related to what are read by Mac as socially violating experiences? Unforgiving normative and hegemonic presence on the part of educators can create scenarios for HDV children and youth like Mac to perform cultural meanings while also creating conditions for resistive identities to emerge. This may be a difficult notion for educators to understand, especially if their childhood cultures and thus identities were not forged out of childhood domestic violence and/or historical trauma.

For children and youth with histories of domestic violence and racialized trauma, these moments of violation may come to feel like impossible scenarios of negotiation forcing ruptures between the hidden and public transcripts (Scott, 1990) or what we have referred to as resistive ambivalence (Pyscher, in press, 2015b; Pyscher and Lozenski, 2014). For Mac, there was not a single liberating option outside of her tactics of resistance. Her every action felt (and was) scrutinized, and in necessary response, her resistively ambivalent tactics included refusing to reenter the classroom and refusing to interact in pretense like raising her hand. What more do we expect from HDV children and historically traumatized youth who know how to read social violence in nuanced ways and respond accordingly?

It became clear that the constructed identities of resistance were central to Mac's navigation of violating interactions in school. At times, the ruptures—resistive ambivalence—become necessary for her. It was also clear that the resistive identities that Mac performed emerged out of her cultural repertoires of practice (Gutierrez and Rogoff, 2003). These repertoires are developed as children interact individually and communally with their social worlds. In order to understand a child's repertoires, one must know their individual and community history. Pyscher (2015a, 2015b) suggested that HDV youth have developed their own low and high forms of liberatory-resistive repertoires of practice that have proven successful for them in handling socially violating experiences.

For Mac, her language and actions were often "misread" as deficit rather than as strategic and/or liberatory by educators who fell back on problematic deficit narratives of "troubled youth" when tensions arose. Liberation for HDV youth like Mac then becomes a necessity. It is difficult to disrupt the ideologies shaping educators' practices during these tension-filled interactions. These ideologies are promoted on a micro level through educators' own schooling biographies that do not typically include HDV or racialized trauma, teacher education programs based in developmental psychology that maintain rigidity in how youth are constructed, and their initiation into the teaching field with little power to change the mechanisms for discipline and dealing with resistance (Britzman, 2003; Pyscher, 2015a, 2015b). On a macro level, these ideologies remain tied to historical colonial relationships based in eugenicist sciences of measurement and paternalistic Enlightenment thinking embedded into the market-based constructs that continue to dictate the purpose of schools.

MAC'S TRAJECTORY: CONCLUDING THOUGHTS

At the time of this writing Mac is in high school. We do not know where her path will lead. Perhaps—and it is our sincere hope—she will be able to maneuver her way to a diploma and beyond. One may ask why we chose to focus on Mac and Makita's story not knowing if Mac will be caught in the school-to-prison pipeline. The reality is that Mac is already in the pipeline. Whether or not incarceration is inevitable for her is beside the point. Our purpose in using Mac's story is to demonstrate that if she, or the numerous youth like her, were to become entangled in the criminal justice system it would already be rationalized as acceptable due to the discursive constructions of who she was projected to be. It would not be a far cry for Makita to receive a call from the precinct rather than the school office "just to let her know." Mac's schools were positioning Makita as well as the rest of us to rationalize Mac's "deficiencies" in preparation for further consequences. Makita, like many black parents, refused to accept this problematic construction of her child and tried to help Mac cope despite living in unacceptable conditions of poverty.

However, Mac's discursive construction as a "throwaway" is not without interruption. As Pyscher's (2015a) larger study shows, eventually Mac and Makita came into contact with a schooling environment (middle school) that positioned her differently, was able to see her resistive acts as desire-based, and supported her—though not perfectly—in ways that positively impacted her path. It is important to highlight this disruption because it demonstrates that schools are not incapable of seeing through and reimagining how youth are positioned. Our worry is that schools overwhelmingly lack the political will to reject the labeling practices that reify the predictability of the social hierarchy and mask ineffective pedagogy and superficial constructions of youth coming from difficult circumstances. Instead of viewing Mac and all of the other "Macs" in their entirety, teachers are asked to refer to simplistic tools for diagnosis such as the Positive Behavioral Interventions and Supports (PBIS) website, and other similar protocols, where they can enter in "symptoms" like Web MD and receive quick solutions of how to either "fix" Mac or further diagnose her deficiencies. This technical approach to behavior management aligns with the medicalization of "pathology" that labels youth as disordered "emotionally" and "behaviorally," ignoring the deeper meaning of the low and high levels of resistance that youth perform when confronted by threatening structures and pedagogies (Pyscher, 2015a, 2015b; Pyscher and Lozenski, 2014).

Mac's sophisticated proclamation that "she got in trouble, but didn't get caught" highlights the agency in her performance. It shows that she recognizes the farce, the hegemony, and the inadequacies of schooling. Her choice to "break the tools" should be understood as a desire for liberation rather than a symptom of brokenness. To know that you will get in trouble for your actions, but that the underlying reason for your resistance lies tucked away in the confines of your inner conscience is liberating. It is something like Malcolm X's (1992) suggestion that he was never freer than when he was in prison because he knew they could not touch his mind (Malcolm X). These are the victories of those who are "thrown away." We do not want to romanticize these acts, because as Willis (1977), Tuck and Yang (2012), and other resistance theorists have documented, they are "penetrations" into oppressive structures, yet the social and economic position of the resistors is often reified by these very acts. If schools truly decide to become spaces of learning, development, and self-reflection for all youth, then they must begin by looking inward and not pathologizing youth. Duncan-Andrade (2007) highlights this "Socratic sensibility" or form of self-reflection and critique as a necessity for educators who are willing to "ride or die" with their students. Drawing from West (2001), he writes, "West describes the person with this sensibility as someone that understands both Socrates's statement that "the unexamined life is not worth living" (Plato, 1966, p. 38a) and Malcolm X's statement that the "examined life is painful" (West, 2001) (p. 632). Schools and the educators who constitute them may feel that self-examination is too painful because they may not like what they see. But youth like Mac represent the mirror that schools often refuse to look at for more than a quick moment.

In her (2015) keynote address to the Literacy Research Association, Gloria Ladson-Billings argued that an overlooked tenet of culturally relevant pedagogy is that educators must have a disproportionate focus on youth with the most tenuous life circumstances. HDV youth and youth who contend with lived and historical racialized violence are among this group. Rather than continue to construct a matrix of brokenness around these youth, we suggest educators take up a reparative stance. Ladson-Billings is arguing for schools to become sites for reparations. This means not being afraid to push forth practices and policies that disproportionately benefit those who have been most harmed by society. We continue to ask educators to think about and move to enact practices that will disproportionately benefit youth like Mac, and refuse to allow more constructions of "throwaway youth."

Chapter Five

Lyrical Interventions

Hip Hop, Counseling Education, and School-to-Prison

Arash Daneshzadeh and Ahmad Washington

In Lewis Carroll's famous children's story, *Through the Looking-Glass* (1871), a demure Alice is found encroaching in the despotic Queen's coveted and palatial lair, a space only reserved for royalty. At the first glance of Alice, the Queen placates an incensed King by advising that he make an acute memorandum, chronicling every detail of Alice's unlawful entry, to ensure that it never recurs. Despite being written well over a century ago, this story provides an important and timely parable about the role of hyper-surveillance in today's schools. The selective triage and caustic treatment of youth was not exclusive to the eighteenth century. Neither is the need to monitor every move students make, especially youth from communities of color, whose presence in the classroom is appraised as an existential threat.

The contradiction, of punishing students for daring to quest into spaces of inquiry and socially sanctioned adulthood, flies directly against the pillar of "educated hope" (Giroux, 2011, p. 120). According to Giroux, schools are designed to magnify hope, described as promise for a better future. This promise is predicated upon the critical pedagogy that equips students for changing their social conditions. As the Greek-French philosopher Cornelius Castoriadis reiterates, schools are community hubs that should educate students "in every aspect (of leadership and politics) in order to be able to participate" (Giroux, p. 24) in creating an image of society that mirrors their backgrounds, knowledge, and ambitions. In the field of education, disrupting the status quo is quelled by a compulsory school system in which measurements of academic performance, hyper-surveillance of student behavior, and draconian discipline policies reveal the institution's greatest fear: A self-defining contingency of Black students. Bell (1992) insists that despite the grave costs of retribution, once a student, "determined to resist her oppression, she [is] triumphant" (p. 90). As scholar-activists tackle an academic apparatus whose dysfunctional projections of White-racial framing (Feagin, 2013) and anti-Blackness (Rios, 2011) create an "othered" category of unwanted and exploited students, they must remember that critical storytelling is vanguard to changing a narrative from criminality to self-definition. The modern poet Tupac Shakur captures this need for insurgent storytelling in *Holler if Ya Hear Me* (1993). Shakur makes a clarion call for the collective wisdom of community members to synthesize a pedagogy of resistance, one that interrogates the warrants for criminalized Blackness. He states, *And now I'm like a major threat/Cause I remind you of the things/You were made to forget*, describing the role of counter-narratives as central to reframing the constructs of criminality in the classroom.

RE-HUMANIZATION OF LEARNING COMMUNITIES

Now fast-forward to our schools today. Donzel's eyes struggled to make direct contact with the unflinching stares of the entire school faculty. He found himself at the nucleus of the circle that kept him closed in, ten to fifteen paces away from the door at which he intermittently glanced with waning familiarity. His teachers' piercing gazes matched only in static glow by the white, chilled tiles during one rainy November first period in a vacant classroom of John O'Connell High School.

The high school was located in an economically embattled community called The Mission of San Francisco. This geopolitical enclave has long been romanticized for its family-owned vendors, murals of socialist and artistic luminaries, and pedigree of diasporic Afro-Latino traditions—it now faces an active insurgency that has shifted the balance from public trust and social compacts, by hyper-commerce demarcated by Google buses, three-thousand dollar studio apartments, and Whole Foods.

The insecurity across Donzel's face was emblematic of the six other students who were subjugated to the "Hot Seat"—a newfangled incarnation of shaming students who were identified as "at risk" based on burgeoning truancy, behavior referrals, and academic struggles. The idea was simple: a) identify a student who was labeled "at risk" of failing an academic term; b) provide them with the choice of either suspension or intervention; c) invite faculty to sit in a circle, surrounding the student and take turns lambasting the student's academic and interpersonal performance into submission. The principal was a former dean at a continuation school for incarcerated juveniles, and this was his first year serving this particular population of students. Shame replaced safety as the persisting dream of opportunity is removed for students, particularly black students in this version of restorative justice that renders students in great need of "restoration." However, the myopic focus is on reducing what's considered a disorder fraught with terminology steeped in misbehavior and impertinence among students of color, commonly referred to as Oppositional Defiance Disorder (Burke, Loeber, and Birmaher, 2002). In response to the pathologization of students, coupled with fears of student safety, schools have adopted extreme measures to prevent tragedies like the Columbine High School massacre of 1999. What is revealed is a parallel between the Safe Schools Act of 1999 and implementation of zero-tolerance policies that operate under a racially neutral auspice. Unfortunately, despite the dramatic decrease in violent offenses by students in recent years (Smith and Harper, 2015), the hiring of school resource officers and sum-zero policies that trigger exclusionary responses to perceived "threats," have turned campuses into supplemental law enforcement agencies. In Texas, 23 percent of students who were subjected to even one suspension during their high school tenure were later involved in the juvenile justice system (Carmichael, Booth, and Patnaik, 2010). This makes discipline far more consequential for public schools that serve a large number of Black youth whose cultural knowledge and experiences are untapped.

According to the Equity Project of Indiana University (Skiba, Shure, and Williams, 2011) students are suspended for non-safety concerns that are subjective in nature. Of particular concern is the over-representation of Black students in school arrests despite comprising less than 10 percent of our overall K–12 populace (Theriot, 2010). As a way of counteracting the forces that inched Donzel closer to the precipice of expulsion, the principal inculcated a mode of pedagogy meant to "teach" the student how to behave through a public brand of discipline that resembled a firing squad. As recently as 2013, in San Francisco, California, Black and Latino students constituted merely 23 percent of the public K–12 school population, yet accounted for 77 percent of all students in regional public schools.

This is especially disturbing in a city long hailed as a bastion of progressivism. These statistics underpin a growing flux of students being hauled from classrooms, missing critical opportunities for academic development. Noguera (2008) indicated these data were an early hallmark of the school-to-prison "pipeline." The name suggests linearity and a positivist rationale that Black males are disciplined disproportionately and thus find themselves in juvenile prison. This fails to account for the marginalization faced by a largely forgotten population of young women of color. Black and Latina girls represent the fastest growing subcategory of over-disciplined students in the American schools. Citing research from the Department of Education for the 2011–2012 academic school year, the African American Policy Forum of Columbia Law School found Black girls are six times as likely to be subjected to "exclusionary" suspension practices than their White counterparts. These practices mandate time out of school where students receive no direct educational service. By comparison, Black males are suspended three times as often as their White male counterparts. Perhaps not surprisingly, the surge in exclusionary discipline has operated in lockstep with a justice system that has experienced a dramatic increase in its numbers of incarcerated women.

The Bureau of Justice Statistics reported in 2011 that the number of Black women incarcerated between 1980 and 2010 jumped 646 percent. This displacement of Black girls from schools, through adulthood, is exacerbated by cultural "deficit" framing (Museus and Jayakumar, 2012) that perceives Black students' families as disinterested in the educational process, thereby justifying harsh penalties for behaviors routinely defined as "willful defiance." Deficit frameworks of children of color are inculcated in criminogenic terms schools use to justify punishments. Hyper-policed schools and student surveillance has a stultifying effect on the long-term academic prospects for youth, particularly those who garner suspension and criminal records as a result of minor infractions. For example, when swiping headphones is classified as "grand larceny," and a playful shoving match between peers is recorded as "assault and battery," students are more likely to garner police records (Skiba, Michael, Nardo, and Peterson, 2002). These findings indicate a common narrative—that Black and Brown youth are more harshly punished for subjective offenses. Willful defiance makes up 48 percent of the 710,000 suspensions in California during the 2011–2012 academic year (Lewin, 2012). We must examine the cost of violating rules whose bedrock is grounded in racialized segregation and Eurocentric normativity.

Many schools and juvenile halls have doubled down on their retributive and exclusionary modes of discipline. The TV show *Scared Straight* popularized the get-tough method of shaming "delinquents" into submission so that they are readied for mainstream education systems. The basic premise of this show is to deter juvenile offenders by interfacing them with adult prisoners. The assumption is that by introducing them to the adult world of incarceration, youth will not reoffend. However, research strongly suggests these scared straight interventions have unintended and deleterious consequences on the psychosocial growth of students (Lilienfield, Lynn, Ruscio, and Beyerstein, 2010). Stressors associated with discipline have shown to impact learning and cognitive function. A 2005 meta-analysis of these programs showed that shaming interventions could exacerbate student academic disengagement (Lilienfield, 2005). Disengagement cropped by *Scared Straight* tactics also includes a substantial increase of juvenile recidivism (Aos, Phillips, Barnoski, and Lieb, 2001).

Scholars are now referring to this phenomena as the school-to-prison "nexus" to account for the intersections of issues that parlay into draconian outcomes (Krueger-Henney, 2013). This attack on youth has manifested into a relentless string of exclusionary suspensions and expulsions that reveal a heavy slant against students of color. This sum-zero policy that pits students in direct opposition to the schools that purport to serve the best interest of youth has recalibrated education with criminalization. For example, in April of 2015, two Black girls attending the Milwaukee High School for the Arts were suspended for reciting a poem about police brutality in their community and recording the performance in the school's cafeteria. In 2014, a twelve-year-old girl in a Georgian middle school was booked on criminal charges and faced expulsion after writing "hi" on a locker-room wall. One-year prior, another 12-year-old Black girl faced expulsion at a private middle school in Florida, unless she altered the look of her natural hair (Crenshaw, Ocen, and Nanda, 2015). These are merely three examples of a barrage of reframing youth, especially Black girls, as in need of behavior modification. Unfortunately, there is very little dialogue around changing the parameters of criminality as it pertains to the intersection of race and gender. While there is an ongoing, public discussion to transmogrify the burgeoning issue of student misbehavior as a "discipline gap," much of the response from schools centers upon the personal responsibility of students (Losen, Hodson, Keith, Morrison, and Belway, 2015). This is a failure to stretch analysis of punishment on a continuum of sociopolitical influence. Bronfenbrenner (1992) insists that academic institutions assess any problem through a panoramic lens. This lens expands from the microsystem that blames individual students for disproportionate discipline rates, communities, and families, to the macrosystem of school policy, cultural values, and the vast political landscape. Adams (1995) calls this form of cultural repression "education for extinction." This education has systemically removed students of color over generations, ever since the first Indian Boarding School punished indigenous students for speaking in their native tongues. White academic imperialism has continually reconfigured itself to maintain distance from Blackness. The fissures between what schools are and what they purport to be are grounded in resistance that upholds the social promotion of hierarchy in lieu of resistance that undercuts the convenient perch from which hegemony operates.

PROBLEMATIZING YOUTH/FRAMING THE PANDEMIC

For 2016–2017, California has budgeted 4.4 billion dollars into reentry programs, incarceration coffers, and prevention interventions to support youth offenders. But force-feeding money into a youth-control machine without examining the merits of its structure, fails to recognize the school-to-prison "nexus" as part of a larger educational gap between teachers and students. Part of the solution to school-to-prison must be to reframe students as sole proprietors of the problem.

While it is important to be diligent in critiquing how teachers and administrators, as purveyors of schools' institutional culture, are complicit with educational structures, we must not ignore how other educational leaders, like school counselors, also contribute to the removal of large numbers of culturally different students through the school-to-prison pipeline. This is a consideration because school counselors are ideally positioned to deliver empathetic therapeutic alternatives to suspensions and expulsions. If more school counselors are to serve students in this capacity, they must first un-pack how they have been socialized to perceive themselves, oriented to their roles in schools, and, most importantly, their relationship to the culturally diverse students most often ensnared by the school-to-prison pipeline.

In many ways, the school counseling profession operates in accordance with the tenets of traditional functionalism. Functionalism posits that social institutions play an invaluable role in helping societies operate at optimum efficiency by imbuing members of the citizenry with essential beliefs, values, and competencies. From this perspective, schools not only mechanistically teach students, they also imbue dispositions and character traits (i.e., respect for authority, punctuality, etc.) that are indispensable in society and the workplace (McMahon, Mason, Daluga-Guenther, and Ruiz, 2014). Because functionalism theorizes that institutions act in the best interest of the entire social organism, schools can ill afford to be anything other than paragons of objectivity in regard to teaching and evaluating students. The ways schools "do business"; meaning how they teach and socialize students, is conceptual-ized as being in everyone's best interests.

With increasing regularity within the school counseling discourse, schools are being theorized as sites of contestation between teachers, admin-istrators, and school counselors who attempt, often unconsciously, to impose the dominant cultural worldview on culturally different students who experi-ence oppression and marginalization (Hipolito-Delgado and Lee, 2007; Mitcham-Smith, 2007). Critical discourses like these within the school coun-seling literature demand that school counseling students be challenged to use interrogative deductive reasoning to make plausible connections between the ideological and economic interests of the dominant class and disparities in suspensions and expulsions between racially and ethnically diverse students and their White classmates. The predominant tendency has been to frame educational and behavioral differences between white and racial minority students through deficit-lenses that construe the struggles of individual stu-dents or entire communities as self-inflicted. It is implied that if racial and ethnic minority students, and students for poor and working-class commu-nities were less impulsive, delayed gratification, or exhibited more resilience or grit, their educational and behavioral difficulties would disappear (Parikh, Post, and Flowers, 2011).

According to Giroux (1981) uncritical and ahistorical explanations for academic successes and failures such as these rely on and reproduce "a form of tunnel vision in which only a small segment of social reality is open to examination" (p. 46). Giroux continues: "More importantly, it [tunnel vision] leaves unquestioned those economic, political, and social structures that shape our lives. Divorced from history, these structures appear to have acquired their present character naturally, rather than having been constructed by historically specific interests" (p. 46). In other words, more consistent critical discourses around education equip school counseling students with an orientation to parse the school-to-prison pipeline in radical and transformative ways.

School counseling programs are expected to design curricula that empower school counseling students to act as social justice advocates that combat systemic oppression (Bemak and Chung, 2005; Dixon, Tucker, Clark, 2010). Although national school counseling accreditation standards (e.g., CACREP, 2016) encompass language about school counselors needing to eliminate barriers that block student success, more can be done to teach social justice competencies to school counseling students (Evans, Zambrano, Cook, Moyer and Duffey, 2011). To this point Holcomb-McCoy (2004) suggested a major shortcoming is the fact school counselor education does not "take on a more interdisciplinary approach" (p. 181). For Holcomb-McCoy, this interdisciplinary approach would include forays into cultural and ethnic studies so school counseling students could receive a richer understanding of the historical and contemporary examples of oppression students have encountered.

The primary impetus for a more radical social justice approach to school counseling is the realization reform strategies have been largely ineffective at ameliorating the school-to-prison pipeline and other educational inequalities racial and ethnic minority students experience (Griffin and Steen, 2011). Griffin and Steen (2011) write:

> If our educational system intends to fulfill its commitment to serving all students, especially on the fringes of society, and intends to live up to its promise of providing vital avenues to access and opportunity, school counselors, in conjunction with other important school stakeholders, must use their unique educational backgrounds and strategic position in schools to make meaningful change in their schools. (p. 75)

The fact the school-to-prison pipeline exists as just one facet in a matrix of barriers obstructing the path to educational equality for scores of racially, ethnically, culturally, and linguistically diverse students (Ratts, Dekruyf, and Chen-Hayes, 2007) necessitates a social justice school counseling approach that examines how schools reproduce the existing social order (Bemak and Chung, 2005). School counselors who evade this mandate function "as gatekeepers of the status quo . . . sorters and selectors rather than advocates" and "dream-breakers" rather than "dream-makers and dream-keepers" to large numbers of children in schools" (House and Martin, 1998, p. 286).

This urgency is reflected throughout the school counseling profession (Trusty and Brown, 2005). The American School Counselor Association (ASCA, 2012) expects school counselors to adhere to the principles of social justice, and develop counseling and social advocacy skills that catalyze educational equity and create more egalitarian schools. This more active engagement with students by school counselors reflects a distancing from the historical functioning of the profession (Bemak and Chung, 2005, 2008) and the recognition counselors "can no longer operate solely from the comfort of their offices if they wish to better serve their constituencies" (Ratts and Hutchins, 2009, p. 269). With social justice serving as a guiding framework, school counselors can discern how the purportedly race neutral ideologies, policies, and practices that insulate the school-to-prison pipeline are but the most recent iteration of nefariously oppressive sociopolitical and educational systems that have privileged White middle-class American culture while simultaneously marginalizing students from racially, ethnically, and culturally diverse backgrounds (Evans, Zambrano, Cook, Moyer and Duffey, 2011; Hipolito-Delgado and Lee, 2007; Nieto, 2004; Potts, 2003). Therefore, schools are not pristine bastions of meritocracy but rather institutions designed to surreptitiously reproduce a preexisting interlocking sociocultural, political, and economic system that reflects the interests of the dominant cultural group (Bowles and Gintis, 1976). Additionally, this means that for countless school counselors, the overwhelming majority being White middle-class women with limited personal, academic, and professional exposure to culturally different people (Erford, 2014), an important first step in becoming social justice advocates involves self-awareness and understanding (Astramovich and Harris, 2007; Griffin and Steen, 2011; Ratts, 2011). Through this reflexive practice, it is believed school counselors are more likely to stand in solidarity alongside marginalized students as they carve out spaces where culturally affirming counterhegemonic practices are fostered even if it means experiencing ostracism and alienation from professional colleagues (Bemak and Chung, 2008; Griffin and Steen, 2011).

The sociopolitical distance in curriculum and punishment must be bridged by interventions that center communication and the cultural wealth of student experiences. Yasso's six-part Cultural Wealth Model (2005) illustrates how schools can frame student experiences as assets to the learning process, rather than ontological threats to class management. However, it is important to note that very little is being done to address teacher and counselor education. Too often, students are placed in full custody of the discipline gap, and as a result, they are unable to offer counternarratives about unfair practices, policies, and stereotypes about their race, class, and gender. School discipline is rooted in a historical bedrock of cultural, physical, emotional, and social genocide. Until educators can openly interrogate these foundations, the school-to-prison pipeline will be framed in mythical language like meritocracy and personal responsibility over ugly truths like systemic racism and colonization.

SCHOOL SPACE AS CULTURAL SPACE

Hipolito-Delgado and Lee (2007) believe one the most effective strategies for engaging marginalized students in dialogue about empowerment was through "the art, culture, and history" of these groups (p. 330). Contemporarily, not only does it appear that for "many youth of today's generation, rap and hip-hop seem to be the music of choice" (Gonzalez and Hayes, 2009, p. 165), hip-hop culture can facilitate powerfully emotive and authentic discussions between disenfranchised youth and school counselors about how the school-to-prison pipeline infringes on life opportunities (Washington, 2015). Rideout, Roberts, and Foehr's (2005) research on the media consumption among eight- to eighteen year-olds indicates the salience of hip-hop culture in young people's lives:

> Rap/Hip Hop account for most of the adolescent music listening: on any given day 65 percent of junior and senior high school kids reporting [sic] listening— over twice the portion that listens to any other single type of music. . . . Although Rap/Hip Hop is the most popular genre among all three ethnic groups, African Americans are still significantly more likely than Whites or Hispanic kids to listen to it. Over three-quarters of African American kids report listening to Rap/Hip Hop (81 percent), vs. 60 percent of Whites and 70 percent of Hispanics. (p. 28–29)

Interestingly, school counselor educators and school counselors were some of the first to contemplate how integrating hip-hop culture might benefit racial and ethnic minority students (e.g., Lee and Lindsey, 1985; Lee, 1987; Lee and Simmons, 1988). Lee and Lindsey (1985) endorsed the use of rap music in group counseling with Black elementary school students because they believed rap music represented an authentic Black cultural expression that could help guidance counselors develop "an understanding and appreciation of Black culture, development of motivation to achieve, development of positive and responsible behavior, and modeling of positive Black images" (p. 229). Lee and Lindsey surmised school counselors could use the lyrics from "The Message" to:

> Develop a series of situations for group members to role play that involve problems of Black people, both in the school setting and in society at large. . . . Using these role plays, help the students develop strategies for dealing effectively with these problems. (p. 231)

"The Message" was also later recommended as a component in "a comprehensive life planning counseling model for assisting Black adolescents in setting career, educational, and marriage and family goals" (Lee and Simmons, 1988, p. 5). By using this song, Lee and his colleagues thought school counselors could create culturally relevant interventions to help Black children navigate critical developmental milestones through childhood and into adolescence.

We believe hip-hop culture can be mobilized with students as an analytical tool to examine how rampant mischaracterizations of culturally different students as disruptive and uninterested in learning legitimates policies which feed the school-to-prison pipeline.

Prioritizing punishment over mutually beneficial relationships between teachers and students fails to live up to the standards of democratic schooling, popularized by the landmark *Brown vs. Board of Education* (1954) decision. In 2015, a proposed bill (TX HB868) entitled the Teacher's Protection Act was put forth in Texas that would authorize teachers' use of lethal force in cases where they felt "threatened" by a student. As Black students are assessed in "cultural deficit" frameworks, implicit bias is strongly implicated as a determining factor of punishment. Consequentially, Black youth receive more suspensions for subjective violations in which teachers felt "threatened" for their safety, in contrast to their White peers, who are more likely to be suspended for concrete violations of school policies such as bringing weapons or drugs to campus.

The presumption that Black families lack structure or interest in educational opportunities combined with the assumption of Black youth as inherently violent creates a stereotype that propels implicit bias toward harsher punishment. This implicit bias is demonstrated as a contributing factor to the discipline gap that embodied by the school-to-prison nexus. In other words, racialized Blackness is othered. We define "otherness" as social distance that operates in a pretense of sociopolitical power. Moore (1993) describes the chasm of communication and cultural understanding between teachers and students in educational settings, as Transactional Distance. This margin is often perceived as indicative of students' cognitive dysfunction. Nonetheless, transactional distance between teachers and students is another explanation for the value systems that essentializes Black youth as disinterested or irritable. Lowered expectations of Black youth have been shown to create a contentious climate between teachers and students. One staggering example from 2003, found that students who displayed a "Black walking style" were perceived by "their teachers as lower in academic achievement, highly aggressive, and more in need of special education services" (Neal et al., 2003), which illustrates why teachers and students should be equal stakeholders in the teaching process who learn about one another's cultural and communication styles to dismantle barriers that reinforce structural bias.

In response to the cultural gaps between educators and students, some school districts have subscribed to ethnic studies curricula that teach historical literacy, cultural wealth, and oppression, centering students from historically dehumanized contexts (e.g., first-generation, indigenous, Black, Latino). Recently, San Francisco, California, decided to pilot mandatory "culturally-relevant" (Ladson-Billings, 1995) ethnic studies curricula across its entire school district. Ethnic studies was assessed by the Stanford Graduate School of Education for its academic benefits (Dee and Penner, 2016). Findings demonstrated gains in attendance and grade point average by "at-risk" students, but it is importance to note a key caveat of the program. That is, enrollment in ethnic studies was only required for students who had grade point average of 2.0 or below, and voluntary for those students with grade point averages above a 2.0. Despite tokenizing of cultural relevancy as a class best reserved for "at-risk" students, positive findings are consistent with the notion "that culturally relevant teaching, when implemented in a supportive, high-fidelity context, can provide effective support to at-risk students." It is important to reorient the epistemology of school discipline from individual student behavior to the cultural and sociopolitical distance between schools and youth.

Chapter Six

Crapitalism

Toward a Fantasyland in the Wal-Martization of America's Education and Criminal Justice System

Dari Green, Melinda Jackson, and Tifanie Pulley

America is currently faced with a national epidemic of selling education and prisons to private companies. These institutions have become "profit machines" run by multinational corporations which often resembles the Wal-Mart business model, placing more emphasis on profits than the lives that are wrapped in them. One of the major tenets, which drive this pipeline, is the rise in zero-tolerance policies. These policies often impose severe punishments, such as suspension and expulsion on students, for nonviolent offenses (Fasching-Varner, Mitchell, Martin, and Bennett-Haron, 2014). Most of these policies are enforced in inner city, majority minority communities. The Orleans Parish School Board located in New Orleans, for example, enforced zero-tolerance policies where 100 percent of students faced with expulsion were Black. Additionally, 67 percent of those faced with school-related arrests were Black students. In the transition from the public school system to the RSD-Algiers Charter School Association 100 percent of both those expelled and confronted with school-related arrests were Black pupils.

Many of these arrests ensue after law enforcement randomly drug test, have detection dogs sniff out substances in lockers, or search the student's person without cause. As a result, these students may not be afforded their right to due process. Additionally, once the juvenile offender enters the system, which is premised on rehabilitating youth, these students often find it increasingly difficult to reenter traditional educational institutions—many ending up with a criminal record instead of a high school diploma.

Nationally, students of color represent only 16 percent of the total youth population; however, they constitute 28 percent of all youth arrests. Of those, 58 percent of juveniles are admitted to adult prisons. African American youth are six times more likely to be incarcerated for the same offense committed by white youth with no prior charges (Kim, Losen, and Hewitt, 2010). As Bell (1992) notes, "racism is a permanent component of American life" (p. 13). We are living in a society where systemic patterns exist of referring students to law enforcement; these practices are indeed, intentional (Fasching-Varner et al., 2014). In other words, America's children are being socialized to adhere to America's tough on crime model (i.e., zero-tolerance policies and broken windows theory) within a K–12 educational system. The educational system in America cannot afford to be a microcosm of its prison system, which currently holds the largest prison population in the world (Bureau of Justice Statistics, 2013).

This chapter aims to fill an important gap in the school-to-prison pipeline research by examining the complex configuration of this "crapitalism" that exists in America society, which represents a system of "crap" that is controlled by privileged whites whose major focus is imprisonment and exploitation of labor. These systems or institutions are often controlled by private owners for profit based on a contractual agreement with a government agency, and oftentimes a third party. Crapitalism removes marginalized people from society while protecting white supremacy. We explore the challenges facing students of color in the education and prison system from a critical perspective. This chapter begins with an analysis of the Wal-martization of America's education and penal system to provide an overview of some of the aspects of the system.

THE WAL-MARTIZATION OF AMERICA'S SCHOOL SYSTEM

While the phrase "Wal-martization of education" may appear to be metaphorical, the Walton family has actually been one of the major supporters and a major source of private funding for charter-school alternatives to public schools. The Walton family is *the* largest private donor to Teach for America, which places many of its corps members in charter schools. The Walton family has subsidized one in four of every new charter school fueling a major growth in moving public school pupils to charter schools. As a result, taxpayers' dollars move to privately operated hands. The classroom, like Wal-Mart, is also intended to run more like a business.

Much like its business model, the Waltons may fail to consult the community where the charter school is entering, while driving out existing schools, and leaving the most vulnerable children and families behind. It is described by Dr. Lori Martin as a model with three features: 1) destroying any local competition for their enterprises, 2) controlling mass media, and 3) preventing any independent organization of their employees. The school system then gives more control to corporations, private hands receive more profit, and workers are given even lower pay. New Orleans has been a prime example of this, in that the public education system was starved of funding, overwhelmed with underperforming students, and ultimately overtaken by the Charter School Movement.

Still the media has until recently avoided serious analysis of treatment among students and fiscal mismanagement, only reporting those things that were favorable in the system. Last but not least, the charters resemble Wal-Mart in that CEOs are highly paid while teachers are not allowed to unionize and work under strict surveillance and heavy protocol. If this model, which has destroyed the lives of many of America's workers who identify as Wal-Mart employees, continues to multiply in the educational setting, this may eventually prove to be as disastrous for the students involved. Children of color are disproportionately affected by this crapitalism due to the education system's failure to meet both the educational and social needs of those most at risk. Furthermore, the commodification of education through the use of human capital by exploiting children of color is pedagogical suicide. For example, both academically and systematically, charter schools comparatively have more resources, but have not shown a significant difference in academic performance than public schools (Russakoff, 2015). If the ideology is the same, then the same problems exist but at a different location. Children of color don't change their ascribed statuses because the school has undergone a name change and acquired more teachers. The public school systems that are heavily populated by Black and Brown youth are not transformed due to a transference of bodies under the direction and guidance of leaders that view their pupils as "problems" that need to be fixed. In other words, these students are often seen as those "in need" based on a deficit narrative often interwoven in the public school narrative. The education reform industry seeks to implement a transformative model for "underperforming" public schools across the United States (Russakoff, 2015). The dismantling of public schools is generating a narrative that further exacerbates race and class debates in terms of social inequality as crapitalism highlights the thorny existence of charter schools or private education over public school education.

THE WAL-MARTIZATION OF AMERICA'S PENAL SYSTEM

What is the purpose of prisons, to rehabilitate inmates or to exploit prison labor (Smith and Hattery 2007)? Though outlawed in the twentieth century, private corporations are once again claiming ownership of prisons. States have turned to private investment or venture capital to run or build new prisons for profit, as voters refused to use state funds to uphold mass incarceration. The term "prison industrial complex" is used to describe a network of individuals, organizations, and social institutions involved with the incarceration of millions of Americans. The individuals, organizations, and social institutions involved in the prison industrial complex include law enforcement officials, courts, and correctional facilities, but also include under-resourced schools, private corporations, and state and local governments. The prison industrial complex is a multi-billion-dollar industry that often harms instead of helps efforts to protect individual rights and maintain public safety and preserve order.

In this chapter we focus our attention on one central component within this system, the school-to-prison pipeline. The school-to-prison pipeline is a theory, which suggests that children (who happen to be disproportionately minority and/or disabled youth) are being pushed out of the school system and into the criminal justice system. This all happens as a result of zero-tolerance policies and the overuse of police officers in schools. This pipeline is only a small part of a complex system, however.

Over 2.4 million American people work, eat and sleep behind bars, a 500 percent increase in population over the past three decades (Alexander, 2012). Inmates, 60 percent of whom identify as men of Color, are highly susceptible to exploitable labor, which many corporations profit from (Alexander, 2012). These men are not only excluded from politics, but due to the fact that they are laboring on farms and in assemblies for very low wages, crapitalism continues to fuel the system. There is a cycle of building for-profit prisons that fail to rehabilitate inmates and provide cheap labor to corporations. The more prisons that crop up, the more people they need to incarcerate.

Juvenile justice and detention centers are not exempt in this web of networks. The exclusionary disciplinary policies that remove students from the school environment increase the likelihood of youth coming into contact with the criminal justice system. Suspensions and expulsions have high correlations not only in regard to juvenile systems, but also high correlations with dropout rates (Nelson and Lind, 2015). After a child drops out from school the likelihood of them being incarcerated increases eight times that of a child that is able to receive a high school diploma. Additionally, youths who become involved with the court increase their likelihood of future interaction with the criminal justice system. In communities of deep social and economic inequities, students who have early contact with the police sets them on a path of alienation, suspension, expulsion, and arrest (Nelson and Lind, 2015).

Prisons not only aim to detain, penalize, and correct behaviors that society considers unlawful but they also create a pedagogical tactic of misconduct and punishment. Such tactics serve as a guide which informs educators' pedagogical decision-making processes in settings with underrepresented populations, which we know are incarcerated at a highly disproportionate rate (Blumstein, 1982, 1988, 1993; Frase, 2009; Garland, Sphon, Wodahl, 2008). In the southern part of the United States, teachers of students of color residing in poor urban settings, spend a great deal of their instructional time applying these arbitrary behavioral expectations, and harshly penalizing children who do not follow their instructions; thus, controlling bodies while sedating young thinkers (Foucault, 1977; Robinson, 2001).

COUNTER-STORY: ABD

ABD, or Adolescent Behavioral Disorder, is an epidemic plaguing the nation's youth. A staggering 50 million of America's adolescents between the ages of ten and nineteen have been diagnosed with this condition. These youths display behaviors such as speaking loudly, rejecting parental and other forms of authority, preferring to walk or talk instead of sit at a desk for eight hours without dialogue, and lacking control of impulses—especially after eating chemically laden foods. These children refuse to walk in straight lines; they struggle with keeping their hands behind their backs, and cannot sit quietly during meals. Children who are "treated" for ABD are much less likely to display such radical behaviors.

Let's take the example of Tyrone, a sixteen-year-old Black male who suffered from the ABD and as a result came into contact with the criminal justice system. Tyrone's first-grade teacher sat down with his mother over a decade earlier with him in the midst expressing concerns about his mental capacity and normalcy. The teacher, Ms. Sally said: "Tyrone is disruptive in class, and though he completes assignments in the allotted amount of time, he is often overzealous and asks too many questions. He refuses to stay seated and often talks during class, I'm beginning to think that a traditional school setting may not be the best learning environment for your child."

Tyrone's mother walked away feeling hopeless, knowing that she had exhausted every option that she'd known. She has scolded, beaten, taken all strict control of his diet allowing no sugars, none of the "Southhampton Six" and no more than two hours of electronics a day. No matter what, however, his mother knew that as an only child, Tyrone became overly excited when he came into contact with children his age. Up until middle school, Tyrone had been able to make passing grades, but his behavior was always questionable. Constantly labeled and branded from the second grade, by middle school Tyrone began to feel hopeless and internalize all of the things that each of his teacher's had told him over the years. His memory replayed: "You'll never amount to anything." "Were you a crack baby?"; "Does your father live at home?"; "You should get more beatings, that'd solve this problem."

Tyrone started to self-medicate at the age of twelve. His cousin told him that marijuana could help him to focus and "chill." His mother had never explored other medicinal options, as she thought the problem to be unique to her child, so to change his reputation as he moved into middle school he went to desperate measures. Each morning before his mother would wake, Tyrone would smoke and spray, ready for his day. During lunch one day, his eighth grade year, he was called over the intercom because dogs had sniffed out his locker. Tyrone was devastated as he was only trying to make his situation better. Tyrone was expelled from school and taken to the police station where his mother was to pick him up. Encountering this system was intended to scare him straight.

Tyrone had to finish the school year out in an alternative school setting and could no longer self-medicate due to regular drug testing. The alternative school suggested that his mother have Tyrone tested for ABD, as most of the students in their facility suffered from the problem. After testing positive for the disorder, Tyrone's mom felt a sense of relief as the diagnosis helped her to know that neither she nor her child was the problem, rather it was a disorder that the universe had prescribed to not only her child but millions of others. After taking the medication, Tyrone would complain to his mother about the way that it made him feel. He often described feeling zombie-like and asked not to take it. His mother insisted that it was the best way to go. Tyrone failed the year at the alternative school, feeling that there was no instruction taking place and that "his brain was not present."

Tyrone's mother transferred him to the local high school the following year. He was now sixteen and decided to no longer follow his mother's strict rules. He did not take his medicine; he ate things not conducive to his mother's diet plan, and spoke out of turn in the classroom. One day after interrupting the lesson, the teacher asked him to leave the classroom. Tyrone refused and remained seated quietly. Instead of moving on in the lesson, however, the teacher called in Officer Stern. Mr. Stern asked Tyrone to move out of the seat, to which Tyrone stated he'd behave. Mr. Stern proceeded to tackle Tyrone to the floor. As Tyrone tried to get up the officer insisted he had resisted arrest. Only Tyrone was never told he was under arrest, he was never read his rights, and never a right of due process. He felt no hope and upon release, decided that school was not the place for him. His fate was now in his hands.

FANTASYLAND

While Tyrone and his mother are fictional characters, stories like these occur every day in the academic setting—labeling, stereotyping, pushing students out of the school system, and leaving them with very few life choices. To remedy such practices and dismantle the pipeline, schools, and administrators should be:

1. Protecting the rights of the students when they are subject to interrogation, searches and seizures by school authority and law enforcement.
2. Re-investing in community-based schooling and rejecting the "McDonaldization" of education.
3. Providing adequate social and emotional resources.
4. Offering a restorative approach to those in need, instead of demonizing and alienating students.
5. Desensitizing the educational system to recognize misconduct or under performance is not the gateway for implementing crime models as normalcy for K-12 education.

In using these and like restorative approaches, the populations most often affected by this pipeline may see fewer citizens locked in cages and social problems could be solved instead of buried. Limitation on law enforcement in schools and the tactics they use for minor offenses would make an enormous impact in the system. The educational system is where scholarship is birthed, nurtured, and reproduced for the greater good of our society. It should not become highly policed. The cropping up of School Resource Officers (SRO) to arrest students for arbitrary misconduct is a flawed process in terms of school reform.

Increase the use of positive behavior interventions and supports. Having data available to parents and members of the public on how race, gender, class, and sexual orientation affect the actions taken when students are disciplined, could cut back on discrimination. Training staff and administration to handle matters of school codes and infractions instead of law enforcement could end the criminalization of students and not only bring back the humanity of these students, but also present age-appropriate solutions to the problems they present; be explicit.

DISCUSSION

The threshold question is, why aren't all children afforded the same right to education? That is the question that should be asked by all minorities in a white male-dominated society. Unfortunately, for African Americans, this question is largely ignored. In a capitalistic, male-dominated, and highly racialized society like the United States of America, students of color have little to no chance of avoiding the school-to-prison pipeline. This piece serves to demonstrate the absurdity of what is happening in the educational system on a massive scale. Children are labeled, stereotyped, drugged, or removed from school settings for what in many situations may be considered common misbehavior. To address these problems and a host of other social challenges, children of color are disproportionately faced with expulsion from school and sent to live in cages where illiteracy, poverty, unemployment, and health care issues persist. Nevertheless, these schooling and prison practices are intentional (Fasching-Varner et al., 2014). Instead of providing our nation's at-risk youth with the services they are entitled to, school officials refer children to law enforcement. An increasing number of youth in the juvenile court are typically referred to law enforcement for behaviors that, a generation ago, were handled easily and appropriately by school administrators. Generally speaking, a child may be referred to the juvenile justice system for an offense that would not be considered criminal if committed by an adult. For example, these offenses include curfew violations, truancy, running away, and underage drinking (Kim, Losen, and Hewitt, 2010). Perhaps the most effective and straightforward method for dismantling the school-to-prison pipeline is very simple—"Keep youth out of the hands of law enforcement!"

Chapter Seven

Loving to Read . . . And Other Things of Which I Have Become Ashamed

Michael J. Seaberry

Bright eyed and bushy tailed, I would enter the library weekly to make sure I left with at least three books. They weren't the normal *Aesop's Fables* that my peers were reading; instead, I searched for the novels and nonfiction thrillers that offered me a real challenge, something that would push my reading limits. I pushed them as far as they could go, becoming the only third grader who read on a ninth grade level. That is, until the librarian pushed back. Without hesitation, she made the conscious decision to limit the amount of books I was able to checkout per week. At one point, the library was a refuge where I was able to search for my history and culture, where I was able to actively open my mind, allowing creativeness and knowledge to flow within. She took that away from me, indefinitely.

When my mother recounts the story, she fills with anger as she recalls the moment that this mid-fifties, white, female librarian pulled her aside as she arrived to pick me up from a well-known magnet elementary school, one in which I was tested to get into. Ms. T, as we will call the librarian, told her that I could no longer check out books that were considered "thick" or above my grade-level. Now, as I presently assess the situation, denoting that a book is "thick" is subjective and gives Ms. T full authority to decide the rules on any given day. The only books that I was allowed to check out from this point on are Accelerated Reader-approved books and those that are considered "fun and playful," again, subjective. In our eyes, she was afraid. She grew fearful of a young, Black male, who recently transferred from an all-Black school, and was accelerating past his white counterparts at the city's most prized magnet elementary school. I had been relegated to a level far beneath my ability. In retrospect, Ms. T had options; she could have taken this moment to assist in dismantling the marginalization of Black youth in public schools. She could have assisted in the rest of my peers working harder to attain my level of reading. She even could have discussed a plan of action with my mother to ensure that I was not "getting ahead of myself," but I guess that option is allowing her a scapegoat for institutionalized racism. The problem is that she did not do any of these. She decided to be blatantly against my education. She set out to immediately stop any chances I had of finding my creativity, finding myself, within those books. Of course, my mother had a hard time explaining that one of my teachers felt that I should not be as far ahead as I am, leaving me to find out these details at the age of twenty-three, but I cannot blame her for not completely divulging the details to me at the age of eight or nine. I am sure it was confusing for her and I know it was confusing for me. At that moment, when my mother was pulled aside, I had a mark placed on me that eventually would make me ashamed of the things that made me who I am: a reader, a lover of arts, and a scholar.

Education in America's public schooling system has taught me that not only am I a Black male, but also that I must accept and adhere to the standards of what being Black and what being a male means, as defined by the dominance of white male leadership. This narrative is the story of many who seemed to be trapped within a system of oppression that actively seeks to marginalize minority populations for the benefit of the free market—the benefit of the school-to-prison pipeline. The NAACP, as quoted by Heitzeg (2009), eloquently defines this pipeline in their attempt to interrupt or dismantle the effects of it as early as 2005. They say,

> In the last decade, the punitive and overzealous tools and approaches of the modern criminal justice system have seeped into our schools, serving to remove children from mainstream educational environments and funnel them onto a one-way path toward prison. . . . The School-To-Prison Pipeline is one of the most urgent challenges in education today (p. 1).

For at least a decade, scholars and researchers have been working toward dismantling the school-to-prison pipeline in various ways. As most research does, however, the attention given to this issue has its key limitations. The current literature focuses, almost exclusively, on macro-level causes, ignoring the minute details that can perpetuate such a pipeline. There is ample literature on macro-level causes such as bullying and zero-tolerance policies (Aull, 2012; Berlowitz, Frye, and Jette, 2015; Heitzeg, 2009) and capitalistic views of the pipeline (Fasching-Varner, et. al, 2014; Porter, 2015). While this research is needed and welcomed, especially within the education realm, there still remains a need to examine micro-level causes that are certainly linked to larger structural issues. These micro-level causes include, but are not limited to, the words and acts of whites in working- and middle- class positions that, quite literally, extinguish the flames of curiosity and creativity in far too many young black males.

In her book, *We Real Cool: Black Men and Masculinity*, hooks (2004) addresses the fact that black boys are stuck within a dichotomy of their outward expression conforming to male stereotypes, while their inward emotions are not being accepted by the patriarchal views continually perpetuated in primary education. There are Black boys in classrooms that want to read, dance, sing, and participate in many things that mainstream society tells them they cannot participate in for fear that they may become far too advanced. The more they are told that they do not fit in, the more ashamed they become of their interests. This shameful feeling can cause insecurities in their masculinity. On one hand, they teach that each child should read and read abundantly; on the other hand, they limit the amount and types of books that Black boys read. hooks laments that this dichotomy seeps within the minds of black boys and renders them powerless and hopeless.

However, the feeling of powerlessness and hopelessness within the minds of Black boys is nothing new under the sun. In this chapter, I aim to address the positioning of antagonizing figures within school systems as an integral part of the school-to-prison pipeline. Furthermore, this chapter will address the de-masculinization of Black boys in schools. This is done in an effort to not only acknowledge the existence of macro-level issues, but to also shed light on the micro-level issues that are not discussed in this context. We often hear about zero-tolerance policies labeling Black bodies as criminals (Heitzeg, 2009), the removal of students who do not fit the norms of the dominant student populations (Fenning and Rose, 2007), and the public policies set in place over-emphasizing juvenile misconduct into adult sanctions (Wald and Losen, 2003); however, the analysis of these issues does not often delve into the psychological harm done to little Black boys in elementary schools who do not fully understand the war waged against them. These macro-level analyses forget the micro-level assaults that are inflicted on Black boys in America. These assaults must be dealt with. We must get to a point where educators, parents, and students understand ". . . the increased application of force is not an expression of powerful dominance; it is, rather, a sign of weakness and a proof of impotence—the pitiful helpless giant beached by its own arrogance (Ayers and Ayers, 2015)."

CURIOSITY KILLED THE BLACK BOY

In the recently released book *Black Male Student Success From Preschool Through Ph.D.*, Chezare A. Warren eloquently penned a chapter assessing elementary schools that serve our Black boys. He focuses on the relationships between what he calls "stakeholders" in the school—students/parents,

teachers, and administrators. In doing so, he references Kunjufu's "conspiracy to destroy Black boys" when he says that the failure of our Black boys is
not only a response to their behaviors, but it is a response to the interactions
had with other social factors, especially teachers and administrators (Warren,
2015). It is time that everyone who has interactions with these schools work
together for the betterment of the Black males within the school. Warren
offers exemplary responses to ameliorating the relationships between these
stakeholders, aiding our Black boys' ability to succeed both at home and in
their schools. He asserts the importance of communication within the school
walls and between neighborhoods as an underlying concern for those of
African descent. Warren (2015) says,

> Learning to read and write has always been a priority for African Americans,
> as evidenced by the examples of slaves who yearned to be literate at any cost
> and the formerly enslaved community's insistence on starting their own
> schools immediately following emancipation (Anderson, 1988). The abun-
> dance of literature documenting Black males' persistent academic under-
> achievement could give the perception that Black boys and Black families do
> not care about school, which is simply not true. (pp. 26–27)

I agree with Warren and the scholars he has cited. If Black parents and
students have always been in favor of literature and learning, then why is it
that this picture has been painted of our students not caring? As an emerging
scholar and survivor of America's school systems, I must pose one more
question to him and his colleagues: When these relationships are mended and
the stakeholders begin to work together, what do we do about the bad eggs
that remain in the system, the wolves in sheep's clothing?

According to the National Center for Education Statistics (2015), in 2011
approximately 76 percent of public school teachers were female and predominately white. In 2012, they released an analysis that shows that 45 percent of
the PK-12 population is made up of students of color, whereas only 17.5
percent of the same population consists of teachers of color (Deruy, 2013).
The problem here is that we cannot outright assume that every educator is
trained effectively and efficiently in culturally relevant pedagogical skills.
We cannot hope that those teaching our young Black boys understand and
associate with the community from which they come. And we surely cannot
look forward to the day that the wolves in sheep's clothing accept our boys
with open arms and no mal-intent. Fasching-Varner and Seriki (2012) eloquently stated, "By having disproportionate access to all children white
teachers become the main socializing force for children of all colors" (p. 2).
And it seems that some of the white teachers mentioned are living as if we
are in South Carolina in the 1700s where an act of Congress fines them for
assisting a person of color to learn to read and write (Martin, 2015). Historically, our boys cannot afford to be socialized by any other race or gender.

Nor can we expect their success when they are subjected to such socialization within the school system. This is not a mistake. Of course, there are many factors that play into the whiteness today's school systems exhibit, but let us remember that these antagonists are set in place for a reason, to weaken the minds of Black boys, confusing them enough so that they do not know who they are and building them back up to what the system wants them to be—illiterate troublemakers. The idea and purpose for Southern schools has historically been to educate Blacks in preparation for living in the lowest of the economic and social totem poles (Martin, 2015). *This is not a mistake.* Rather, this is an attempt to benefit a market that needs people to drive the free market economy. The school, and prison, system is working just as it has been initially designed to work (Fasching-Varner, Mitchell, Martin, and Bennet-Haron, 2014). Dr. Roy Jones, director of the Call Me MISTER Program that seeks to place minority male teachers in deserving schools, says,

> Too often educators aren't well-prepared or equipped with how to deal with the challenges and nuances of the people who come into their classroom that are not as well-prepared academically, socially, intellectually, and emotionally as they should be. So having teachers that are culturally sensitive and that have similar backgrounds has always been viewed as value added to any school situation. (as quoted in Deruy, 2013)

Ta-Nehisi Coates (2015) pens in *Between The World And Me* that schools were never truly about education for young Black boys. He quotes, "When our elders presented school to us, they did not present it as a place of higher learning but as a means of escape from death and penal warehousing" (p. 26). We have allowed teachers to force more compliance than curiosity out of our Black boys and, quite frankly, our boys are losing trust in their teachers (Coates, 2015).

BROADWAY DREAMS DEFERRED

Weinraub et al. (1984) cite Walter Mischel's social learning research when they say that children exhibit behaviors associated with sex as a result of reinforcement from parents and modeled behavior of the parents. It is not until later (ages two to four) that they realize the reality of boys versus girls and the characteristics associated with the respective sex. In other words, children are born with gender fluidity and are able to become whomever and whatever they so decide (should their surroundings match their decisions). Naturally, once the doctor assigns a sex, the family or guardian proceeds to socialize the child in the way that they have been labeled, boys wear blue and girls wear pink even before leaving the hospital. This continues on into toddler years and adolescence, but never seeks to take into account the mental roadblocks that are being constructed while this socialization is happening. There are Black boys who have a true and strong passion for the performing arts, whether that includes song, dance, poetry, or rhythmic step. The only issue is that they have been socialized through their families and, unfortunately, their schools that this arena belongs to females, and the few males who do participate are quickly labeled as feminine, less-than, girly, not man enough, and so on and so forth.

It is fact that more than half of our Black boys live in single-parent homes and low-income neighborhoods, but, fortunately, the parents are not the problems. The students are succeeding academically (Toldson, 2013), but my fear is that some of them are failing emotionally, socially, and spiritually due to the stifling of their true selves in public elementary schools. In Los Angeles, only 35 out of more than 700 schools received an "A" from the governing board on art integration within schools. There are elementary schools that have never offered music or art classes until 2015. This is a sign that there is a severe issue with student creativity not being integrated within a system that already teaches assimilation into white women's lives as discussed earlier. The *LA Times* mentions that the elementary schools that are the hardest hit when it comes to school arts programs are in poor neighborhoods, the communities where most of our Black boys live (Torres and Menezes, 2015).

As stated, Black boys are stripped of their own definitions of Black male masculinity in elementary school through shaming what they deem as important. Teachers then push them to middle and high school campuses where they suffer further division through disproportionate tracking into classrooms that are of lower academic-ability than their white, male counterparts. Classes such as Advanced Placement, Honors, and Schools-within-Schools are preparing their counterparts for college, while Black boys are being prepared for prison (Dancy, 2014). By not readily allowing access to these sectors for Black males it causes a trend of the "token" Black male to become the undesirable person in the room. According the National Education Association (2011), Black boys are 2.5 times less likely to be placed in "upper-level" courses such as talented and gifted. However, they constitute over 80 percent of the students in special education programs. What are we telling our boys? Once a human being feels undesirable, they may seek to do any and everything possible to blend into their surroundings and assimilate as easily as possible to the dominant culture. Henceforth, Black male masculinity issues can stem from such a case where the "undesirable" Black male in the room is working to rid himself of his own culture and characteristics. He is trying to fit within the dominant culture, much like chasing a carrot on a stick attached to a moving train. He will never catch it. Again, Ta-Nehisi Coates (2015) discusses this complex best in his book-long letter to his son where he details the perils of being stuck between not violent enough with his friend and too violent with his teacher. He says, "I was a capable boy, intelligent, well-liked, but powerfully afraid. And I felt, vaguely, wordlessly, that for a child to be marked off for such a life, to be forced to live in fear was a great injustice" (p. 28). How long will we allow our Black boys to live in fear of being rejected from dominant society for doing what they love?

When their reading and learning capabilities are stifled, yes, they lose interest. When their creativity is limited, yes, they lose interest. However, this loss of interest is in reaction to the systematic unwanted feeling surrounding them on a daily basis; the beginnings of what we can clearly see should be labeled as racial battle fatigue. Let's make it a little simpler:

> Cutting off a third grader's reading habits or telling a Black boy that participating in dance is girly → Loss of Interest → Failing Grades → Powerlessness/ Hopelessness → Trouble-Making → Zero-Tolerance Policies/Removal From School → Prison → Enhancing Free Market Benefits.

According to Fasching-Varner et al. (2014), neither schools nor prisons were designed to aid the needs of those populations that are marginalized and under represented, but they were designed to aid the needs of those from the majority populations. Now that we have an understanding of the position of who most schools in America aim to please, we can begin to address it, making those who perpetuate the design uncomfortable, calling for change.

Chapter Eight

Chronicle of a Superpredator

Master Narratives and Counternarratives in the School-to-Prison Pipeline

Michael E. Jennings

Discrimination in schooling is nothing new for African American males. Several decades of educational research has discussed the discrimination and disenfranchisement of African American males in schools and the resulting measures of underachievement attributed to their alleged shortcomings (Goings, Smith, Harris, Wilson and Lancaster, 2015; Noguera, 2009; Hrabowski, Maton, and Greif, 1998; Kunjufu, 1985). Running parallel to this disenfranchisement has been the existence of a criminal justice system that has disproportionally adjudicated and incarcerated African American males in ever increasing numbers (Weatherspoon, 2014; Hartlep and Ball, 2014). While rates of incarceration have increased across the entire population, the rise of incarceration rates among African American men has been particularly high and resulted in devastating consequences for African American families and communities (Hattery and Smith, 2014; Roberts, 2004). It is at this juncture of schooling and incarceration that the School to Prison Pipeline (STPP) has emerged. Heitzeg (2009) succinctly describes the STPP as a merger of outcomes and inequities that connect schools and prisons based largely on constructs of power and inequality:

> Rather than creating an atmosphere of learning, engagement and opportunity, current educational practices have increasingly blurred the distinction between school and jail. The school to prison pipeline refers to this growing pattern of tracking students out of educational institutions, primarily via "zero tolerance" policies, and tracking them directly and/or indirectly into the juvenile and adult criminal justice systems." (p. 1)

This blending of inequity between two of society's most powerful institutions has relied, at least in part, on perceptions of school aged African American males as the byproducts of a predatory culture that encourages aggressive hypermasculine behavior within the context of school identities labeled as oppositional and defiant. This chapter seeks to explore the role of race and discipline in a secondary school setting by constructing a critical race counternarrative regarding an African American boy who encounters the STPP in a public high school during the mid-1990s.

ON NARRATIVES, MASTER NARRATIVES, AND COUNTERNARRATIVES

The importance of narrative in education has been growing over the past thirty years (Huber, Caine, Huber, and Steeves, 2013). Narrative has been described as ". . . the study of how humans make meaning by endlessly telling and retelling stories about themselves that both refigure the past and create purpose in the future" (Calandin and Connelley, 1986, p. 385). These stories are of particular importance in educational research because narratives around schooling and education move beyond technocratic conceptions of education and represent potential links to "fundamental qualities of (the) human experience" (Calandin and Connelley, 1986, p. 385).

Of particular note in the growing importance of narrative in education has been the rise of Critical Race Theory (CRT) as a major theoretical construct for the study of race in education (Lynn and Parker, 2006). CRT strongly asserts the primacy of race as a factor in the development and maintenance of educational institutions while grounding its conceptual framework in a distinctive historical context that places an emphasis on the experiences of people of color (Taylor, 1998). In conducting this type of research, CRT scholars often use "non-traditional" methods of research such as narrative and storytelling to challenge the existing social construction of race (Ladson-Billings, 1998, 2013). Utilizing these methodologies challenges the status quo by questioning prevailing ideas and assumptions and by highlighting the untold and unheard stories that emphasize the experiences of people of color (Solórzano and Yosso, 2002). These stories do not merely communicate facts and opinions but instead they represent an important "counternarrative" that challenges racist ideologies that create, maintain, and justify oppressive master narratives (Delgado and Stefancic, 2001; Solórzano and Yosso, 2002).

The phrase "master narrative" comes from the term "metanarrative" first described by Jean-Francois Lyotard (1979) as part of his critique of the Enlightenment (Stanley, 2007). Stanley (2007) describes "master narrative" as "a script that specifies and controls how some social processes are carried out" (p. 14). For Stanley (2007), these scripts go beyond the grand narratives described by Lyotard (1979) by also including what he described as the "official" narratives of everyday life. These master narratives represent legitimating stories that are propagated for specific political purposes and which manipulate public consciousness by claiming a set of common cultural ideas and beliefs (Giroux, Lankshear, McLaren, and Peters, 1996).

Solórzano and Yosso (2002) assert that master narratives are utilized to create, maintain, and justify racism. Racism forms a context that allows "monovocal" stories to be told about academic disengagement by African American male students and a lack of caring by African American families and communities. Gause, Okun, Stalnaker, Nix-Stevenson, and Chapman (2007) further delineate the power of master narratives by asserting that the "master narrative serves to keep our focus on that which serves entrenched power, reinforcing it in unseen but powerful ways" (p. 42). Given that the concept of racism is central to the dilemma facing African American males, it is necessary to utilize a theoretical lens (CRT) and a methodology (critical race narrative) that together can construct a counternarrative reflecting a story that goes beyond the master narratives that often perpetuate the subordination of African American males in schools.

Just as the master narrative of schooling legitimates stories of neutrality, meritocracy, and equal opportunity, there are also master narratives that mask the connections between schools and jails and their devastating effect on the lives of African American men (Meiners, 2010). At the heart of this racialized linkage between schools and prisons is the concept of "educational and penal realism" (Fasching-Varner, Mitchell, Martin, and Bennett-Haron, 2014). This concept borrows from Bell's (1992) work on "racial realism." Bell (1992) describes the reality of racial discrimination for African Americans by stating that:

> Black people will never gain full equality in this country. Even those herculean efforts we hail as successful will produce no more than temporary "peaks of progress," short-lived victories that slide into irrelevance as racial patterns adapt in ways that maintain white dominance. This is a hard-to-accept fact that all history verifies. We must acknowledge it, not as a sign of submission, but as an act of ultimate defiance (p. 12).

In discussing the STPP, Fasching-Varner, Mitchell, Martin, and Bennett-Haron (2014) pick up on Bell's (1992) theme of defiance in the face of oppression by delineating several tenets of educational and penal realism that explicitly name and describe the realities of institutional oppression that exist in both schools and penal institutions. It is beyond the scope of this work to discuss each of the tenets espoused in the concepts of educational and penal realism. However, taken together, these concepts represent a potential for developing new theoretical models that combine Critical Race Theory and

Critical Prison Studies in ways that explore the continued existence of the STPP.

MORAL PANIC AND THE MYTH OF THE SUPERPREDATOR

One of the most startling examples of a destructive master narrative aimed at African American male students is represented in the ideological origins of the punitive policies that began in the 1980s and reached their zenith in the 1990s (Castillo, 2013). These policies were fueled largely by racialized fears of a rise violent juvenile crime, particularly in urban areas. Dr. John J. Dilulio (1995), then a professor at Princeton University, tapped into these fears and provided a name for this particular vision of young African American men. His research about the impending tide of juvenile offenders became known as the "super-predator" thesis. This thesis hypothesized that a dangerous group of young male criminals (most of whom were African American) would wreak havoc on American society as they matured into adulthood over the next ten years. Bennett, Dilulio, and Walters (1996) further explain that,

> America is now home to thickening ranks of juvenile "super-predators"— radically impulsive, brutally remorseless youngsters, including ever more teenage boys, who murder, assault, rape, rob, burglarize, deal deadly drugs, join gun toting gangs, and create serious communal disorders, They do not fear the stigma of arrest, the pains of imprisonment, or the pangs of conscience. They perceive hardly any relationship between doing right (or wrong) now and being rewarded (or punished) for it later. To these mean street youngsters, the words "right" and "wrong" have no fixed moral meaning. (p. 27)

This rise of the superpredator was widely discussed in both print and television media (Muschert, 2007) and was also supported by both criminologists (Dilulio, 1995) and law enforcement officials (Baer and Chambliss, 1997; Elikann, 2007). This widespread support confirmed the long-held belief that African American school-aged males represented a serious threat to the moral and physical well-being of society. As a reaction to this myth, states revamped their juvenile justice systems to allow more juvenile offenders to be tried as adults and potentially incarcerated for longer periods of time in facilities often intended for adult offenders (Miller, Potter & Kappeler, 2006).

These frenzied perceptions of African American youth violence in the early to mid-1990s and the resulting policy changes were part of what can best be described as a "moral panic." The term "moral panic" represents widespread feelings of fear or dread regarding an evil that threatens the well-being of society (Bonn, 2010). In regard to alleged group criminal activity, a moral panic is constituted when there is an "arousal of public concern, intense hostility toward a particular group of people, inflated language used to portray the group blamed for the crime and exaggerated fear in proportion to potential threat. . . . " (Farmer, 2010, p. 371). The moral panic around the fear of African American males contributed to the increased implementation of zero-tolerance policies and the criminalization of schools in the 1990s (Skiba and Knesting, 2001) that in turn hastened the creation, growth, and maintenance of the STPP (Farmer, 2010).

THE CHRONICLE OF A SUPERPREDATOR

Dr. James Edward Bell often reflected on his own experiences in schooling when he researched and wrote about African Americans and education. He had recently received tenure and he was excited about the opportunity to continue doing his work without the distraction of worrying about the all-consuming tenure process. As one of only a handful of African American professors at the small liberal arts university that he worked at, he felt that the time was right to take a few risks with his work.

A few years back he had written extensively about his schooling experiences as an African American male who had achieved success despite having problems in school and with the law. Writing the article was actually more difficult than he thought it would be. He talked to his mother about things that happened in the past and dug down deep within himself to unearth memories about things that happened throughout his childhood. Some of the memories were pleasant and elicited a smile from that came from deep within. He thought about fun days and carefree times playing with friends on the streets of his working-class neighborhood until the street lights came on. In the school he attended most of his teachers had some connection with his community. Some of the teachers had grown up there and returned to teach during the week and to attend church or community events on weekends. A few of the older teachers at the school actually lived in James's community. One of them had taught James's mother when she was a student at the same school. The teachers at school made him feel cared for and he felt "at home" in their classrooms. With their support and the support of his family, he excelled as a student from his earliest days of Kindergarten all the way through eighth grade.

However, in continuing his reflections on school, James reflected on memories that were very different. They could only be described as painful. His experiences in school changed drastically when he made the transition from middle school to high school. Because of his excellent grades and test scores his parents pushed him to attend a prestigious district-wide magnet school. He didn't want any parts of the magnet school. He wanted to stay near home and going to the nearby neighborhood high school meant being able to see his friends every day and not having to rise early to catch a bus across town every morning. His mother had gone to the local high school, as had several of his aunts and uncles. It was a familiar place, so why go somewhere else? His mother told him that there better opportunities at the district magnet school, but he wasn't sure that he believed her. She said that many of the students from the magnet school got scholarships and went on to very good colleges. This made James think. College was important to him and his mother because no one in his family had gone to college, so being the first was very important to him.

For the first time in his life, he attended a large school, where he only knew a handful of kids and where none of the teachers seemed to have connections to his community. For the first time ever, he remembered being called the "n-word" and being questioned about how he managed to gain admission to the school's magnet program. The assumption was that he got in through some type of affirmative action program. Although no type of affirmative action program existed, its alleged existence remained a source of suspicion for his white classmates. James's memories of high school re-flected feelings of being excluded, ostracized, and silenced because of his race.

The African American kids at the school banded together to support one another against the hostilities of a school that didn't welcome them. As a result, they had very little contact with the white students outside of class. James's teachers seemed to view him and the other African American males in the school as a menace. They seemed to be merely a loose collection of problematic individuals whom the teachers didn't really want to deal with in any way, shape, or form. Some of the teachers were afraid of the boys, others merely felt pity for them. The one thing that most of the teachers and admin-istrators seemed to have in common was a belief that the boys didn't belong at the school. Some wanted to fix the boys, others just wanted them to go away. The idea that the school's African American boys would go away didn't seem realistic to James. After all, he reasoned, they made up at least 10 percent of the school's population and probably about 60 percent of the athletic teams that the school was so well known for.

As bad as things may have been, they changed for the worst during James's sophomore year in high school. It was the mid-1990s, and the eve-ning news constantly informed the public about the epidemic of drugs and violence that was sweeping the city. He knew things were going to change for the worse when he attended an assembly at school where the principal talked about the new zero-tolerance policies that were going into effect. This principal said that "no more foolishness would be tolerated" and that any rule breakers would be immediately held accountable. It didn't take long for James to find himself in the assistant principal's office on a regular basis. The first time was for being late to class. The next two times it was for violations of the dress policy. After the third infraction, James was given an in-school suspension. Although his teachers sent assignments for him to complete while serving his suspension, he still missed several important concepts that were being taught in his math and science classes. Two days later he failed a quiz in his math class. He was frustrated because the quiz covered concepts that were taught while he was on in-school suspension. James questioned the teacher about his grade and asked why he even had to take the quiz since he wasn't in class for part of the week. She told him that missing what was taught was his own fault because he had been serving an in-school suspension. James had seen this happen with at least two of his classmates in other classes. He wondered aloud as to why this seemed to only happen to the African American male students at the school. "After all," he said, "being tested on something that he had not been taught was unfair and that's why black kids at the school hate being here." By now, other students in the class were egging him on and laughing at the obvious discomfort registered on the teacher's face. She told James to sit down and be quiet, but that just angered him further. "Why can't we just go to school here and be who we are," he said loudly. The teacher quickly replied in sarcastic tone, "if you would shut your mouth, do your work and follow the rules you might just learn something." James took this comment as question of his intelligence and said, "well if you would stop treating black kids like crap then maybe we actually would learn something." The teacher did not respond but instead immediately sent him to the AP's office for what she labeled as insubordination and disruption.

After waiting in the main office areas for a short while he noticed two police officers come in and speak with the receptionist. The receptionist motioned toward James and the officers walked over to his chair. "Have you been having a problem with your teacher today?" one of them asked. James was stunned by the question and scared by the close physical presence of the officers. He muttered a tepid response but was interrupted by the second officer, "Listen this is serious business. You've been disrupting the class and yelling at your teacher so you're in violation of school policy." James responded excitedly, "I wasn't disrupting anything and I wasn't yelling. I was just telling her that she was wrong. . . . " Before he could finish, the principal stepped briskly out of his office and toward the three of them. "James, I'm sorry but you're going to have to go with these officers. We can't have people causing a disturbance and threatening teachers. We have zero tolerance for that kind of thing." James leapt to his feet, "that's a lie, I never threatened anybody, what is she talking about?" The two officers grabbed him on each side and forced him to the ground face first. One had his knee in James's back while the other pressed his face into the tiled floor. He began to cry and sob knowing that he was being arrested. He had never been in trouble with the police has whole life. What would his parents think? Would his hopes and dreams of going to college be shattered? He cried and sobbed uncontrollably under the weight of the officer's knee pressing down on his back, "this ain't right, I didn't do anything!" he yelled. "Stop resisting!" one of the officers shouted. "You're only making this harder on yourself son," the second officer said, as he violently yanked James's arm across his back.

Once James was handcuffed they rolled him over on his back and quickly yanked him to his feet. He couldn't seem to catch his breath and he was dazed, confused, and scared from what had just happened. His mind reeled, "was this really happening, or was it just some crazy nightmare?" he wondered. His feet seemed to barely touch the floor as the officers dragged him down the school's main hall, one holding each of his arms. As they walked him out of the building through the main doors he thought that he heard them chuckle as they read him his rights: *"You have the right to remain black, anything you say, do or think will be held against you. . . ."*

CONCLUSION

This chronicle offers a brief look at a phenomenon that has become an unfortunate part of the experiences of many African American boys in schools across the country. However, it should be noted that this story is not meant to be seen as representative of the entirety of experiences of African American boys in schools. There are many stories to be told of the success achieved by African American boys in schools and universities across the country (Stinson, 2008). Ironically, the predictions regarding the rise of the superpredator in American society proved to be false. Rather than experiencing an explosion of violent juvenile crime with the onset of the new millennium, America actually witnessed a precipitous decline in juvenile violent crime in the late 1990s and into the twenty-first century (Rhineberger-Dunn, 2013).

However, this chronicle represents a counternarrative to the view of schooling as a societal institution that functions in a fair and neutral manner by offering equal opportunities and supports to all students (Oakes, 1996). This prevailing belief in the power of racelessness as a feature of American schooling represents a "hegemonic fantasy" (Higgin, 2009) that extends the concept of meritocracy in ways that embody a "master narrative" of school success casting African-American males as unworthy and unwilling to achieve success (Harris and Marsh, 2010; Lundy, 2003; Stinson, 2011).

This accusation of unworthiness makes it conceivable that some African American boys would "push back" against what they perceive as a racist institution that has required their participation since a very young age. The rise of zero-tolerance policies and the increase in surveillance has ensured that educational institutions are operating in ways similar to penal institutions

(Hirschfield, 2008). In addition to increased surveillance, students (particularly "students of color") are often subject to increasingly harsh consequences for a host of minor rules and regulations.

Given the pervasive stereotypes around African American males as juvenile offenders and the continued disenfranchisement of African American males in schools, it is no surprise that the surveillance and control of the African American male body has become an important concern within a variety of school contexts. Smith (2005) has identified this concern as a combination of both fear and hatred which he labels as "Black misandry" (p. 58) and describes as "an exaggerated pathological aversion toward Black men created and reinforced in societal, institutional, and individual ideologies and practices" (p. 558). The operation and maintenance of the School to Prison Pipeline strongly reinforces this notion of Black misandry and reifies Foucault's (1995) discussion of disciplinary power and its influence on knowledge production and behavior. If the ultimate goal of institutional discipline and its systems of surveillance reflects an attempt to instill self-discipline and orderly behavior, then the School to Prison Pipeline can be viewed alongside the plantation and the ghetto as a powerful sites of Black misandry that has thrived for at least the past twenty years (Mendieta, 2004; Wacquant, 2002).

Chapter Nine

Breaking the Pipeline

Using Restorative Justice to Lead the Way

Kerii Landry-Thomas

As I sit down to write this chapter, I struggle with my introduction, not in the everyday writing manner of how and what to write, but more with the tone of what I want to convey. I immediately think of my audience and how best to discuss this issue in a manner that (1) will be clear and (2) will invoke change. I initially want to reference the light-hearted, coming-of-age movies of my youth such as *Fast Times at Ridgemont High*, *The Breakfast Club*, and *Ferris Bueller's Day Off.* You know the ones where young, white students behaved badly and were reprimanded not by going to jail, but by facing in-school detentions or irate yet understanding teachers, administrators, and even police officers. I mean who does not remember Sean Penn as Jeff Spicoli going head up with his teacher, Mr. Hand. In those interactions between the two of them, there was a lot going on, but never a time of calling in the police. In addition, *The Breakfast Club* was premised on this notion of conflict between adolescent and the teacher authority figure, yet no police officers were called in. I can go on, but at this point you have likely recalled similar movies regarding the way in which American culture viewed adolescent behavior in formal school spaces. In using the context of American culture, it is imperative to understand that there is a normative view of what that means. Specifically, the idea that when you recall those movies, you recall white students and their experiences, indicative of the white racial framing that occurs in America. Importantly, as I recall these early movies there was a dearth of coming-of-age movies featuring Black youths that carried the same themes that did not feature police officers being called in. For example, *Cooley High*, which follows the antics of two Black high school boys on the north side of Chicago, are intertwined with teachers, police officers, and the criminal justice system. It is the weight of this difference that changes the tone of my chapter. Moreover, the data showing that Black and Hispanic students are disproportionally suspended and expelled from schools and are more likely to be exposed to the juvenile justice system because of behavior that their white peers also engage in, further moves me in a different direction. The disheartening notion that children as young as five are subjected to suspensions and expulsions further directs me to a more terse tone (Smith and Harper, 2015; Wood, 2014; U.S. Department of Education, 2014). The U.S. Department of Education (2014) found that during the 2011–2012 academic year, Black kids made up only 18 percent of preschoolers in the U.S., but were 42 percent of students suspended once and 48 percent of students suspended multiple times from preschools. These numbers should give anyone pause; research has shown that expulsions and out-of-school suspensions are strongly associated with subsequent participation in juvenile and criminal justice systems (Fabelo et. al, 2011; Noguera, 2003; Toldson, 2011). Thus, there is a school-to-prison pipeline that is being fed by young children of color.

Fasching-Varner et al. (2014), in their provocative work on the school-to-prison pipeline, argue that the education system and penal system in the United States are working as planned. Additionally, they find that the school-to-prison pipeline is a substantial tool of an economic system that makes money off of the stratification of people in a society. Their article sets forth seven tenets of this educational and penal realism, which perfectly sums up the complexity of the issue but offers up no solutions. I explore, consequently, the complex nature of the school-to-prison pipeline and discuss one possible alternative that in recent years has shown to be effective in dismantling the pipeline, restorative justice practices. In addition, this chapter looks at the theory and history of restorative justice practices, and how they are currently being implemented in some U.S. schools. Finally, I conclude the chapter with a discussion of the paradigm shift that will need to occur in our public policy discourse in order for restorative justice practices in school to be effective for students of color.

WHY RESTORATIVE JUSTICE PRACTICES?

While I do not believe that restorative justice practices are the only solutions to dismantling the school-to-prison pipeline, I do assert that they are good alternatives and tools in the toolbox to help move American educational and criminal justice policies away from punitive practices and more toward inclusive practices. My belief in restorative justice practices is in fact a response to the policies and laws that have detrimental effects on students of color. For example, in South Carolina where a young, black, female student was thrown out of her chair by a school resources officer, the often ignored aspect of that case is that the young student was criminally charged for whatever her role is in the incident (Craven, 2015). While many people believe that the officer is wrong and that the young girl did nothing to warrant the actions against her, the fact remains that this young girl allegedly violated a law. In fact, she was not only arrested, but charged under a provision of South Carolina state law that prohibits *any person* from "willfully, unlawfully, and unnecessarily from interfering with and disturbing" students and teachers (S.C. Code Ann. § 16–17–420). It should be noted that the law actually goes further and prohibits a person from acting in an "obnoxious manner" on a school campus. Really? If convicted of this "crime," a person faces a fine of "not more than $1,000" or "be imprisoned for not more than ninety days." This means one can face ninety days in jail or pay a fine of $1,000. So, this teenager faces these consequences if convicted for being a normal teenager. Actions that were once considered normal adolescent behaviors and were in the purview of school administrators have now become criminally liable actions that are codified in laws of the states. I argue in this paper that the policies and the laws are wrong and need to be changed. However, I argue further that the law is a reflection of what our society values and as such, while the law needs to be changed so does the underlying philosophy of criminalization of adolescent behaviors. This change will not be easy since this is not an effort that the federal government has direct control of as most of the policies or laws are developed by states. Thus, change requires each state to participate. However, this is not impossible. In thinking about those feel good coming-of-age movies that I mentioned earlier, one reflects on the time when it was not a criminal offense to be young and immature and a time when students were counseled by teachers and administrators and were almost never exposed to the criminal justice system. Whereas in the past "delinquent" behaviors were found to be normal adolescent behaviors and would be handled by school administrators now school officials outsource discipline to police officers (Henning, 2013; Payne and Welch, 2015). School-yard fights now become felony assaults, and students who refuse to "listen" are charged with disorderly conduct at school (Henning, 2013). This shift started to occur in the early 1990s as strict school policies were implemented in response to a growing concern about school safety. In addition, the federal government passed the Gun-Free Schools Act, which provided funding for schools that expelled a student for at least a year or referred students to criminal justice authorities for bringing weapons onto school grounds (Wood, 2014). As the mood of the country stayed focused on a "tough on crime" mindset, many school districts expanded their policies beyond just possession of weapons and included other violations. By 1997, 79 percent of schools across America had developed zero-tolerance policies (Wood, 2014). Critics argue that zero-tolerance policies do not necessarily make schools any safer than they were before the implementation of such harsh policies. In addition, the punitive responses have a negative effect on students (Payne and Welch, 2015). The policies increase the risk of future delinquency and also increase the likelihood of exposure to the criminal justice system (Fabelo et. al, 2011; Nichols, 2004; Schiraldi and Zeidenberg, 2001).

The school-to-prison pipeline is further complicated by the role that race plays in who is thrust into the spokes of the machine. Research indicates that Black students are disproportionally subject to harsh school discipline and harsh treatment by both school officials and law enforcement (Smith and Harper, 2015; Wood, 2014; U.S. Department of Education, 2014; Henning, 2013; The Civil Rights Project, 2000). As studies have consistently shown, Black students are more likely to be penalized for "subjective" offenses, such as disrespect, defiance of authority, and excessive noise (Skiba et al., 2000; Wood, 2014). This allows room for racial bias to play a role in disciplinary actions. Research has consistently found that zero-tolerance disciplinary practices in schools not only harm students by depriving them of educational opportunities, but also fails to make schools safer places (Gonzales, 2012). In addition, the outcomes of these practices indicate that they disproportionally effect minority students and students with disabilities (America's Cradle to Prison Pipeline, 2007). Moreover, data indicates that zero-tolerance policies are more likely to be present in schools with a higher proportion of Black and Latino students (Welch and Payne, 2010; Civil Rights Project, 2000). Welch and Payne (2010) theorize that the influence of racial threat plays a role in the impact that racial composition has on discipline. They suggest that more Blacks in an area intensify public punitiveness because of the perceived threat that a large minority population presents to a White majority (Crawford, Chiricos, and Kleck, 1998). Additionally, research has found that a higher population of Black students decreased the odds that a school would incorporate restorative justice practices such as student conferences, peer mediation, restitution, or community service (Payne and Welch, 2015; Welch and Payne, 2010). This indicates that the way we discipline in our schools can be tainted by racial bias. A call for the use of restorative justice practices by school districts is twofold: (1) they reduce the likelihood that subjective and racially biased thoughts will dictate how discipline is administered; and (2) they create an environment where we humanize and not dehumanize children. Furthermore, restorative justice practices are useful for preventing children from getting in the pipeline and are tools for the many that are already in the pipeline to dismantle it.

WHAT ARE RESTORATIVE JUSTICE PRACTICES?

Restorative justice practices are a broad set of approaches that help students reintegrate into the school community through the use of mediation circles and other holistic approaches. In addition, the practices are inclusionary and not exclusionary and are completely opposite of the punitive zero-tolerance practices that use suspension, expulsion, and police force to remove students from learning environments (Wood, 2014). Overall, this approach recognizes the humanity in all students and works to dismantle the school-to-prison pipeline by shutting down the rotating belt of students. In an effort to work within an inclusive framework and to find solutions that work for the students, restorative justice practices vary in the ways in which they are implemented. Some include peer mediation, community service, student conferences, and other methods of communicating. While there are different variations of restorative justice practices, the key principles represented in much of the literature focuses on promoting healthy, caring communication and fostering nurturing relationships. In addition, there is a focus on addressing harm done and not rules broken (Vaandering, 2014). Importantly, restorative justice practices can be located on a continuum, on one end individualized behavior is addressed and on the other end punitive, managerial structures of schooling can also be changed (Hopkins, 2004). In my view, these methods are a way of returning to a time when students were recognized as being young and still developing. Yet, the individualized practice simply is reactive and should be coupled with the broader cultural shift of the school managerial practices. Morrison, Blood, and Thorsborne (2005) argue that restorative conferencing to deal with harmful behavior is effective, but limited, and suggest that schools should utilize a more comprehensive approach. They argue that this approach should utilize a range of practices that integrate the restorative philosophy, practices, and principles into the wider school culture in order to be more holistic and proactive (Morrison et al., 2005). These methods would not only remove resource officers from a school campus and return social workers, counselors, and additional support into schools, but would also humanize students and assist with social and emotional learning. Restorative justice practices require a paradigm shift in the way the United States approaches not only school discipline, but the way we see our youth, particularly youth of color. For example, in May 2015, a lawsuit was filed in the federal court in Central California alleging among other things that students of color with behavior issues related to "complex trauma" were disproportionately subject to harsh discipline practices that found them suspended, expelled, involuntarily transferred to other schools, or put in contact with the juvenile justice system. In their petition, the plaintiffs in the case argue for a remedy that implements "restorative practices" that seek to "prevent, address and heal after conflict" (*Peter P. et al. v. Compton Unified School District, et al.*). This case is important to watch because if the plaintiffs prevail then it will set a model that encourages school districts to look seriously at restorative justice practices as the means to discipline students or they could face liability for their lack of appropriate disciplinary practices. Moreover, this case could signify a paradigm shift in the way society as a whole views adolescent behavior. Thus, there could be a trickle-down effect on the way the criminal justice system also responds to adolescent behavior.

Notwithstanding the fact that movement away from zero-tolerance policies and laws is an effective tool, it must be acknowledged that this will not happen in a vacuum. Many scholars who study race in education as well as race in the criminal justice system find that there are clear racial biases involved (Alexander, 2010; Fasching-Varner et al., 2014; Henning, 2013). Recently, research has shown that Black youths are viewed as older than they are and viewed as less innocent as compared to White youths. In addition, Black children were not only viewed in a prejudiced light, but also in a dehumanizing light (Goff et al., 2014). Thus, without a paradigm shift, Black youths are viewed as incapable of benefiting from restorative justice practices in either school or the criminal justice system. As noted before, the data show that the more populated a school is with Black youths, the more likely that zero-tolerance policies will be in place and the less likely that restorative justice practices will be utilized (Payne and Welch, 2015). However, restorative justice practices have been found to be an effective strategy in decreasing suspensions of Black males as well as reducing dropout rates in the schools were restorative justice practices have been implemented (Jain et. al, 2014). In addition, after Oakland Unified School District implemented whole-school restorative justice practices, as well as peer restorative models, they found improved conflict resolution skills, improved emotional and social skills of their students, and positive interaction between teachers and their students (U.S. Department of Education/Civil Rights, 2014). Thus, it is in the best interest of society to start to dismantle the school-to-prison pipeline. It is time for all involved to acknowledge the role that racism, white supremacy, and our economic system play in the keeping the school-to-prison pipeline going. It's time for the United States to recognize "educational and penal realism" and begin the process to break away from this model (Fasching et al., 2014). While I acknowledge that this process won't be easy, I refuse to acknowledge that it is impossible. I recognize the historical foundations of racism in our education system, one in which Blacks were never intended to receive the same quality education as the ruling class (Anderson, 1988). In addition, I recognize not only the historical foundations of racism in our criminal justice system, but also the current manifestation of racial disparities in arrests, charging, convictions, and sentencing (Alexander, 2010; Kennedy, 1997). Racial realism (Bell, 1992) requires me to acknowledge the uphill battle that will accompany the attempt to dismantle the school-to-prison pipeline, but it also requires us to "implement racial strategies that can bring fulfillment and even triumph" (Bell, 1992, pp. 373–374). Restorative justice practices are such strategies because at the core of the framework is the humanization of our youth. These practices begin the process of American society changing the way we look at criminalization and call us to have a culture of inclusivity.

Chapter Ten

In and of Itself a Risk Factor

Exclusionary Discipline and the School-to-Prison Pipeline

Russell J. Skiba, Mariella I. Arredondo, and Natasha T. Williams

The term "school-to-prison pipeline"[1] (STPP) has become common in the literature and public discourse. Widely-used by advocates (Advancement Project, 2011; ACLU, 2008), researchers (Christle, Jolivette, and Nelson, 2005; Nicholson-Crotty, Birchmeire, and Valentine, 2009), and policy makers (St. George, 2012), the term refers to policies and practices, often focusing on school discipline, that decrease the probability of school success, and are associated with a variety of negative life outcomes, particularly juvenile justice involvement.[2]

Although the school-to-prison pipeline construct has provided a useful frame for focusing on the possible contribution of school discipline to juvenile justice outcomes, it is also true that the increased currency of the term does not guarantee that all those who use the term school-to-prison pipeline are describing the same process. Indeed, some critics have argued that the construct is more a "political movement than a scientifically-validated term" (see, e.g., James, 2013; Resmovits, 2013). Given a range of interpretations, and challenges to the validity of the term, it is important to examine the state of evidence with respect to the STPP. What is the extent of empirical support for connections between school-based disciplinary procedures and negative school and life outcomes, including juvenile justice involvement?

In this chapter, we examine the strength of the data documenting the school-to-prison pipeline, that is, the short- and long-term effects of exclusionary school discipline: out-of-school suspension and expulsion. First, we identify the components that have been described as characterizing the school-to-prison pipeline. We then review available research on suspension, expulsion, and discipline disparities and their association with a range of short- and long-term outcomes, assessing a series of four claims (see below) made about the school-to-prison pipeline. In the process, we propose a model tracking the benchmarks that may mediate the connection between school disciplinary events (i.e., suspension or expulsion) and juvenile justice outcomes in a STPP; we examine the extent of research support for each of these links. Finally, we consider the extent to which there is support for claims concerning the directionality of the pipeline from school disciplinary actions to negative school and life outcomes (e.g., dropout or juvenile justice involvement). Ultimately, examination of the evidence indicates strong empirical support for links between school-based disciplinary procedures and negative school and life outcomes, including juvenile justice involvement.

WHAT IS THE SCHOOL-TO-PRISON PIPELINE? THEMES IN THE STPP

In order to capture a range of definitions of the term *school-to-prison pipeline*, we conducted searches using computerized bibliographic databases and collected research, policy, or advocacy reports addressing the STPP, supplemented by personal inquiries to researchers engaged in the topic in order to track down in snowball fashion, other references to the term.

Table 10.1 presents a representative sample of the use of the term, as are drawn from published research, advocacy, and policy reports. Four consistent themes emerged. First, exclusionary school discipline—the use of out-of-school suspension and expulsion—is widespread (ACLU, 2011; Burris, 2012; Pane and Rocco, 2014), systematic (Kim, 2003; Smith, 2009), and increasing in usage (Heitzeg, 2009; Wald and Losen, 2003). Second, school exclusion for disciplinary purposes increases the likelihood of long-term negative outcomes, in particular involvement with juvenile justice (Darensbourg, Perez, and Blake, 2010). Third, these practices and outcomes fall disproportionately on particular populations (Wald and Losen, 2003), especially youth of color. Finally, the term "school-to-prison pipeline" implies a certain direction of causality—that policies and practices of schools, rather than solely the characteristics of students themselves, are to some degree responsible for those negative outcomes (Advancement Project et al., 2011; ACLU, 2011). Some have emphasized the intentionality of the school-to-prison pipeline in stronger terms, including "pushout" (Kim, 2003; Smith, 2009) or "by design" (Burris, 2012).

For this chapter, we examined the evidence base in order to assess the extent of empirical support for the components of an STPP. We address four research questions based on the identified themes:

1. Can the use of school exclusion be characterized as widespread, systematic, and increasing?
2. To what extent does the usage of school exclusion affect certain groups differently? Which groups appear to be most affected?
3. To what extent have links between school suspension/expulsion and further negative educational and life outcomes, including juvenile justice, been empirically demonstrated?
4. Is the literature strong enough to justify a claim of directionality or intentionality? Have available studies controlled for alternative hypotheses sufficiently to suggest that school practices themselves are a risk factor for future negative outcomes?

We begin with an assessment of the status of school exclusionary discipline as we examine each of these four questions.

Approach and Methodology

To examine these questions, we conducted searches for peer-reviewed journal articles and dissertations using the online databases of ERIC, PsycInfo, JSTOR, Academic Search Premier, Education Full Text (H. W. Wilson), Psych Articles, Criminal Justice Abstracts, Sociological Abstracts, and the Google Scholar search engine. The search terms "school-to-prison pipeline," "suspension," "expulsion," and "exclusionary discipline" were crossed with outcomes such as "academic engagement," "school climate," "achievement," "dropout," "graduation," "juvenile justice," and "arrests."

The key criteria for article inclusion were that the articles were: (a) based on empirical data specific to school discipline (b) included measures of school discipline and short- or long-term outcomes such as academic engagement, achievement, climate, dropout, or juvenile justice involvement; and (c) disaggregated the school discipline data in order to measure the differential impact of suspension or expulsion by group. Articles or other documents excluded were those not in English, not supported by empirical findings, and not focused on K-12 education. In the following four sections we describe the results of the review, exploring the four research questions of the study.

Table 10.1.   School to Prison Definitions Drawn from the Literature

The School to Prison Pipeline proposes that exclusionary discipline techniques (e.g., detention, out of school suspension, disciplinary alternative education placements) experienced by African American males alienate them from the learning process by steering them from the classroom and academic attainment and toward the criminal justice system.	Darensbourg, Perez, and Blake, 2010, p. 197
"School-to-Prison Pipeline"—the use of educational policies and practices that have the effect of pushing students, especially students of color and students with disabilities, out of schools and toward the juvenile and criminal justice systems.	Advancement Project et al., 2011, p. 2
These phrases refer to a journey through school that is increasingly punitive and isolating for its travelers—many of whom will be placed in restrictive special education programs, repeatedly suspended, held back in grade, and banished to alternative, "outplacements" before finally dropping or getting "pushed out" of school altogether.	Wald & Losen, 2003, p. 3
The "school-to-prison pipeline" refers to the policies and practices that push our nation's schoolchildren, especially our most at-risk children, out of classrooms and into the juvenile and criminal justice systems.	ACLU, 2008
The school-to-prison pipeline is the collection of education and public safety policies and practices that push our nation's schoolchildren out of the classroom and into the streets, the juvenile justice system, or the criminal justice system.	Archer, 2010, p. 868
Research on both the overuse of, and disproportionality in, punitive consequences in school discipline and juvenile justice has been identified under the rubric of the *school-to-prison* pipeline.	Kim, Losen, & Hewitt, 2010
The pipeline metaphor exists to describe the collective system of local, state, and federal policies and procedures that siphons children out of school and into prison.	Swain & Noblit, 2011, p. 466
The 'pipeline' refers to a disturbing pattern of school disciplinary problems escalating from suspension to removal from school, juvenile justice system involvement, and school dropout.	Fowler et al., 2010, p. 1

The term "school-to-prison pipeline" aims to highlight a complex network of relations that naturalize the movement of youth of color from our schools and communities into under- or unemployment and permanent detention.	Meiners, 2011, p. 550
The phrase "school-to-prison pipeline" conceptually categorizes an ambiguous, yet seemingly systematic, process through which a wide range of education and criminal justice policies and practices collectively result in students of color being disparately pushed out of school and into prison.	Smith, 2009, p. 1012
The school-to-prison pipeline represents the widely accepted process of disciplining a student, removing that student from the classroom as punishment, wondering at that student's decreasing academic interest and skills, and watching that student flounder and eventually enter the judicial system.	Pane & Rocco, 2014, p. 3
Academic failure, exclusionary discipline practices, and dropout have been identified as key elements in a "school-to-prison pipeline."	Christle, Jolivette, & Nelson, 2005, p. 69
The school-to-prison pipeline refers to this growing pattern of tracking students out of educational institutions, primarily via 'zero tolerance' policies, and, directly and/or indirectly, into the juvenile and adult criminal justice systems.	Heitzeg, 2009, p. 1
The devastating end result of these intertwined punitive policies [zero tolerance and high stakes testing] is a "school-to-prison pipeline," in which huge numbers of students throughout the country are treated as if they are disposable, and are being routinely pushed out of school and toward the juvenile and criminal justice systems.	Advancement Project, 2010, p. 6
The "school-to-prison pipeline" refers to policies and practices that systemically push at-risk youth out of mainstream public schools and into the juvenile or criminal justice systems	Kim, 2003, p.956

HOW WIDESPREAD IS THE USE OF EXCLUSIONARY DISCIPLINE? IS IT INCREASING?

Examination of the literature across a wide range of studies show out-of-school suspension to be among the most frequently used response to disciplinary infractions (Fabelo, Thompson, Plotkin, Carmichael, Marchbanks, and Booth, 2011; Lewis, Butler, Bonner, and Joubert, 2010). In a longitudinal investigation of suspension and expulsion, Fabelo et al. (2011) found that 59.6 percent of students in Texas public schools received a suspension or expulsion at least once between seventh and twelfth grade. Over time, the use of exclusionary discipline has increased substantially. According to data collected by the U.S. Department of Education's Office for Civil Rights (OCR), in the span of thirty-six years the rate almost doubled at which students across the country were suspended and expelled from schools from 3.7 percent (1.7 million students) suspended in 1974 (Wald and Losen, 2003) to 6.6 percent (over 3 million students) suspended in 2009–2010 (Losen and Gillespie, 2012).

The usage of out-of-school suspension is not restricted to serious, safety-threatening behaviors, but is used in response to a variety of offenses. Studies have consistently found it to be used primarily as a consequence for non-violent, minor to moderate student infractions, such as disobedience and disrespect (Raffaele Mendez and Knoff, 2003; Skiba, Peterson, and Williams, 1997), defiance and insubordination (Gregory and Weinstein, 2008; American Association of School Administrators & Children's Defense Fund, 2014), attendance problems (Morgan-D'Atrio, Northrup, LaFleur, and Spera, 1996), failing to report to detention (Rosen, 1997), and general classroom disruption (Brooks, Schiraldi, and Ziedenberg, 1999). School expulsion, on the other hand, appears to be used less frequently, more likely to be reserved for situations when the offenses are seriously disruptive, violent, or involving criminal behavior (Heaviside, Rowand, Williams, and Farris, 1998).

DIFFERENTIAL EFFECTS: WHO IS AT RISK FOR EXCLUSIONARY DISCIPLINE?

Racial and ethnic disciplinary disparities have been found at all school levels and locales (e.g., elementary vs. secondary; rural, suburban, and urban), and documented in both peer-reviewed journals (Bradshaw, Mitchell, O'Brennan, and Leaf, 2010; Eitle and Eitle, 2004; Lewis, Butler, Bonner, and Joubert, 2010; Raffaele Mendez, Knoff, and Ferron, 2002; Skiba, Horner, Chung, Rausch, May, and Tobin, 2011) and advocacy reports (e.g., Advancement Project/Civil Rights Project, 2000; Fabelo, Thompson, Plotkin, Carmichael, Marchbanks, and Booth, 2011). African American disproportionality has been found in office referrals (Bradshaw, Mitchell, O'Brennan, and Leaf, 2010; Rocque, 2010; Skiba, Horner, Chung, Rausch, May, and Tobin, 2011), suspension and expulsion (Eitle and Eitle, 2004; Gregory and Weinstein, 2008; Walsh, 2015), school arrests (Theriot, 2009), and corporal punishment (Shaw and Braden, 1990). Black students receive fewer mild disciplinary sanctions (McFadden, Marsh, Price, and Hwang, 1992; Payne and Welch, 2010) and more severe disciplinary consequences (Skiba, Horner, Chung, Rausch, May, and Tobin, 2011) for comparable infractions.

African American disciplinary disparities have not been found to be caused by poverty status nor differential rates of disruptive behavior (see, e.g., Bradshaw, Mitchell, O'Brennan, and Leaf, 2010; Skiba, Michael, Nardo, and Peterson, 2002; Wallace, Goodkind, Wallace, and Bachman, 2008; Wu, Pink, Crain, and Moles, 1982).

Disciplinary disparities for other racial/ethnic categories have been less-well studied. While Peguero and Shekarkhar (2011) found disparities in discipline for first- and third-generation Latino students, others have reported rates of out-of-school suspension for Latino students not significantly different from White students (Horner, Fireman, and Wang, 2010; McFadden et al., 1992; Skiba, Peterson, and Williams, 1997). Patterns are beginning to emerge, however, showing disproportionate rates of suspension and expulsion in middle and high school, but little or no disproportionality at the elementary level (Losen and Gillespie, 2012; Skiba et al., 2011). In a national examination of self-reported data concerning discipline outcomes, reported that Native American students were over-represented and Asian students under-represented in school discipline, in general, and suspension in particular (Wallace, Goodkind, Wallace, and Bachman, 2008; Whitford and Levine-Donnerstein, 2014). Students with disabilities[3] are at risk for disproportionate discipline (Krezmien, Leone, and Achilles, 2006; Raffaele Mendez, 2003). According to the most recent CRDC data, students with disabilities are more than twice as likely to receive out-of-school suspension as their peers without disabilities (U.S. Department of Education, 2014).

Disproportionality in discipline, particularly suspension and expulsion, extends to girls of color as well. Wallace, Goodkind, Wallace, and Bachman (2008) found that African American girls were over five times more likely than White girls to be suspended or expelled. Other research has found high rates of disciplinary disparities for Black females at both the elementary and secondary school levels (Blake, Butler, Lewis, and Darensbourg, 2011; Raffaele Mendez and Knoff, 2003; Toldson, McGee, and Lemmons, 2015), and in some instances higher than White and Latino males (Finn and Servoss, 2015; Toldson et al., 2015).

Finally, new research drawing from national, district, and local level data suggest that Lesbian, Gay, Bisexual, and Transgender (LGBT) students are disproportionately disciplined in school. Himmelstein and Bruckner (2011), using a nationally representative, population-based sample of adolescents in grades 7 through 12, found that same-sex-attracted youth, particularly girls, were 1.4 more likely to be disciplined at school than their heterosexual peers, even after controlling for self-reported rates of misbehavior. A more recent study examining sexual orientation-based disparities at the county level in the state of Wisconsin, analyzed collected surveys from 13,645 youth across twenty-two high schools and found that LGBT youth (self-identified) were more than twice as likely as heterosexual students to report that they had been suspended from school (Poteat, Scheer, and Chong, 2015). Lastly, in a mixed-methods study also examining discipline experiences for LGBT and gender non-conforming youth, students reported experiencing exclusionary discipline at higher rates than their heterosexual peers (Snapp, Burdge, Licona, Moody, and Russell, 2015).

EMPIRICAL SUPPORT FOR PATHWAYS FROM SCHOOL PRACTICE TO SHORT- AND LONG-TERM CONSEQUENCES

Figure 10.1 represents a model for the STPP in its most basic form. Available data suggest that school exclusion in the form of suspensions and expulsions are associated with increased rates of juvenile justice involvement (Fabelo et al., 2011; Vanderhaar, Petrosko, and Muñoz, in 2015); yet it seems likely that the effects of suspension and expulsion on juvenile justice involvement and outcomes are most likely mediated by a number of short-term negative outcomes. A more articulated model of the paths created by excessive use of out-of-school suspension and expulsion is presented in Figure 10.2. Although the use of exclusionary discipline is intended to improve the quality of the school climate by removing disrupting students from the learning environment (Skiba and Rausch, 2006), emerging research suggests that it may instead be associated with perceptions for a lower quality school climate (Steinberg, Allensworth, and Johnson, 2015). Given a consistent connection between opportunities to learn and achievement (Greenwood, Horton, and Utley, 2002), the use of suspension and expulsion might also be expected to have a negative impact on school achievement by reducing academic engagement. One would expect that these short-term outcomes could prove to be strong predictors of both school dropout and eventual involvement in the juvenile justice system. In the succeeding sections, we examine and evaluate the extent and strength of the data documenting each of the links between exclusionary discipline and the benchmarks in a school-to-prison pipeline.

School Climate

School climate refers to the way an educational community perceives its environment, including safety, emotional, and socioeconomic well-being, and how these factors affect student learning (Nava Delgado, 2014). Positive perceptions of school climate have been found to be associated with improvements in academic achievement (see, e.g., Brand, Felner, Shim, Seitsinger, and Dumas, 2003), lower student involvement in risk-taking and violent behaviors (Resnick et al., 1997), and a lower probability of engaging in problem behavior (Brand, Felner, Shim, Seitsinger, and Dumas, 2003; Wang, Selman, Dishion, and Stormshak, 2010).

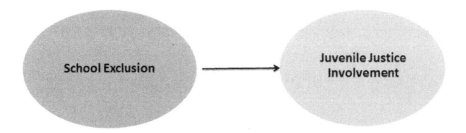

Figure 10.1.   Simplest representation of school exclusion as a component of the school-to-prison pipeline, the focus is primarily on the direct contribution that suspension and expulsion may make to juvenile justice involvement.

Research suggests that the use of exclusionary discipline in schools is associated with more negative perceptions of school climate (see, e.g., Rausch and Skiba, 2006; Steinberg, Allensworth, and Johnson, 2015; Wallace, Goodkind, Wallace and Bachman, 2008), and perceptions of the school climate vary by race. Gregory, Cornell, and Fan (2011) examined school practices and rates of suspension in 199 schools and found that schools rated by students as having the lowest levels of support and academic expectations had the highest rates of suspension, and the largest Black-White suspension gap. Black students rate school climate more negatively than their White peers, and report more experiences with racism and lack of racial fairness at school; such ratings have been found to be associated with higher rates of detention and suspension (Kupchik and Ellis, 2008; Mattison and Aber, 2007; Watkins and Aber, 2009).

School Engagement/Lost Educational Opportunity

Two of the strongest predictors of academic achievement have found to be educational opportunity and academic engagement (see, e.g., Brophy, 1988; Greenwood, Horton, and Utley, 2002), and research has documented a consistent association between school alienation/school bonding and subsequent delinquency (Christle, Jolivette, and Nelson, 2005; Welsh, Greene, and Jenkins, 1999). For African American male students, school disengagement has been found to be a strong predictor of truancy in the long term (Toldson, 2011).

Disciplinary removal has been found to have a negative effect on both educational opportunity and school engagement. Examining time lost to Office Disciplinary Referrals (ODRs), Muscott, Mann, and LeBrun (2008) reported an average of 15–45 minutes of instructional time lost due to each referral. Lewis, Butler, and Joubert (2010) examined loss of time due to suspensions out of school and found that in one urban school district, 3,587

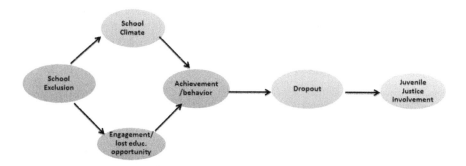

Figure 10.2.   A more articulated model of a school-to-prison pipeline, assuming that possible risks created by school suspension and expulsion are moderated by the effects of those consequences on a series of shorter-term outcomes that are presumably additive in increasing the ultimate risk of juvenile justice involvement.

African American males missed a collective 3,714 school days in one academic year. Such losses seem to predict a concomitant loss in school engagement and bonding. McNeely, Nonemaker, and Blum (2002), found that school connectedness tends to be lower in schools that use expulsion for minor infractions, while Davis and Jordan (1994) reported that the number of suspensions received was negatively related to school engagement among tenth-grade African American male students.

Achievement and Behavior

While removing disruptive students is intended to deter further misbehavior and improve behavior and achievement outcomes by removing the most disruptive students, available evidence suggests that school exclusion is associated with increased negative academic and behavioral outcomes. School exclusion has been found to be negatively associated with multiple measures of student academic achievement, including state accountability examinations (Rausch and Skiba, 2005), reading achievement (Arcia, 2006; Perry and Morris, 2014), math achievement (Morris and Perry, 2016), school grades (Rocque, 2010), and writing achievement (Raffaele Mendez, Knoff, and Ferron, 2002). In a three-year longitudinal study of a matched sample of suspended and non-suspended middle school students, Arcia (2006) found that number of days suspended was negatively associated with growth in reading achievement. These relationships appear to be especially salient for students of color. Most recently, Morris and Perry (2016) found evidence that disproportionate school suspension lowers school performance and contributes to racial disparities gap in achievement. In their longitudinal study examining the impact of student suspension rates on racial differences in reading and math achievement, they reported that Black and Latino students are more likely to be suspended than White students and suspensions are a strong predictor of significantly lower reading and math scores. Davis and Jordan (1994) in a multivariate model controlling for a number of student demographic variables, found that a school's emphasis on discipline and the number of suspensions a student received negatively predicted achievement in eighth grade for African American males.

Based on the classic operant definition of punishment (Alberto and Troutman, 2003; Skinner, 1953), exclusionary discipline could be defined as an effective punisher if it reduced future rates of disruptive behavior. Yet rather than reducing the likelihood of future suspensions, being suspended appears to predict higher future rates of repeat offending (Bowditch, 1993; Costenbader and Markson, 1998). In a longitudinal study examining predictors of suspension rates and effects of suspension on student's educational achievement, Raffaele Mendez (2003) found that the number of out-of-school suspensions a student receives in fourth or fifth grade significantly predicts the number of suspensions in middle school. This negative effect on behavioral trajectory has led some to conclude that, in many cases, "suspension functions as a reinforcer . . . rather than as a punisher" (Tobin, Sugai, and Colvin, 1996, p. 91).

Dropout

Extensive evidence shows that suspension increases the probability of dropout or failure to graduate on time (Balfanz, Byrnes, and Fox, 2015; Christle, Jolivette, and Nelson, 2005; Raffaele Mendez, 2003). Balfanz and colleagues (2015), in an eight-year longitudinal study, found that being suspended one time in ninth grade increased the risk of dropping out from 16 percent to 32 percent, while being suspended twice increased the risk of dropout to 43 percent. Analyzing data from the National Longitudinal Survey of Youth (NLSY97), Suh and Suh (2007) found that being suspended at least once increased the likelihood of dropping out of school by nearly 77.5 percent, and that suspensions are a stronger predictor of dropout than either grade point average (GPA) or socio-economic status (SES). Again, this relationship appears to be stronger for students of color. Raffaele Mendez (2003) found the number of out-of-school suspensions received in sixth grade was associated with a lower probability of on-time graduation, and that relationship was even more significant for African American students.

Juvenile Justice Involvement

Retrospective studies of youth already incarcerated have found a strong link between suspension/expulsion and involvement in the criminal justice system. Sedlak and McPherson (2010) found that 61 percent of youth detained in juvenile justice facilities reported being expelled or suspended from school the year prior to entering juvenile justice custody. In a sample of over 500 males in a juvenile correctional facility, Krezmien, Leone, and Achilles (2006) reported that more than four in five had been suspended from school and more than one in two had been expelled from school. The retrospective nature of this research, however, precludes strong statements about the extent to which suspension and expulsion may represent a predictive risk factor for involvement in juvenile justice.

Longitudinal studies tracking students at school from disciplinary encounters to contact with the juvenile justice may provide stronger conceptual links. The *Breaking Schools' Rules* study, tracking students from seventh grade through twelfth in the state of Texas, found that being suspended or expelled for a discretionary school offense nearly tripled a student's likelihood of contact with the juvenile justice within the following year (Fabelo et al., 2011). Vanderhaar et al. (2015) examined ten years of data on a cohort of students entering third grade and reported that students who received one to two suspensions were eight times more likely to be placed in an alternative school, and those with three or more suspensions were twenty-five times more likely to be placed in an alternative school.

It is no surprise that school exclusion and juvenile justice involvement seem to affect students of color, particularly African Americans more than other students. Nicholson-Crotty, Birchmeire, and Valentine (2009), examining school discipline and juvenile justice data for African American and White youth aged ten to seventeen in fifty-three counties in Missouri, reported that racial disproportionality in out-of-school suspensions was strongly associated with racial disparity in juvenile court referrals, even after controlling for delinquent behavior, poverty, and other demographic variables. Vanderhaar et al., (2015) reported that, of students receiving an alternative school placement in middle school for disciplinary reasons, 50 percent of Black students were eventually detained, compared to 32 percent of White students.

EVIDENCE OF CAUSALITY OR INTENTIONALITY IN THE STPP

The phrase "school-to-prison pipeline" in and of itself suggests a direction of causality, namely that school exclusion initiates a process that puts students at increased risk for a gamut of negative developmental outcomes. Yet finding correlations between exclusionary school discipline and short- and long-term negative outcomes does not prove that exclusion is responsible for those events. A reasonable alternative hypothesis might suggest that higher suspension rates and a higher likelihood of dropout are both caused by poverty, that low-achieving students are at increased risk for a wide range of negative outcomes, including suspension and expulsion, academic disengagement, dropout, and even incarceration (see, e.g., Harlow, 2003), or students engaging in more disruptive behavior will be more likely to be both suspended and eventually involved with the legal system. To what extent do the data support a claim of directionality, that school practices and expulsion themselves create further risk for negative school and life outcomes?

Fortunately, more sophisticated multivariate and longitudinal designs that can better rule out alternate explanations are relatively common in the school discipline literature. Studies investigating disciplinary outcomes and disproportionality have controlled for level of student behavior (Bradshaw, Mitchell, O'Brennan, and Leaf, 2010; Skiba, Horner, Chung, Rausch, May, and Tobin, 2011), socioeconomic status (Noltemeyer and McLoughlin, 2010; Wallace, Goodkind, Wallace, and Bachman, 2008; Wu, Pink, Crain, and Moles, 1982), or prior achievement levels (Fabelo et al., 2011). Examinations of the relationship between school suspension and school dropout (Suh and Suh, 2007) or juvenile justice involvement (Fabelo et al., 2011) have typically utilized multivariate analyses that include a variety of covariates. The logistic analyses in *Breaking Schools' Rules* (Fabelo et al., 2011) exploring the association between school discipline and school dropout and increased juvenile justice involvement included eighty-three control variables, including disability status, economic disadvantage, achievement rate, and attendance rate. Prospective longitudinal studies also have shown increases in risk over time due to suspension and expulsion for achievement (Arcia, 2006), further disciplinary involvement (Raffaele Mendez, 2003), dropout (Balfanz et al., 2015), and delinquency/juvenile justice involvement (Fabelo et al., 2011; Shollenberger, 2015). Tracking suspended students over time, Shollenberger (2015) found that a significant proportion of suspended youth who later became delinquent had not engaged in serious delinquency until after their first suspension. These studies have consistently found that exclusionary school discipline makes a significant contribution, above and beyond individual, family, and community risk factors, to a range of negative developmental outcomes that predict increased juvenile justice involvement.

Some definitions of the STPP go beyond mere directionality to suggest that the movement of students out of school toward more restrictive alternatives through disciplinary exclusion is intentional or by design (Burris, 2012). Only limited data exists in this regard, however, Bowditch (1993), in a qualitative case study examining disciplinary procedures of a public inner-city high school, reported that school policies and procedures encouraged disciplinarians to use suspensions, transfers, and involuntary "drops" as a method of pushout for students perceived to be troublemakers or less likely to succeed academically. Figlio (2006), measuring a three-way interaction among high-stakes assessment, student achievement, and school exclusion in a subset of school districts in Florida, found that schools reduced their suspension penalties for higher-achieving students in high-stakes grades (grades four, five, eight, and ten) during the testing window, while simultaneously raising suspension penalties for lower achieving students in those same grades. Although such data suggest a possible relationship between academic achievement, high-stakes testing, and disciplinary exclusion, there are no studies we are aware of suggesting that this illustrates an intention on the part of school personnel to accelerate students' progress towards juvenile justice involvement.

DISCUSSION

Advocates, researchers, and policy makers have used the term "school-to-prison pipeline" to describe a pathway or pathways, beginning with out-of-school suspension and expulsion, that place students at risk for further negative outcomes, including involvement in the juvenile justice system. Yet some have claimed that there is no empirical validation of the STPP and the use of the term serves political, more than scientific, ends (James, 2013). The range of literature we examined enables a test of the extent to which the central assertions of an STPP model are grounded in empirical findings, and in the end provides solid empirical support for each of the four themes that run through previous definitions of the STPP.

School Exclusion is Widely Used and Increasing in Frequency

In our nation's schools, the use of out-of-school suspension and expulsion continue to be central components of disciplinary practice. For African American students, in particular, the use of exclusionary alternatives in schools continues to increase, and out-of-school suspension is used most frequently used for day-to-day disruptions, especially defiance and non-compliance, rather than being restricted to serious or dangerous behavior.

School Exclusion Falls Disproportionally on Certain Groups

For over forty years, the over-representation of African American students in discipline has been documented extensively, and continues to increase. In order to understand patterns of disproportionality for other racial/ethnic groups, especially Latino and Native American students, more research is needed; however, both gender and disability status have been found to be consistent predictors of disciplinary removal. Finally, new studies (Himmelstein and Bruckner, 2011; Poteat et al., 2015) suggest that differences in sexual orientation or gender identity also may place students at risk for higher rates of discipline and exclusion.

School Exclusion is, in and of itself, a Risk Factor for Further Negative Outcomes

For some proportion of students it is entirely plausible that a first suspension or expulsion could lead to a delinquent event; in general, however, the school-to-prison pipeline might better be described as a set of possible pathways toward increasingly negative school and life outcomes. Thus, exclusionary school discipline has been consistently been found to be associated with short-term negative outcomes, such as academic disengagement and depressed academic achievement that may be additive over time, accelerating the risk for eventual contact with law enforcement and juvenile justice.

This chapter reviewed a substantial body of research demonstrating an association between exclusionary school discipline and short- and long-term negative outcomes. Suspension and expulsion rates are associated with both qualitative (Sheets, 1996) and quantitative (Mattison and Aber, 2007) indicators of school climate. Exclusion from school for disciplinary purposes also appears to pose a threat to factors, such as educational opportunity (Muscott, Mann, and LeBrun, 2008) and student engagement, that are strongly predictive of both academic and behavioral outcomes. Thus, it comes as no surprise that exclusionary discipline is associated with decreases in academic achievement for both the overall school (Davis and Jordan, 1994; Rausch and Skiba, 2005) and individual levels (Morris, and Perry, 2016; Rocque, 2010), and an increased risk of negative behavior over time (Hemphill et al., 2008; Tobin, Sugai, and Colvin, 1996). Academic disengagement and deteriorating academic and social outcomes are most likely mutually reinforcing, eventually increasing the likelihood of failure to graduate or school dropout; in fact there is substantial evidence documenting a link between out-of-school suspension and school dropout (e.g., Suh and Suh, 2007). Given that associations between school disengagement, dropout, and juvenile justice involvement have been well established (e.g., Christle, Jolivette, and Nelson, 2005; Hawkins, Guo, Hill, Battin-Pearson, and Abbott, 2001), findings of a significant relationship between exclusionary discipline and juvenile justice (Fabelo et al., 2011; Nicholson-Crotty et al., 2009) are not surprising.

Is There a Directionality or Intentionality to the STPP?

Use of the term "school-to-prison pipeline" inherently implies a direction of causation—that school-level processes and events create increased risk for future negative outcomes. Simple correlations or descriptive research show-

ing that suspensions are related to further negative outcomes are not sufficient to prove that school practices are the first step in a causal sequence,
without controlling for a host of other covariates. At each point in our proposed STPP model, multivariate and multi-level models have tested those
relationships while including controls for a variety of demographic and behavioral characteristics and prospective longitudinal studies have better been
able to ascertain direction of causation. Together, this body of research supports the conclusions of the American Academy of Pediatrics (2013) that
suspension and expulsion are, in and of themselves, a developmental risk
factor, above and beyond demographic or student behavioral risk factors.
Some (e.g., Burris, 2012) have suggested that the pipeline is not merely
causal but intentional. Although some limited data supports the notion of
pushout for academic reasons, further research would be necessary to support
the notion of intentionality in the school-to-prison pipeline.

CONCLUSION

It is becoming increasingly clear that the school-to-prison pipeline is more
than simply a metaphorical or political concept. Rather, research evidence
consistently supports the claims most frequently made concerning the STPP.
Simply put, disciplinary removal through out-of-school suspension and expulsion increases student risk for a variety of serious negative outcomes, and
such risks are not distributed equally, but rather fall disproportionately upon
students depending on their race, gender, disability status, and, most likely,
by their sexual orientation/gender identity. Regardless of other factors that
may increase the risk of negative short- and long-term outcomes, these data
consistently indicate that out-of-school suspensions or expulsions *in and of
themselves* increase student risk for school disengagement, poor school outcomes, dropout, and involvement with juvenile justice, especially among
those groups who are disproportionately disciplined.

Such findings have contributed to a national reconsideration of the use of
out-of-school suspension and expulsion as school disciplinary measures.
Across the nation, a number of major urban school districts, including the
Los Angeles Unified School District (Jones, 2013) and Broward County,
Florida (Alvarez, 2013), have revised their codes of conduct shifting the
focus to preventive alternatives, and using suspension and expulsion only as
a last resort. A national initiative to supporting disciplinary reform by the
U.S. Departments of Justice and Education has resulted in new federal guidelines aimed at reducing the use of, and disproportionality in, suspension and
expulsion, highlighting the discriminatory nature of disparities in school discipline (U.S. Department of Education/Department of Justice, 2014).

Thus, a national consensus appears to be emerging, focusing on the need to replace ineffective and inequitable exclusionary practices with more preventive and instructional strategies for developing safe and healthy school climates. Yet, it is also true that many schools still consider suspension and expulsion to be essential tools in maintaining school order; demands for sudden and wholesale changes in school discipline will likely generate resistance and even create a risk for increased school disorder, unless school personnel are adequately supported with training and resources that enable them to effectively implement new approaches. In 2014, the Discipline Disparities Research-to-Practice Collaborative, a national consortium of researchers, educators, advocates, and policy analysts, released a series of recommendations for reducing the use of exclusionary discipline, and especially for addressing disciplinary disparities, in the areas of school-based intervention (Gregory, Bell, and Pollock, 2014), policy (Losen, Hewitt, and Toldson, 2014), and research (Skiba, Arredondo, and Rausch, 2014).[4] Those recommendations include:

School-Based Intervention

- Develop interventions that approach issues of discipline as issues of equity, and educational opportunity, inextricable from issues of student instruction.
- Prevent conflict by supporting student-teacher relationships, increasing academic rigor, implementing culturally responsive instruction and classroom interaction, and establishing bias-free classrooms and respectful school environments.
- When conflict does occur, make use effective and pre-planned responses, including structured inquiry into the causes of conflict through analysis of disaggregated discipline data, problem-solving approaches to discipline, recognizing and including student and family voices, and reintegrating students after conflict.

Policy

- Ensure that states and school districts collect, publicly report, and use disaggregated discipline data to guide disciplinary practices.
- Revise federal and state accountability structures to include measures of exclusionary discipline levels and disparities, require schools in turnaround status to address disciplinary as well as achievement gaps, and include incentives in federally supported programs for reducing disciplinary gaps.

- Expand the availability of evidence-based disciplinary alternatives by supporting increased research on the effects of alternatives to suspension and expulsion.
- Support teacher training and professional development aimed at promoting higher levels of student engagement and improved student-teacher relationships.

Research

- Increase examination of the extent of and reasons for disciplinary disparities, especially for groups that have been under-represented in that research, such as Native American, LGBT, and English language–learning students.
- Increase research on the impact of security personnel and technology on disciplinary outcomes, school arrests, and disparities.
- Continue to build the knowledge base of effective interventions and programs that can enable schools to reduce their use of exclusionary discipline and reduce disciplinary disparities.
- Identify a range of resources that schools and districts can access in order to create effective disciplinary reform.

To create successful reform in school discipline, resources in the domains of practice, policy, and research will need to be mobilized to implement more effective and equitable methods of school discipline. As our nation increasingly comes to a shared consensus that it is time to reducing the risk and disproportionality created by exclusionary discipline through the implementation of more comprehensive and preventive approaches, a key challenge will be to ensure that all school personnel are provided with the tools they require to preserve both the integrity of the school learning climate and student learning opportunity.

ACKNOWLEDGMENTS

The authors gratefully acknowledge Atlantic Foundations and the Open Societies Foundation for their generous support of this research.

NOTES

1. Significant portions of this chapter appeared in: Skiba, R. J., Arredondo, M. I., and Williams, N. T. (2014). More than a metaphor: The contribution of exclusionary discipline to a school-to-prison pipeline. *Equity and Excellence in Education, 47*(4), 546–564; and are used with express permission of the Taylor & Francis Group.

2. Although definitions of the school-to-prison pipeline may include police presence or school arrests as components of that model (see, e.g., Price, 2009; Thurau and Wald, 2009/2010), due to space limitations, this chapter will focus only on the extent to which exclusionary discipline practices contribute to a set of negative developmental outcomes that might be considered pathways in an STPP model.

3. Students with disabilities are those served under the Individuals with Disabilities Education Improvement Act (2014).

4. The complete set of recommendations contained in those briefing papers, as well as supplementary materials pertaining to disciplinary disparities, can be found on the Discipline Disparities Research-to-Practice Collaborative website: http://rtpcollaborative.indiana.edu.

Chapter Eleven

Unpacking Classroom Discipline Pedagogy

Intent vs. Impact

Tonya Walls, Janessa Schilmoeller, Irvin Guerrero, and Christine Clark

The headline, "[Desert] County Schools See Rise in Discipline for Bullying" (KLAS-TV, 2014), coupled with a report that the Desert County School District (DCSD) suspended or expelled 1,736 students for bullying or intimidation during the 2012–2013 school year, 9.6 percent more than the 1,584 pupils disciplined for those acts in 2011–2012 ([State] Department of Education, 2012–2013a, p. 3; 2011–2012, p. 6), captures one of the many disciplinary dilemmas that embattled DCSD school leaders have to confront. On the one hand, school leaders may feel a need to address school safety concerns in humanizing ways, and, on the other hand, they may feel obligated to adhere to the district's no tolerance policy, supported by national, state, and local regulations. In the face of such a dichotomy, policy and related regulatory actions typically win (Gregory, Clawson, Davis, and Gerewitz, 2014). As a result, the disciplinary procedures and practices enacted within PK-12 schools often lead to exclusionary and punitive approaches, increasing suspensions and expulsions in general, and the over-representation of students of color who are suspended, expelled, or otherwise punitively reprimanded for discipline matters overall (American Civil Liberties Union of Nevada, 2012). Such disproportionality in disciplinary practices raises concerns about how discipline is being employed in schools and provides the context for DCSD educators to engage in critical dialogue around this topic, particularly as it is connected to the national debate around racial justice and the proliferation of the School-to-Prison Pipeline (STPP). In fact, top district officials have already begun such dialogue. In an opinion piece titled "Rethinking Discipline to Increase Academic Achievement," Denson (2013), a former DCSD associate superintendent and co-chair of the superintendent's Educational Opportunities Advisory Council (SEOAC), explains that, "DCSD must do all that it can to ensure that schools are safe places to learn, so that students are ready to compete in college or career without remediation" (para. 1). Denson's piece marks the beginning of a district-wide initiative to unpack and address the question lingering within the headline posed by local television station, KLAS-TV (2014):

> How might school leaders, and classroom teachers address the need for disciplinary practices that decrease violence, while simultaneously maximizing student opportunities to learn and thrive in an environment that is safe, inclusive, academically challenging, and ensures equity in access to effective teaching and learning for all students?

Denson's piece seeks to answer this question using the ten points put forth by SEOAC to address the committee's concerns about racial disproportionality in disciplinary action impact. One point explicitly calls for the reduction in the over-representation of students of color being disciplined using exclusionary methods, and two other points suggest that this reduction can best be done by providing professional development focused on helping teachers and school leaders develop *cultural competency*, or as DCSD has come to define it, the ability to develop effective relationships with people who are culturally and socially diverse by recognizing, reflecting on, and suspending the impact of preconceptions, stereotypes, and personal biases on educational issues related to diversity (DCSD, 2014). These three points make clear the priority DCSD has made in regard to these concerns, and provide a pathway for school leaders and teachers to begin to develop the ability to enact Culturally Responsive Pedagogy (CRP) that district leadership appears to believe will help it more proactively, fairly, and, ultimately, effectively address disciplinary challenges. What is of controversy is whether or not these proposed solutions employed as a result of this initiative, can actually achieve these goals.

RESEARCH CONTEXT

The research documented and discussed in this chapter was undertaken as a part of the requirements for a graduate course on the STPP, described in the course as the formal and informal educational and law enforcement processes and policies (and the prejudices—acknowledged, covert, and denied—that underlie both) that have the effect of pushing PK-12 students, predominantly Black and Latino males, out of school and into the juvenile and adult criminal justice systems (Clark, 2012). Using pre-existing connections (familiarity sampling) within a single, large, school district in the urban southwestern United States (DCSD), graduate student research teams were directed to examine the STPP through analysis of teacher disciplinary practices, broadly considered to include the nature of their relationships with students, non/engagement with parents, pedagogical approaches, and classroom management techniques). Teams were to develop a critical ethnographic research-based framework (Fettermen, 1998; Frank, 1999; Hammerseley, 1990; Madison, 2013; Spradley, 1980) to structure their classroom observations. While these observations were to be the focus of the research, educational practices not exclusively at the classroom level, nor solely related to teacher instructional habits, that fed the STPP were also to be considered. In short, teacher classroom management strategies, whether they fed or starved the STPP, were to be examined in the context of the larger school climate and culture.

The focus of our research team's critical ethnographic inquiry was to explore the ways in which proposed solutions for discipline, articulated in the SEOAC's ten-point proposal, entitled *[Desert] County School District Final Report on Overrepresentation by Gender, Race/Ethnicity, or Disability in Discipline-Related Actions and/or Special Education Placement*, and enacted by elementary school leaders, show up in teacher practice at the classroom level (SEOAC, 2013). We entered into this critical ethnographic inquiry with the understanding that Culturally Responsive Classroom Management (CRCM), discussed further later (Ladson-Billings, 1995; Haberman, 1995; Weinstein, Tomlinson-Clarke, and Curran, 2004; Brown, 2004; Bondy, Ross, Gallingane, and Hambacher, 2007; Gay, 2010; Dahlgren, 2015), can be used as a powerful tool to combat the social inequities in school discipline, and, thus, begin to disrupt and/or dismantle the first point of contact for students being shuffled into the STPP (Clark, 2011). In an effort to determine whether or not this premise is sound, we examined the classroom management and disciplinary practices of two elementary school teachers. We asked ourselves the following questions as we observed: 1) *In what ways do the school discipline policies and procedures and/or classroom management practices enacted by elementary school teachers align with the characteristics of CRCM, if at all?*; and, 2) *Do these practices reproduce or disrupt and dismantle the social inequities in school discipline evident in the national and local data?* What follows is our explication of the inquiry. We begin with an overview of the conceptual framework used to conduct the inquiry, followed by a description of the observational site. This is succeeded by a summary of our observational experiences, including the outlining of key findings coupled with relevant connections to literature in the field. We close with a summary of conclusions and a discussion of the implications these may have for classroom management, teacher professional development, and school discipline.

CONCEPTUAL AND OBSERVATIONAL FRAMEWORK

The national debate around the effectiveness of zero-tolerance policies is a significant one for DCSD generally, and, more specifically, for its teachers and school leaders who are charged with enacting these policies within their classrooms and schools. Statistics released from the U.S. Department of Education (NCES, 2014) reveal that within DCSD, African American students and students receiving special education services are over-represented in statistics for students receiving disciplinary action, and under-represented in statistics for students receiving an education that might prepare them for college or career once they graduate. As the report details, African American children and youth account for 14.4 percent of the student population, yet represented 32.8 percent of expelled students, 25.8 percent of those given out-of-school suspensions, and 25.2 percent of those given in-school suspensions (para. 4). In 2009, DCSD also reported 670 students were referred to law enforcement: 220 students with school-related arrests, and 550 students who were expelled under zero-tolerance policies, for infractions such as bringing squirt guns (toy water pistols) to school because they "look like" weapons (American Civil Liberties Union of Nevada, 2012, p. 8). It is clear that, like school districts across the nation, DCSD finds itself grappling with a policy initiative that: 1) criminalizes even minor disciplinary infractions, 2) negates the ability of adults within the school to develop trusting, caring, and supportive relationships with students (in part because the policy initiative strips these adults of discretionary decision-making authority relative to the imposition of disciplinary measures); thus, 3) fails to promote conflict resolution and problem-solving; and, 4) cultivates a climate that is exclusionary, punitive, and reactive, while also failing to preserve the safety and integrity of the learning environment that it claims to promote. Accordingly, DCSD schools, and the educators and school leaders within them—including those at our observational site—are tasked with finding new and creative ways to address discipline.

The Observational Site

Let's Go Innovative Elementary School (pseudonym) is a small, public, PK-5 school located in the city's historically African American community. According to the latest accountability report published by the [State] Department of Education (2015), the school has 519 students (p. 2). The school's mission statement conveys a family-friendly sentiment and to stress the school's focus on the arts and technology. Though the school has historically maintained a primarily African American student body, most of whom live in the area immediately surrounding the school, this area has recently undergone a demographic shift, and thus, so too has the school.

The students and instructional staff. Today, 279 (53 percent) Let's Go students identify themselves as Hispanic, 190 (36 percent) identify as Black, 20 (3 percent) identify as White, and 16 (3 percent) identify as two or more races, with 14 (2.6 percent) identifying as other ([State] Department of Education, 2015, p. 2, para. 1). Additionally, 268 (51 percent) Let's Go students are female, while 251 (48 percent) are males. 58 (11 percent) Let's Go students have an individualized education program or IEP, 182 (35 percent) qualify for English Language Learner supports, and 470 (90 percent) qualify for free/reduced price lunch ([State] Department of Education, 2015, p. 2).

Though demographic data on DCSD teachers and administrators is not easily made public, ethnographic and informal survey data reveal that the Let's Go instructional staff, which includes PK-5 classroom teachers and specialists, is not as diverse as the student body. 15, or 48 percent of faculty, identify as White, 11 (35 percent) identify as Black, and 5 (16 percent) identify as Hispanic/non-Black (Walls, 2015). There are 4 male teachers, 2 African American and 2 White; the rest are female. All but 7 teachers range in age from early twenties to late-thirties, and approximately 80 percent are new to the school and have been teaching for less than ten years (Walls, 2015). Thus, the teaching faculty at Let's Go Innovative Elementary school is primarily new-to-the-profession, young, female, and White, and the student body is best characterized as racially and ethnically diverse, working class, and characteristic of those disproportionally over-represented in STPP. These demographics reflect national data from research in teacher education and on the STPP that the least prepared/experienced teachers end up in the highest-need schools (Gay, 2010; Harry and Klingner, 2006; Howard, 2006; Irizarry, 2011).

School leaders. Let's Go Innovative Elementary is led by two charismatic, middle-age African American administrators, the principal, who is male, and the assistant principal, who is female. Both are aware of the district's focus on disrupting the pattern of disproportionality in discipline, and both express being highly committed to taking up this challenge. When interviewed, both conveyed the desire to create and nurture a safe, positive, and productive learning environment where students develop the personal and interpersonal skills they need to be successful in school and society. Each also stated that they hoped to create spaces where teachers and students developed strategies and tools to resolve problems and conflict, as a part of developing strong relationships. "We must have a connection to the student and we must be proactive; by connections, I mean that the kids need to know that we care for them, and that we are here for them, and finally that we will go the extra step for them" (S. Cunningham [pseudonym], personal communication, November 5, 2015). These words, shared during an interview of the assistant principal, illustrate Let's Go leadership's desire to create a school environment built on strong relationships and an ethic of care. The principal echoed this sentiment and connected it to discipline in sharing that:

> Building relationships and developing a system of logical consequences is important in discipline. We must find out what the child was trying to avoid or gain or how s/he was thinking before we apply discipline or make decisions. If we don't know our students, we won't be able to do this. (D. Dawson [pseudo-nym], personal communication, November 5, 2015).

Both school leaders acknowledged the importance of valuing each student's cultural capital and felt it was an important to consider this capital when applying disciplinary consequences. Finally, both school leaders were aware of the STPP, acknowledged their roles as school leaders in disrupting and dismantling it, and were verbally supportive of the district's initiatives to explore culturally responsive pedagogical and classroom management practices as one way to begin this disruption/dismantling process.

Reported behaviors and school-wide discipline approach. When we turned our attention to the school's approach to discipline and related behaviors, we found that Let's Go Innovative Elementary School reported eight incidents of violence between students, and three from student toward staff during the 2014–2015 school year ([State] Department of Education, 2015, p. 3). Thirteen incidents of bullying were reported with only two of the incidents leading to student suspension/expulsion (p. 3). The school reported no instances of cyber bullying, and both administrators reported that while conflict between students is an issue, discipline problems that lead to police involvement and exclusionary practices are minimal. The principal attributed minimal police involvement to small class sizes (the school reported a 21:1 student to teacher ratio in grades PK-4, and 30:1 in fifth grade ([State] Department of Education, 2015, p. 3), the development of a community of care, and leadership ability to navigate the district's "no tolerance" policy directives in critically conscious ways, as well as with intentionality toward disrupting the STPP. When asked how a community of care is developed across classrooms, the principal shared, "We are still working on that. We (meaning administration) have been going through 'Cultural Competence' training to learn how to relate to our students better and now we have to find ways to help teachers develop those skills" (D. Dawson, personal communication, November 5, 2015). While neither he, nor the assistant principal, could share explicit ways in which school-wide discipline was addressed using non-exclusionary practices, they did both express a desire to share what they had learned about CRP with their teachers, and explained that they had already begun to discuss possible strategies for undertaking this sharing that would, ideally, lead to their teachers being able to actualize CRP. Both believed that the implementation of CRP would help the school to decrease bullying complaints, as well as help them to handle other discipline issues in culturally responsive ways. We believe this is the reason these school leaders were such willing participants in our team's research inquiry. They, too, wanted to explore our premise that CRCM might be a powerful tool in disrupting and, eventually, dismantling the STPP.

A Pragmatic Solution: Culturally Responsive Classroom Management

We assert that CRCM can be used as a strategic tool to disrupt and dismantle the STPP. Drawing from Black feminist thought, Matthew Lynch (2011) summarizes CRP as, "a student centered approach to teaching in which the students' unique cultural strengths are identified and nurtured to promote student achievement and a sense of well-being about the student's cultural place in the world" (p. 1). Teachers who employ CRP to enact what we codify herein as CRCM value the culture, language, beliefs, interests, and personal experiences that students bring to school, view these experiences as resources—what some researchers have called *cultural capital* or *funds of knowledge*—and use these resources as assets on which to build, rather than seeing them as barriers to learning (Aceves and Orosco, 2014; Moll, Amanti, Neff, & González, 1992; Yosso, 2005). A major theme emerges from a review and synthesis of research on the use of CRP; it can help create safe, inclusive, and culturally responsive learning environments, eliminate and/or disrupt the need to employ punitive and exclusionary discipline practices, and positively impact student engagement and achievement (Ladson-Billings, 1995; Haberman, 1995; Weinstein, Tomlinson-Clarke, and Curran, 2004; Brown, 2004; Bondy, Ross, Gallingane, and Hambacher, 2007; Gay, 2010; Dahlgren, 2015). Further, Haberman (1995) explains, "Whatever the reasons for children's behavior—whether poverty, personality, a handicapping condition, a dysfunctional home, or an abusive environment—classroom teachers are responsible for managing children, seeing that they work together in a confined space for long periods, and ensuring that they learn" (p. 22). This explanation emphasizes the requirement for teachers to create learning environments that meet and sustain the needs of all students, with appreciative understanding of all students' diverse backgrounds. CRCM may be one way to accomplish this goal.

CRCM builds from the understanding that expectations for behaviors are culturally influenced, and that conflicts around behavior are more likely to happen when teachers and students come from different cultural backgrounds (Weinstein, Tomlinson-Clarke, and Curran, 2004). Rather than being an approach, CRCM is a mindset and a disposition with its ultimate goal not being to achieve compliance or control, but, rather, to provide all students with equitable opportunities for learning (Weinstein, Tomlinson-Clarke, and Curran, 2004). Further, when teachers use classroom management techniques that reflect the needs of their culturally diverse learners and that support CRP, they are more likely to develop strong relationships with students and are non-punitive with their students when administering discipline measures (Brown, 2004). Through CRCM a mutual respect is established between teachers and students, which, in turn, helps to create a caring learning community in which teachers' authentic interest in the success of their students is ever-present. Teachers who successfully practice CRCM, demonstrate assertiveness in interactions with students by setting clear expectations for achievement and behavior (Brown, 2004). What is not clear from the research in this area is if these habits of practice were developed in the studied teachers' educational training, something they learned from trial and error in their own classroom practice, and/or a function of specific teacher personalities; this information gap notwithstanding, there is ample evidence to support the claim that educators seeking to disrupt the STPP will be supported in this effort by the adoption of a CRCM posture.

CRCM is a viable tool to improve classroom management, and thus students' engagement within schools (Brown, 2004; Weinstein, Tomlinson-Clarke, and Curran, 2004). Use of CRCM requires teachers to have a clear understanding of "self" and the values, priorities, and/or biases that impact their teaching praxis and, ultimately, student success. This means teachers must employ a self-critical lens when managing student behaviors and making disciplinary decisions. It is essential for teachers to acknowledge and consider that cultural differences exist among people generally, and that schools, as societal institutions/systems, perpetuate biased and discriminatory practices based on cultural differences, differentially negatively impacting students from non-dominant cultural groups. Accordingly, teachers must develop techniques to combat biased and discriminatory practices that minimally include: 1) organizing the physical space in their classrooms in ways that are conducive to the development of respectful relationships with and between students; 2) establishing clear expectations for student behavior and responding immediately when behaviors are off course; 3) creating a community of care with and between students; and, 4) communicating with students in ways that respond to their cultural precepts and values. In school communities where students come from cultural backgrounds that have been traditionally marginalized and are disproportionately represented in those targeted by exclusionary and punitive discipline measures, the incorporation of CRCM on the part of the teacher has proved beneficial, including in disrupting and/or dismantling the STPP, while simultaneously improving student engagement and equitable achievement outcomes in schools (Brown, 2004; Weinstein, Tomlinson-Clarke, and Curran, 2004).

DCSD has already embarked upon a bold professional development effort designed to ensure that every school leader and teacher is *culturally compe-*

tent—able to use CRP with efficiency and toward the goal of addressing racial and gender disproportionality in disciplinary practices and less than satisfactory achievement outcomes (DCSD Pledge of Achievement Strategic Plan, 2014). With this in mind, we sought to determine whether or not this district-wide initiative to provide ongoing professional development training in CRCM, through the development of CRP, had translated to the use of said practices in actual classrooms (it was beyond the scope of this study to also consider impacts on satisfactory achievement outcomes). We also wanted to determine whether or not these practices, once used, did, in fact, disrupt disproportionality in punitive and exclusionary discipline measures, including the STPP. We chose to explore these questions through classroom observations within a single DCSD elementary school with leaders committed to the district's initiative to develop teacher cultural competency. We selected critical ethnography as our inquiry approach, primarily because critical ethnography would allow us to focus our classroom observations through a critical lens focused on unpacking classroom teaching and disciplinary practices and their impact on traditionally marginalized students. We were able to obtain the school leaders', S. Cunningham and D. Dawson, permission to observe two teachers at Let's Go Innovative Elementary School. These teachers were Mr. B., who teaches second grade, and Ms. W. who teaches fifth grade. The teachers and their students also agreed to be observed.

RESEARCH PROCESS

Critical Ethnography and a CRCM Observational Framework

Based on the conceptual understanding that CRCM promotes inclusive learning environments that eliminate and/or disrupt the need for more punitive and exclusionary discipline practices most associated with the STPP, we created a CRCM framework to guide our observations (see Appendix A). Our framework outlines characteristics of teachers who operate with CRCM knowledge, skills, and dispositions. These characteristics include, but are not limited to: recognition of one's own cultural lens; demonstrated knowledge of students' cultural background; understanding of the broader socioeconomic and sociopolitical context of schooling; ability and willingness to use culturally appropriate techniques; and, commitment to building caring classroom communities. A classroom observation protocol form was derived from the CRCM framework for research team members to use to, at least loosely, guide observation note-taking process (see Appendix B). This form included a section for CRCM indicator codes in the analysis of our findings.

Each research team member conducted six hours of classroom observations, three hours with each of the two selected classroom teachers. The first observation was completed by all three researchers at the same time on

October 8, 2015. The purpose of this joint observation was to "calibrate" our observation protocol and discuss our individual observation styles. We each recorded observation notes individually, discussed our observations, compared observation strategies, and recommended ways to align our individual observations moving forward. Two such calibrations were to remember to document times of classroom events, and to describe the specific students involved in noted in teacher-student interactions. At the conclusion of the observation period, we met to discuss and analyze all findings, noting specific connections to the CRCM framework, as well discrepant observations in contrast to the framework.

By rooting this study in the conceptual framework of CRCM, we hoped to implement a critical ethnography that "resist[ed] domestication and move[d] from 'what is' to 'what could be,'" specifically in terms of what strategies and characteristics teachers in urban elementary school classrooms can implement as an alternative to the destructive zero tolerance measures that fuel the STPP (Madison, 2012, p. 5). Madison (2012) describes the meaning of critical ethnographers' attempts to "resist domestication" by using resources, skills, and privileges "to penetrate the borders and break through the confines in defense of—the voices and experiences of subjects whose stories are otherwise restrained and out of reach" (p. 5). Critical ethnographers understand that both empowered and disempowered groups of people exist everywhere—in the case of this study, including within the classroom; accordingly, with this understanding, critical ethnographers attempt to uncover the invisible hegemonic practices that contribute to this power divide through ethnographic observations (Dunbar, 2009).

In line with our specific critical ethnographic study goals, our research team sought to identify and highlight the impact of classroom management on the experiences of students most marginalized and at risk of entering the STPP. In so doing, we felt the research would also assist the school's leaders, who indicated a desire to transform school discipline methods by seeking to better understand students, including their school discipline experiences:

> It is important to understand why students exhibit behaviors. For example, take that girl in the news with the cell phone incident, she was a foster child and probably felt that her cell phone was the only thing that connected her to a sense of value. Of course she wouldn't give that cell phone up, because she needed it. So in her case, the district policies and procedures don't work. You have to do something different. Now I know I have to keep my job and make sure I am doing what I am supposed to do, but I also have to stay true to my convictions. I've learned how to navigate the gray areas of policies and procedures. I have to talk to my students and learn who they are. I have to talk to my teachers and help them connect with our students better. That way, instead of suspending and expelling students, we can investigate because they will talk to us. Together we can figure out solutions that don't lead to kicking students out

of the classroom and the school but before we get there, we have to know what's going on with them. We have to be critical about ourselves too. I am learning that in my classes and professional development. (D. Dawson, personal communication, November 5, 2015)

As this quote illustrates, the principal, himself, takes a critical stance to impacting change within the school; clearly, he wants to make a positive difference. He shared further in this vein stating, "The influence of My Brother's Keeper [Obama-inspired educational initiative to address the STPP] weighs heavily on me as an African American male; I feel compelled to change the pipeline for Hispanic and African American male students. I want to create a pipeline to college, not prison." The African American, female assistant principal echoes his concerns here in reflecting:

The teacher's culture and climate is the real detriment, or not to how behaviors manifest in classrooms. As a teacher, I knew I was a role model for students and I expected them to succeed, so they did. The teacher has to take full responsibility for their environment and try to instill in kids a willingness to want to improve and do better. This means they have to adopt a philosophy, routines and behavioral expectations that say kids can do this! They have to believe it as much as the kids which means they have to listen to and get to know the kids. They have to care and they have to build the relationship. How we get teachers to this place, I don't know exactly. (S. Cunningham, personal communication, November 5, 2015)

With these comments in mind, our research team believed that both leaders would apply relevant findings from our study to help them accomplish their goals for school-wide discipline transformation. For this reason, we included them in our team's discussion and development of our observational approach in this study.

Summary of Observational Experiences

Two classrooms were selected for observation in this study: a second grade classroom and a fifth grade classroom. These classes were selected by the principal upon our request. Our intent was to observe the two teachers that the principal identified as having the "most effective" and "least effective" classroom management skills. Observations were analyzed collaboratively to determine whether any of the CRCM framework indicators were present. Findings are reported by grade level below.

Second grade classroom. The second grade teacher in this observation is referred to as Mr. B. He is a young African American male teacher who is in his first year of teaching, obtaining a preliminary teaching license through the Alternate Route to Licensure program (ARL) at a local university. Mr. B. implemented many "traditional" classroom management strategies that a new teacher seeking to establish control of the classroom might be expected to try, most of which did not align with CRCM framework indicators. Generally, rather than resolving misbehavior using proactive solution-oriented practices, Mr. B. relied on reactive measures. His presence in the classroom and instructional strategies were fractured, students' voices were discouraged in myriad ways, and differentiated treatment toward students based on gender was evident.

Teacher-centered control. According to Winn (2011), urban pedagogies, that prioritize discipline over rigorous education, form a *culture of incarceration* or students as *education's prisoners* in classrooms that, increasingly, resemble prisons as a result of the warped relationship between schooling, political economy, and the prison-industrial complex. "Both students and teachers become imprisoned by the idea that Black and Brown bodies are in need of constant policing and surveillance, and that youth should seldom, if ever, be heard" (Winn, 2011, p. 111). This notion of *ghetto schooling*, which emphasizes discipline and control over quality teaching and learning for urban, poor, underserved communities, was evident in Mr. B.'s classroom, especially in the ways that he opted to silence students who were active and interactive in the classroom in ways that he deemed out of bounds.

In the first classroom observation, Mr. B. questioned a Latino male student about an incident involving a missing iPad® (mobile digital device) that was discovered in the student's possession on the previous day. The student, Sebastian (pseudonym), stood at his desk while all of the other students sat (arranged in an u-shape) and watched. This questioning went on for approximately 15 minutes, in a one-directional teacher-centered manner during which Sebastian did not have an opportunity to meaningfully respond. The teacher told Sebastian that he, the teacher, would have to write a referral to the principal and call his parents regarding the incident; however, Mr. B. also told Sebastian that he had saved himself from further involvement with the police by admitting that he had the iPad. Mr. B. then told the class that they were "not too young for handcuffs" and that, "they have a place for children to go to jail." Though Mr. B. told the class that his goal was for none of them to ever have handcuffs on their wrists, he also said that if this incident had happened outside of his influence, like at a Wal-Mart, Sebastian would be in jail. Mr. B. also emphasized to the class, and more specifically to Sebastian, that "there are cameras everywhere," and that these cameras watch students for bad behavior. It was as if Mr. B. was making a direct connection to Foucault's (1995) concept of *panopticism*, the major effect of which is "to induce in the inmate a state of conscious and permanent visibility that assures the automatic functioning of power" (p. 201). Although Mr. B. used positive language in saying that it was his goal for none of his students to ever have handcuffs on their wrists, his holding of, essentially, a disciplinary hearing on Sebastian during class (witnessed by all), was teacher-centered and -

controlled, as was his suggestion that he had the power to determine the extent to which police might become involved. He did not engage in any student-centered dialogue on reasons for misbehavior or solutions to the root causes of it. Further, Sebastian was never given an opportunity to explain why he took the iPad and there was never any discussion about positive alternative behaviors that Sebastian could enact should he be placed in a similar situation in the future. Instead, Mr. B. portrayed Sebastian as a *spectacle* of what not to do: "to make everyone aware, through the body of the criminal, of the unrestrained presence of the sovereign" (p. 49).

Mr. B.'s teacher-centered and -controlled classroom management style was reiterated later in a curricular connection that he made between Sebastian's actions and those of the "bad" character in a book the class read aloud about a cat bandit who burglarizes a local home. This character could have been used by Mr. B. as an opportunity to help students make connections between their background knowledge and/or prior learning; instead Mr. B. used it to exacerbate the example of Sebastian as *spectacle*.

While Mr. B.'s teaching behavior, as it was just described, seems troubling, it is important to consider a counteranalysis of it as well. We do not have extensive enough qualitative interview data to discern the true intentions of Mr. B. in his exchange with Sebastian. Accordingly, it is possible that Mr. B was attempting to enact a culturally responsive pedagogy in his handling of the missing iPad. For example, if viewed through what Delpit (1988) terms the *culture of power*, it is important to consider the rules, codes, and patterns of behaviors that children from marginalized homes learn in order to operate in mainstream school and societal culture. Delpit argues that teachers from marginalized communities may enact pedagogy based on these rules, codes, and patterns in ways misunderstood by their mainstream peers and educational researchers alike. Thus, it is possible, that Mr. B believed he was disrupting Sebastian's entrée into the STPP by publicly shaming him, rather than allowing others—again outside of Mr. B.'s control—to handle the situation. Perhaps out of care, Mr. B. offered his own brand of firm "real-talk" interrogation inside the classroom, explicitly providing Sebastian and the rest of the class a reminder about the rules, codes, and patterns of behavior that they are expected to follow in mainstream public settings like school, and/or a Wal-mart. Mr. B. also delivered this message in what might be characterized as a decidedly culturally informed manner: with an authoritative stance, and in a strong and animated tone of voice through which he may have intended for all the students to learn from Sebastian's experiences (Ladson-Billings, 1995). By doing this in the presence of Sebastian's peers, Mr. B may have even been exercising a culturally informed brand of restorative justice, in that the iPad theft was a problem rooted in the school and larger community and, thus, it had potential to negatively impact all of his students (especially those who most resembled Sebastian). Accordingly, Mr. B. may have believed the problem needed to be engaged more broadly (Acosta, Chinman, Engberg, and Augustine, 2015). So, instead of pulling Sebastian aside to speak to him privately, perhaps in a softer tone of voice, as is characteristic of Eurocentric culturally informed approach stressing individual communicative confidentiality, Mr. B chose to make the discourse public, perhaps as a teachable moment during which Sebastian was, at least in theory, provided the opportunity to take responsibility for his own actions, especially to take responsibility for their negative impact on his classroom peers. By using this possibly culturally specific praxis, Mr. B was able to teach a lesson to Sebastian and the entire class at the same time. However, it is not clear if Mr. B's approach was, in fact, intentionally embedded culturally responsive praxis. Further, even if it was, it still fell short in that it appeared to perpetuate what such praxis seeks to interrupt: the marginalization of Sebastian and, thus, his subsequent funneling into DCSD's STPP.

Differentiated treatment. In fact, teacher-centered control and reactive discipline arose in every one of our observations in Mr. B.'s classroom, and several observations highlighted especially strict disciplinary reactions toward Black female students. Black girls are often viewed as a "problem" and/ or as disrupting of the normative classroom climate. Winn (2011) argues that these so-called disruptive behaviors of Black girls are actually their culturally informed/performed ways of demonstrating knowledge. Unfortunately, these actions are not understood as such by most teachers and, thus, not only not valued, but devalued, deemed deviant, and disciplined.

On several occasions, Mr. B. "shut down" Black girls in his classroom for perceived "outbursts" during class discussions, as well as for various forms of self-expression (physical and verbal) while working independently. One specific student, Shae (pseudonym), was repeatedly singled out. Mr. B. was hastier to react to her every utterance and movement, and expressed impatience with her in his tone of voice when attempting to redirect her behaviors; he also publicly scolded her for behaviors such as dancing (though he played music in the classroom) or walking to his desk to ask a question. Other students exhibiting similar behaviors were not only not reprimanded, their behaviors went unnoticed as problematic. This is a clear example of what the STPP literature defines and documents as race and/or gender-related disciplinary disparity (Harry and Klingner, 2006). During one observation, though Shae was talking and dancing to the music, she was on task, cutting paper for a math activity. Still, Mr. B. said to her in an exasperated voice, "Shae! You need to do more cutting and less talking!" Meanwhile, a male student next to Shae was never redirected for not doing working on this task at all, and the students with whom Shae was talking were not admonished. When Shae went to the teacher's desk for help in the same manner as several other students before her had, she was told not to dance up to the desk, rather to ask for help the "correct" way; in response to this Shae stomped back to her desk, flopped down in her seat and said to no one in particular, "When I asked for help he just ignored me." Shae raised her hand in the air (to ask for help the "correct" way), but Mr. B. ignored her even when he came near her desk, instead answering the questions of a boy sitting next to her.

Later on, a male student accidently hit Shae with his chair and Shae expressively exclaimed, "Ouch! That hurt!" Mr. B. responded by telling Shae that it was "rude" to talk so loudly, never acknowledged her injury/pain, nor sought to negotiate an apology from the male student toward Shae. As a result, Shae did not subsequently engage with the male who accidentally hit her when he tried to help her with her assignment. Instead she told him, "I don't want your help!" In this instance, it was clear that Shae was still upset that her injury/pain had gone unaddressed. During another observation, Shae was, again, shut down when trying to make a personal connection to a lesson's content. She raised her hand to attempt to share this connection, in response to which Mr. B. told her to "make it quick" and that what she shared had to be in the form of "a question, not a statement." Shae then said she had forgotten the point she was going to make and opted not to share her connection. Later on, during a class transition period, Mr. B. told Shae to go to the back of the line because she was "arguing" with another student. In fact Shae was talking with another student who was not similarly scolded/punished. During another transition period, another African American female student was also scolded and sent to the back of the line, this time for not standing quietly *enough*. She was told that if she continued to "cause problems in line" she would be sent to the office. When this student arrived at the back of the line confusion ensued as to whether she should go to the absolute back of the line be second last, since a Latina student was previously assigned to be the "caboose" of the line. When this Latina student would not allow the African American female student to go behind her, an argument ensued. Mr. B. never acknowledged the conflict that he essentially created, nor the Latina student's part in it, instead he, again, told the African American female student that she would go to the principal's office if she kept arguing.

Mr. B.'s reactive (not proactive) and often silencing disciplinary action toward expressive Black female students, specifically Shae, reflect findings in the emerging, though still limited, STPP research focused on Black girls. This research documents that Black girls are at a higher risk of suspension for subjective behavior because they are perceived by teachers and other school personnel as "unruly," "loud," and "unmanageable." Further, disciplinary actions, like those of Mr. B., are said to be employed to encourage Black girls to "adopt more 'acceptable' qualities of femininity" (Crenshaw, Ocen, and Nanda, 2015, p. 24); qualities typically associated with hegemonic or white notions of femininity, specifically of the (white) female body as self-regulated, polite, docile, and culturally obedient (Crenshaw, 2003; Harris, 2003; and Deliovsky, 2008). Mr. B.'s repeated requests to Shae to lower her voice, to stay in her seat, and raise her hand are particularly illustrative in these regards.

Since Mr. B.'s ethnic/racial identity matched that of Shae and the other African American female students whom he overdisciplined, it is possible that he was attempting to enact a culturally specific praxis, though clearly one lacking critical insight regarding the culture of power as previously discussed. It is also possible that Mr. B. simply lacked consciousness of his own sexism and, thus, that it most clearly manifested in a culturally embedded fashion. Regardless, greater exploration of the intersectional nature of students' marginalization and its connection to the STPP is needed.

Fifth grade classroom. The fifth grade teacher in this study, Ms. W., is a white female teacher in her fifth year of teaching overall, her second year at Let's Go Innovative Elementary School. Like Mr. B, Ms. W. exhibited a reactive rather than proactive approach in response to conflict in the classroom, as well as inequitable treatment of specific students in her classroom, In particular, we observed disparate discipline of Black male students, as well as of students with special needs, in her classroom. While Ms. W. did also exhibit some of the characteristics highlighted in the CRCM framework—such as accessing students' prior learning, allowing students freer movement including in peer engagement in the classroom, using desk clusters to promote student collaboration, and articulating clear expectations for assignments and activity transitions—it was not clear if these characteristics were present in her classroom management because she had knowledge of and a commitment to CRCM (intentionality), or if, instead, she had simply developed these characteristics as part of her classroom management repertoire as a result of her five years of experience in the classroom (incidentally). It is important to stress that the extent to which Ms. W.'s praxis was CRCM aligned, it was so only in the instructional practices arena, not the behavioral management, one in which her associated teaching practices were observed to be still largely teacher-centered as previously noted.

Characteristics of CRCM. In our observations we noted that Ms. W. attempted to create a classroom environment in which students were provided clear expectations and were encouraged to collaborate. For example, we observed that during activity transitions Ms. W. gave students explicit directives for putting away old and taking out new activity materials, usually thirty seconds, followed by detailed instructions for completing the new activity. We also observed that Ms. W. arranged the students' desks into six groups with four to six students in each, and that students were frequently asked to work with their group to complete assignments. During one observation, Ms. W. asked students to recall prior knowledge from a previous lesson on the Great Depression. Students then watched a rap video about the Great Depression that was, perhaps, intended be culturally responsive and otherwise engaging for students. Several students appeared to show engagement by singing along with the video. During another observation, Ms. W. acknowledged that she was, in fact, wrong when a student called her out for the incorrect answer on a math problem, modeling that it was okay to make mistakes, including in the learning environment, as well as how to move on after making them. In sum, these examples illustrate that Ms. W. demonstrated some of the characteristics of CRCM (see Appendix A).

Teacher-centered control. As noted, although Ms. W.'s classroom management revealed some use of CRCM, its use was not consistent nor *meaningfully* connected to students' learning. Accordingly, these practices may have emerged in Ms. W.'s teaching repertoire because she understood them to be simply "best practice" rather than "culturally responsive." While the *adaptation* of so-called best practices to local contexts is argued to make them, in fact, "good practices," there is still a gap to be bridged between good and culturally responsive or relevant (Gay, 2010). For example, although student desks were arranged in groups to encourage collaboration, these groupings led to group members gaining or losing points for behavior as a group, regardless of the individual action of group members, and absent teacher engagement with the groups. As a result, there were several occasions during which Ms. W. deducted points from an entire group for arguing, though we never observed her providing scaffolding for positive group collaboration, nor acting to resolve group conflicts. Ms. W.'s seeming inability to guide students through group dynamics challenges resulted in obvious lack of engagement for the remainder of the observation period among students directly involved in these challenges, as well as uninvolved students who were punished for their group peers' challenges. This suggested to us these students had no expectation that anything they did/did not do would change the course of their classroom experience at that point.

While Ms. W.'s classroom did not physically resemble Mr. B.'s semicircle panopticon, an arrangement Mr. B. used to manage all students through the creation of clear lines of vision to each and direct access and close proximity to each of their desks, her powerful *gaze* (Foucault, 1995) was still present in the use of the arbitrary group point behavior system. According to Foucault, "A relation of surveillance, defined and regulated, is inscribed at the heart of the practice of teaching, not as an additional or adjacent part, but as a mechanism that is inherent to it and which increases its efficiency" (p. 176). So, even though Ms. W. made statements like, "Thank you group two," or "You are ready, you get a point," to affirm positive behavior in her classroom, she also used this system to disaffirm behavior and remove points, often without notice (thus, without affording students a chance to correct or improve behavior) or clear reasoning. In sum, points were inconsistently given and taken, usually without explicit rationale for either action, thereby, again, conveying to the students that they have no agency in their education because no matter how they behave/perform, there is no clear/predictable/reliable path to success.

Despite Ms. W.'s collaborative groupings, her instructional approach was also largely teacher-centered because of the way that classroom conversation was focused on her voice—either as the authority or as a result of its derelict absence. For example, even when groups were allowed to work autonomously in groups, they did so based on ground rules created exclusively by the teacher. Yet when students raised questions to Ms. W., she told them to ask their group members for answers; in fact, in most instances, Ms. W. did not respond to student requests for help. And, even when Ms. W. did directly solicit students' voices, it was only to answer a specific math question or respond to a specific reading prompt, not to cultivate student-generated critical and creative thought and action.

Differentiated treatment. As noted in general terms previously, Ms. W. exhibited a teacher-centered orientation to conflict resolution in her classroom. This orientation was particularly visible to us in several observations of her interacting with two African American male students and a Latino male student. Repeatedly, the two African American male students were disciplined and then redirected by Ms. W. for actions that went undisciplined when exhibited by other students in the class, particularly female students. While these students' behaviors are described as particularly common among African American students—expression through physical movement, spontaneity, animation, and exaggerated forms of bravado—they are also exhibited by non-African American students, though they are often interpreted differently (as less disruptive) in these students by white, female teachers (Monroe, 2006; Delpit, 1995). Further, Monroe cautions against broad generalizations about so-called culturally normative behavior given the heterogeneity of behavior within cultural groups.

More specifically, in two observations, one of the two African American male students commonly overdisciplined by Ms. W., O (pseudonym), was told to read quietly at his desk. When he got up to the bookshelf, ostensibly to get a new book to read quietly, Ms. W. reacted to his movement immediately and loudly from across the room: "Go back to your seat. We are not doing this; we are not changing books every two minutes. *Now.*" Two female Latina students who were already at the bookshelf when O arrived there, and who had gone there without asking permission, were not simultaneously redirected to return to their seats at that, or any subsequent, point during the reading period. Returning to his seat without a new book, O was then scolded by Ms. W. for talking with his desk group members, and then directed to go sit on the floor by her to read, perhaps from a book he had already read or in which he had no interest. Ms. W. never asked O why he was talking with his group members (one of them had taken something from him). Later, during the same observation, O was arguing with another African American male student about the spelling of his name. Ms. W. came over and told the group to keep working. O told her, in an exasperated, louder voice, that the group had misspelled his name and he was trying to correct them. Ms. W. told O that it was fine that they had misspelled his name, that she, too, had misspelled his name before, and that he needed to keep working. O was later scolded, again publicly, for not sitting "correctly" on his chair, Ms. W. questioned O, "Is that the way we should sit in our chairs?" In stark contrast to Ms. W's hypervigilant corrective actions of O, there were only a very few such actions between Ms. W. and all the other students in the classroom, though many other students talked, even argued in their groups, and sat "incorrectly" in their chairs. Following Ms. W.'s stricter and only teacher-centered disciplinary engagement with O, O was visibly disengaged in class-work, worked much more slowly than others in his group, and continued to have behavioral run-ins with Ms. W.

Ms. W.'s manner of questioning O noted above is illustrative of the research findings on white middle-class teachers' use of indirect, rather than direct, speech. According to Monroe (2006), these teachers' use of indirect speech operates in contrast to the more direct communication styles considered to be more culturally responsive and, thus, effective, especially for economically disadvantaged Black students. Delpit (1995) argues that White middle-class teachers' use of indirect commands, perhaps well-intentioned to downplay student-teacher power relationships in the classroom (Freire, 1970), may have the effect of conveying to some students that the teacher is fearful, thus less deserving of respect. Black teachers are more likely to use explicit commands that some students interpret as these teachers having a high degree of personal power in the classroom, making students less inclined to act out (Delpit, 1995). It is important to consider these raced and classed concerns in a highly discrete and otherwise nuanced way relative to the research on CRP as well as CRCM (Ladson-Billings, 1995; Haberman, 1995; Weinstein, Tomlinson-Clarke, and Curran, 2004; Brown, 2004; Bondy, Ross, Gallingane, and Hambacher, 2007; Gay, 2010; Dahlgren, 2015). Otherwise, Ms. W.'s earlier described behavior could be misinterpreted as using more direct communication (e.g., "Go back to your seat . . . "), and the focus on explicit commands as culturally responsive and relevant for a community whose experience has been so significantly, negatively impacted by racialized colonization could be critiqued as deficit-oriented and racist.

During another observation, O and P (pseudonym) (another African American male student who was among the students who had previously misspelled O's name) appeared disengaged from the lesson and were not provided further explanation of, or direction on, it by Ms. W. In fact, Ms. W. never called on O or P, nor any of their other group members, to answer any of the questions she posed to the class during the lesson. Furthermore, they were the only group not asked to participate. At the outset of the observation, P had his head down on his desk as if sleeping. O played with his pencils. At a slightly later point during the lesson, O, who was humming, was scolded by Ms. W.: "Stop, I told you we are not doing this today." A little later, O and P, still disengaged from the lesson, began arguing with the two Latina female students in their group. Ms. W. came over to the group, told O and P to follow her into the hall, and then handed them over to the school's instructional coach. When Ms. W. returned to the classroom, she told the Latina female students next time they needed to ask O and P "nicely" to stop making noises, not in a rude voice; alternatively she told them they could just ignore O and P. Since O and P were not included in this discussion, no meaningful conflict resolution could occur to enable the group to learn to collaborate better.

Observations in Ms. W.'s classroom also revealed similar disparities in the instruction she gave to, and the disciplinary approaches she employed with, students with special learning needs. Nationally, students who have been labeled as having disabilities are at significant risk for entering the STPP, much greater risk that their counterparts without disability labels. "Although only approximately 9 percent of students aged six to twenty-one have been identified as labeled with disabilities that impact their ability to learn, a survey of correctional facilities found that nationally approximately 34 percent of youth in juvenile corrections had been previously identified as eligible for special education pursuant to the Individuals with Disabilities Education Act (IDEA)" (Kim, Losen, and Hewitt, 2010, p. 51). Additionally, where there is overlap between African American students and students with disabilities, these disparities are even greater. In DCSD alone, the Center for Civil Rights Remedies (2012) reported that 6 percent of all students with disabilities in the elementary grades are suspended, with a higher suspension rate of 13.4 percent for all African American students with disabilities in the elementary grades (p. 1).

In Ms. W.'s classroom, students with special learning needs (identified as such based on public statements made by the teacher or because they were seen working with an aide) were all placed in the same group at the back of the room. Two of the three such identified students were African American males. These students were rarely seen on task with curricular activities that were neither modified nor differentiated. Instead, these students were seen organizing their work spaces, reading quietly, and drawing shapes. Although these students were placed in the "least restrictive" environment in the general classroom as required by special education law (U.S. Department of Education, IDEA, 2004), while there they did not appear to be receiving the adequate and equitable education also required by the law. More specifically, one of the African American males in the special learning needs group was scolded (though it was not clear what for) by the aide there to assist with learning tasks; the aide then directed him to clean out his desk, rather than directing and supporting him to work with his group members on the collaborative science activity assigned to all of the class groups. The disproportionate over-representation of students of color, particularly African American males, in special education is well documented, the result of poor classroom management, poor instructional skill, and inconsistent academic and behavioral policies and practices, including biased evaluation (Harry and Klingner, 2006, 2007). Further, when students with special needs are provided inferior educational services, and/or are inaccurately labeled for special educational services, they are more likely to act out, be suspended/ expelled, and end up in the juvenile justice system (Kim, Losen, and Hewitt, 2010). Our observations of Ms. W.'s classroom raised questions not only about whether the services provided to these students adequately met their specialized needs, but also whether their special needs label was even correct/appropriate. At the very least, though these students were socially constructed as "*the* problem" in Ms. W's classroom, it was clear to us that these students were the least of the problem.

SUMMARY DISCUSSION

Our research began in response to the national debate over school disciplinary practices and the proliferation of the STPP. We put forth a premise that CRCM could serve as a powerful tool for teachers, and school leaders when seeking to address the, often conflicting, responsibility of schools to develop discipline practices that decrease violence, maximize student opportunities to learn and thrive in safe, inclusive, and academically challenging spaces allow educators to strategically and successfully navigate restrictive district regulations and policies. We were excited to learn that DCSD had already developed and put into practice an action plan that aligned with our premise, and welcomed the opportunity to observe in classrooms embedded within a school where the leaders were, like us, committed to a vision of CRCM as a pathway for schools to both prevent, and recover from, the STPP. During our inquiry, we found that, while leaders maintained a commitment to CRCM, they were still developing the skill to translate their vision into action, especially by classroom teachers. In fact, there was a clear disconnect between the articulated beliefs, conceptual knowledge, and desired leadership praxis held by school leaders and those employed in classrooms by teachers. While Let's Go Innovative Elementary school leaders demonstrated knowledge of CRP, considered developing cultural competence a priority, and engaged in critical reflection and dialogue about issues such as race and gender disproportionality and the STPP when prompted by us to do so, the school's teachers did not exhibit these traits. The school principal occasionally modeled behaviors and strategies commensurate with CRCM, including developing meaningful relationships with students, demonstrating care for students, sharing cultural capital in interactions with students, and holding high expectations for all students. However, even his use of these practices was not consistent, and these same practices did not show up in our classroom observations of two of the school's teachers. Instead, these teachers exhibited very little CRCM, relying instead on teacher-centered instructional approaches, teacher-controlled discipline systems and interventions. To the extent that classroom observations revealed scant employment of CRCM, its implementation was sporadic, and largely disconnected from a larger context in which meaningful teacher-student relationships and related interactions existed. To the extent that CRCM was evident, it was unclear if its use was a function of the development of CRP, or if it was simply a desirable by-product derivative of the teachers' professional development experiences, especially the fifth grade teacher given her years of teaching experience.

A disconcerting, but not entirely surprising finding of our research relates to both teachers' propensity to treat African American students differently, particularly more punitively. This was especially disconcerting because one of the teachers is African American, and the school's leaders are both African American and have strong grounding in CRP. However, it is important to reiterate that the African American teacher observed treating Black female students differently is male, and the differential treatment of African American males was carried out by the white female teacher. Since our study did not include teacher interviews, we cannot be sure of these teachers' intent, however, our research findings are in alignment with the existing research on race and gender disparities in the STPP. Students with special needs were also treated differently. Though not reprimanded for minor behavioral or disciplinary missteps, they were denied access to quality educational experiences, including being allowed to simply disengage during instructional activities, which can lead to the more serious disciplinary infractions that, in turn, lead to the STPP.

In summary, our research revealed, that while student behavior challenges and teacher punitive disciplinary concerns may not be chronic conditions at Let's Go Innovative Elementary School yet, the approaches to classroom management used by the two teachers at focus in this study forecast the beginnings of a STPP in the school. While the school as a whole and the specific classrooms observed have behavioral management systems in place, the actualization of these systems do not align with the characteristics of CRCM, and, in many instances, are enacted in ways that cause students to disengage, particularly African American students and students with learning challenges. Unless school leaders are able to convey their vision for CRP and expectations for its implementation at the classroom level, the school's and

DCSD's effort's to thwart practices leading to the STPP will prove ineffective.

CONCLUSIONS

The use of disciplinary practices that lead to a disproportionate percentage of students of color experiencing disciplinary action, with African American students and students with special learning needs being particularly overrepresented in these experiences, presents a dilemma for DCSD authorities broadly, and Let's Go Innovative Elementary school leaders especially. In order to address this dilemma, school authorities will need to rethink disciplinary policy and practice using a multi-tiered approach. As revealed in our research, this rethinking has already begun. Both DCSD and its schools' leaders have recognized the need for district-wide culture change concerning race and gender disproportionality in disciplinary action. As also revealed in our research, there is much more to be done. The effective implementation of transformational classroom management strategies that are particularly culturally responsive in considering the cultural capital that all students bring to the classroom are of paramount importance to on-going and long-term success. To achieve this success requires system-wide development of such strategies, coupled with the preparation of school leaders and teachers to ensure their effective, comprehensive implementation. Concomitantly, proactive measures to change student behaviors are also needed. Creating welcoming and affirming school and classroom climates in which all students can affirmatively see themselves are pivotal. While individual critically conscious teachers, enacting CRCM, can disrupt the STPP by significantly reducing and/or completely eliminating their use of discipline referral systems, dismantling the STPP at the school and/or district level and beyond, requires strategic coordination of efforts not only in specific teachers' classroom praxis, but across the sociopolitical contexts within which all districts, all schools, all school leaders, and all teachers and their classroom praxis operates. The STPP is not solely created by the ill-action of a single teacher, nor can it be solely dismantled by the sole pro-action of one. The genesis for its obliteration must take a broader view of schooling, leadership, teaching, and learning as situated within the complex web of systemic oppression that has given rise to the STPP (Alexander, 2010). This broader view recognizes that the local dismantling of the STPP requires intentional, critically conscious investment from state and district leaders willing to take the legislative action, including the commitment of significantly more financial resources for public education, to make this goal a reality. Such action and resources must be dedicated to requiring extensive, critically conscious education and training for teachers and school leaders that ensure their ability to translate

CRCM theory to practices in schools and classrooms. Policy initiatives in teacher education, school leadership preparation, and ongoing in-service professional development for both teachers and school leaders must be designed around, and adequately funded to accomplish, these ends.

The STPP is evident in DCSD. If DCSD hopes to stave off its continued proliferation, it must take action to create and sustain safe, inclusive, and rigorous learning spaces that all its students need to thrive, especially those students who have been persistently marginalized and, thus, are most vulnerable to the STPP.

APPENDIX A

Culturally Responsive Classroom Management (CRCM) Framework: Characteristics of Teachers Operating with CRCM Knowledge, Skills, and Dispositions

Knowledge of Student's Cultural Backgrounds (KSCB)

- attempts to activate all students' prior knowledge through discussion or engaging activity;
- makes connections explicit between student knowledge, previous learning, and new learning;
- makes the purpose of the lesson clear and relevant for students (link past to today);
- provides opportunities for students to build on current knowledge, challenge knowledge, clarify initial understandings, or question relevance and validity of knowledge;
- knowledge co-constructed from a variety of perspectives; and,
- learning task and projects are student centered; environment reflects diversity of *21st Century* communities and schools (wall hangings, books, materials used, curriculum content, videos, etc.).

Recognition of One's Own Cultural Lens and Biases (CLB)

- teacher makes understandings explicit and is not afraid to question own thinking;
- teacher admits when s/he is mistaken;
- teacher provides alternate ways of thinking or completing a task, and affirms student's ways of thinking and knowing;
- steers clear from language that speaks to one right answer or that privileges one way of knowing and doing over another;
- allows students to question teacher;

- students explain their thinking and contrast it to teacher's way of thinking;
- uses progressive discipline methods; allows students to brainstorm consequences and choices;
- norms and rules co-created, posted, and behavioral expectations made clear at the onset of each transition or at the beginning of each new task;
- values more than one learning and communication style; and,
- does not form stereotypes; uses socially just language.

Awareness of the Broader Social, Economic, and Political Context (SEPC)

- classroom practices reinforce equity and social justice and are non-discriminatory;
- respect is co-defined by students and teachers and everyone is clear about what it looks like, feels like, and sounds like in the room;
- students engage with each other across identity borders;
- respectful language used by all in the learning environment;
- conversations incorporate global issues that touch the lives of students;
- policies, rules, etc., are examined for fairness;
- misbehavior is discussed and corrected using positive solution-oriented practices;
- lots of dialogue, problem-posing, critiquing of bias and attitudes; and,
- school and classroom rules are discussed as a collective community.

Ability and Willingness to Use Culturally Appropriate Management Strategies (CAMS)

- physical setting allows for free flow of movement and engagement among students;
- materials are visible and easily accessible for all students;
- instruction is goal-oriented, problem-based and geared to address a variety of learning modalities; differentiation occurs (all students are not doing the same thing at the same time);
- behavioral expectations are clearly established and discussed;
- teacher reinforces expectations with a sense of firm fairness;
- variety of languages used; physical environment reflects diversity of students;
- desks arranged in clusters for engagement, collaboration, and discourse;
- materials shared, small groups work together, discussion oriented;
- affirming messages and positive language used to motivate students;
- inquiry, creativity, and innovation encouraged;

- all children are engaged, regardless of background and learning need; equity not equality reinforced through teacher interaction with students;
- teacher models respectful language, action, and movement;
- teacher moves through the room engaging students in discourse (not in one place); and,
- parents and/or community members present in the room.

Commitment to Building Caring Classroom Communities (CCC)

- kind, positive, and affirming language used;
- lots of discussion, students work interdependently and independently;
- room has a happy buzz from group work or collaboration (not silent);
- positive language flowing from and between all in the room;
- students and teacher are helpful to and with each other; and,
- learning activities reinforce social engagement, even when content based.

APPENDIX B

Table 11.1.

School-to-Prison Pipeline & Classroom Management Classroom Observation Tool	Classroom Context (Grade, Level, and Subject Taught):
School Name:	Teacher's Initials:
Research Team Member's Name:	Teacher's Gender:
Observation Time/Duration:	Visually Discerned Racial Identity of Teacher:

Use this tool to collect evidence throughout the observation.

Table 11.2.

Observation Evidence: *Record the verbal communications and physical actions of teachers and students only.*	Aligned CRCM Indicator(s) and Code(s):
Questions/Comments/Analysis: *Note these as they come up during the observation.*	

Please be prepared to critically reflect on and discuss this observation with research team colleagues and the school site administrator in a follow-up post-observation analysis and calibration conference. Conference discussion will be based on recorded observation evidence and noted questions/comments/analysis, as well as suggestions contained in relevant literature on the

School-to-Prison Pipeline (STPP) and its connection to Culturally Relevant Classroom Management (CRCM).

Post-Observation Conference Date and Time:

Post-Observation Conference Discussion Notes/Analysis:

Chapter Twelve

The Role of Teacher Educators in the School-to-Prison Pipeline

A Critical Look at Both a Traditional Teacher Education Program and an Alternative Certification Route Model

James L. Hollar and Jesslyn R. Hollar

Children of color, children with special needs, and children in foster care disproportionately bear the burden of the climate of school discipline today. In many school districts with harsh disciplinary, "no excuses" policies, there is an inequitable distribution of expulsion sentencing along racial lines wherein young children of color are expelled and suspended from school at alarmingly disproportionate rates than their white counterparts (Skiba and Horner, 2011). For instance, in Seattle, suspension and expulsion data suggests that during the 2012–2013 school year black students were suspended and expelled at five times the rate of white students (Shaw, 2014). Statistics such as this are common throughout the country (U.S. DOE, 2014). When considered side by side with statistics on racial disparities in incarceration rates, which indicate that blacks are incarcerated at six times the rate of whites in the U.S. prison system, a strong suggestion can be made regarding a link between school discipline practices and mass incarceration (NAACP, 2005; Casella, 2003; Irby, 2014; Osher, Woodruf, and Sims, 2002).

This practice of punitive disciplinary policies focuses unduly on punishment for behavior and not enough on addressing the underlying causes for the misbehavior or on practices that encourage children to learn from their mistakes. Termed the school-to-prison pipeline, harsh disciplinary policies come at a time when too many children—many of whom are already academically below grade level and living in conditions of poverty—are forced out of the school learning environment as punishment, further exacerbating academic achievement gaps in contemporary schooling (McNeely and Falci, 2004; Osher et. al., 2002).

In high-stakes classrooms throughout the country where teacher evaluation and job security is increasingly being tied to measurements of student academic performance on standardized tests, teachers are under pressure to maximize every second of classroom instruction for academic learning (e.g., Stecher, Barron, Chung, and Ross, 2000; Taylor, Shepard, Kinner, and Rosenthal, 2003; Abrams, 2004; Vernaza, 2012). Minor misbehaviors that warrant swift, but caring correction by the teacher in the classroom (such as a student looking on her cell phone, per se) are now escalated into office referrals or in at least one instance, resolved by alerting the school resource officer. Teachers may not have the time in a micro-managed, high-stakes learning environment to address the behavior more appropriately. Or, the teacher may have not had the time to build a relationship with the student that moves beyond curricular objectives and learning targets (Hamre and Pianta, 2001; Cornelius-White, 2008). Or, the teacher may lack a broader understanding of students' developmental needs and the factors that affect student behavior (Bergin and Bergin, 2009). Or, the teacher may not have been sufficiently prepared to manage misbehavior in a culturally diverse classroom.

This chapter represents an attempt to address this last concern in ways that will make us proud to be teacher educators. We offer an examination of classroom management curricula delivered at Central Washington University (CWU)—one of the largest public universities preparing teachers in Washington State. The chapter first discusses a classroom management course required for all undergraduate and traditional post-baccalaureate teacher candidates and then focuses on how to frame such a course to more explicitly make students aware of the role of the teacher in perpetuating the school to prison pipeline. This particular section is authored by Jim Hollar as he teaches the classroom management course in the traditional teacher preparation program. From there, Jesslyn Hollar examines embedded curricula within an alternative pathways to teaching program at Central—an accelerated teacher preparation program, composed of a year-long internship experience. It is our hope that this inquiry into the classroom management coursework of two different programs housed within the same university sheds insight on some of the ways in which teacher educators and the structures of teacher preparation play a role in perpetuating or dismantling the school-to-prison pipeline.

A "POVERTY OF CULTURE" IN THE TRADITIONAL CLASSROOM MANAGEMENT COURSE

A central purpose here is to respond to a detachment in teacher education from issues of racial disproportionality in school discipline. Unlike achievement gaps around race and ethnicity, the school-to-prison pipeline seldom comes up in discussions around pre-service teacher preparation. Perhaps more importantly however, this work offers a map for fellow instructors of classroom management courses to prepare preservice teachers to think critically when it comes to concepts like discipline and power in the classroom.

To dig into these issues with some specificity, discussion is limited to the classroom management course I teach as a part of the traditional teacher education program at CWU. After a discussion of some concerns of the current course, I discuss several ways I engage my students in connecting culturally relevant and culturally responsive teaching practices with classroom management. This work is by no means new. Weinstein, Curran, and Tomlinson-Clarke (2003, 2004) explicitly write about such connections. As a teacher educator, then, it is my responsibility to find ways to present their critical scholarship as a counter-narrative to the traditional construction of a classroom management course.

The following is the course description for EFC 350 Classroom Management at CWU: "Development of values, confidence, assertiveness skills, and decision making skills in classroom management. Development of a comprehensive management plan for first year teaching. Includes a field experience component." Most noticeable in this brief description is what is missing: the lack of a descriptive term to center the course on the knowledge essential to the course. The focus of this course as it is constructed through the description is on dispositional traits. If we can agree that "values" are dispositional, then "confidence" and "assertiveness" are as well, just more specific ones. And while skills are also mentioned, nothing in the description sets a focus on knowledge: that is, what pre-service teachers need to know to develop these dispositions and skills.

Despite the lack of attention to knowledge in the course description, at present, the current classroom management course is structured to focus on a collection of knowledge centering on particular authorities in the field. The recommended text for use in teaching the course is C. M. Charles's *Building Classroom Discipline* (2013), which focuses on canonical management and discipline approaches such as Lee and Marlene Canter's "assertive discipline," Fred Jones's "tools for teaching," and William Glasser's "choice theory," among others. Because the school-to-prison pipeline disproportionately affects students of color, teachers and teacher educators must question any list of authorities that is made up of mainly white men, especially considering the widely discussed demographic imperative involving the mainly white teaching force and an increasingly diverse student population (Banks and Banks, 2012).

Another issue with centering the classroom management course on such a text deals with how these theorists construct their particular "management system." In this case, the theorists adopt frameworks based on child and adolescent developmental psychology. Ladson-Billings (2004) considers this "stubborn insistence on suturing the field [of teacher education] to psychology" as problematic (p. 104). She questions the teacher education programs that offer a "strong concentration in psychology that includes courses in child or adolescent development, cognition and learning, and exceptionality" (Ibid). She writes that to "understand teaching in the United States is to understand a wholly 'psychologized' field" (Ibid). The point here is not to say that development psychology shouldn't be a part of the classroom management course, but to once again question what such a focus then excludes. This privileging of psychology—away from other disciplines like sociology and philosophy, and especially anthropology signals what we value in our contemporary educational system. More simply, educational psychology has "stuck." Instead of letting that go unquestioned, it is important to push back on the focus of psychology in classroom management courses because psychology constructs students as individuals irrespective of culture, community, and context. Ladson-Billings is instructive on this point as well:

> American culture maintains a narrative of the individual. Although we are a nation of over 200 million people, we still give primacy to the individual. Despite the way group membership shapes and defines much of our lives, we focus on the individual. . . . Our supreme reliance on individuals means that we look at students as individually responsible for their success in school. We lack complex understandings of how individual, family, community, school, and societal factors interact to create school failure for some students. It is much easier to explain students' failure by looking at something internal to the students than endemic in this thing we call school culture. (pp. 105–106)

Here, the school-to-prison pipeline becomes a way we "create school failure for some students," especially those students who don't fit the mold we have fashioned from our insistence on a deraced (among other erasures) developmental psychology. The effect then is that teacher candidates are ill prepared to understand the ways in which "group membership shapes and defines" their future students of color.

Returning to the course description above, another issue is how the "development of a comprehensive management plan" communicates to pre-service teachers that such a plan can be made "comprehensive" without extensive input from administrators and teacher colleagues of the school in which they will teach, without acknowledging a broader community context, and without seeking input from the parents and students themselves. However, instead of simply blaming course descriptions that can indeed have little connection to actual course content, the intent here is to deemphasize the notion that classroom management is about a plan teachers make in isolation. In place of this then, is a more explicit effort to braid together culture with the knowledge, dispositions, and skills needed to be an effective classroom manager. In order to show one way of making such connections, I discuss how I introduce my pre-service students to these ideas in the first week of our classroom management course.

The first aspect I make clear to my students is how and why I position the classroom management course as a natural extension of the course on multicultural education taken as a prerequisite. This imbrication of the two courses is perhaps the clearest way in which I prepare my students for what is to come. Turning then to issues of racial disproportionality in school discipline directly, we look at a variety of sources from both the federal and state perspective as well as an article from *The Seattle Times* on the school-to-prison pipeline that place such "knowledge" as foundational to our course. For instance, the students and I read and discuss the Winter 2016 issue of *American Educator*, which focuses on the school-to-prison pipeline and several resources from *Teaching Tolerance*. We then discuss how important it is for teachers to care enough about these inequities to work to alleviate them. Then, once this particular knowledge and disposition is introduced, the skills to do such work seem like the natural next step. To make these efforts even clearer, I offer a new course title at the end of our first class meeting: Critical and Culturally Relevant and Responsive Classroom Management.

On day two, the class discusses the importance of the "critical" addition to our course. We begin by looking at the definition of critical thinking and then continue with how both critical pedagogy and critical literacy can be braided into classroom management. A discussion of critical pedagogy helps teacher candidates understand the classroom as a socially constructed space and how both the teacher and student must have the agency to positively impact that space if we hope to create a community of learners. The critical literacy perspective then stresses the need to see any "comprehensive management plan" as a text to be understood through lenses of power and justice (hooks, 2009).

To practice this critical lens, I ask students to consider the following question as a "text": Why do some students continuously create classroom management problems for me? Then, instead of simply responding, I ask them to "talk back" to it by asking their own questions. We eventually get to a set of critical questions like these: What kinds of problems are they creating/causing for you? What kinds of problems are you creating/causing for them? What do you mean by "some"? Who are these students? What do mean by "continuously"? Who benefits by blaming the ones with the least power in a given situation? Such an interrogation of the first question offers pre-service teachers a new way, as Banks (NEA Today Online) would say, to know and care about the students who they might instead reflexively categorize as problems.

Once this knowledge of critical pedagogy and critical literacy is in place, along with the understanding of the dispositions these concepts require of us, the course then shifts to focus on the skills embedded in culturally relevant and culturally responsive pedagogies. To do this, I place Laura Pinto's *From Discipline to Culturally Responsive Engagement* (2013) text as the central one for our course. I spend the rest of the second day reviewing these concepts with the help of Ladson-Billings's (1994) and Geneva Gay's (2000) foundational work with these concepts.

Knowing that these students are already familiar with such concepts is helpful in this work. In our multicultural education course the students and I discuss how important it is to understand and make appropriate use of the various cultures their students bring into the classroom. The link between this work of Ladson-Billings and Gay (and others of course) then to classroom management is much the same: students' cultures enter the room along with them and in order to construct a learning environment for all students, that is both successful and equitable, teachers must critically consider how their "comprehensive management plan" responds to those cultures.

As the course moves forward, I center for my students as well as myself these questions: What is the role of teacher educators in perpetuating the school-to-prison pipeline? How are pre-service teachers prepared to manage students in a culturally diverse classroom? How could the classroom management course be strengthened so future teachers are better prepared to avoid funneling certain students into the school-to-prison pipeline? By holding myself accountable in this way, as perhaps a kind of intake valve within the pipeline system, I am better able to ask these future students to consider themselves accountable as well.

TROUBLING THE CLINICAL TURN IN ONE ALTERNATIVE TEACHER CERTIFICATION PROGRAM

Alternative teacher certification programs are fast becoming a method to fast-track individuals unwilling or unable to invest the time and resources necessary to complete a traditional teacher certification program into poor and minority school systems. As of 2013, one in five teachers is certified through a means other than a four-year undergraduate degree program or a master's degree program (U.S. DOE, 2013). In many of these new programs, teachers complete most of their preparation as teachers of record in schools serving mostly students living in poverty (Zeichner and Hutchinson, 2008). Despite an ambiguous track record about whether alternative route programs are succeeding in improving student achievement (Zeichner and Conklin, 2005), alternative teacher certification is here to stay.

In addressing the role of teacher preparation programs in reinforcing the school-to-prison pipeline, it is important to critically question alternative teacher certification programs' approaches to teaching classroom management. Specifically, does scaled back pre-service course work and the insertion of more practice-relevant teaching tips and tricks, including the techniques of Doug Lemov (2010) in *Teach Like a Champion* promoted in alternative teacher certification programs like the RELAY GSE teacher preparation franchise[1] prepare a new generation of teachers whose classroom discipline policies reinforce the school-to-prison pipeline in the same schools where discipline policies are disproportionately harming poor and minority students? To grapple with this question, I use my experience with the alternative routes to teaching program at Central Washington University to ask how and whether alternative teacher certification programs could instead prepare teachers to dismantle the policies and practices that reinforce the school-to-prison pipeline.

The Alternative Pathways to Teaching (APT) program at Central Washington University came out of a call by the Washington State Legislature for public universities of higher education to develop a plan to offer and eventually implement alternative routes to teacher certification. The APT program is approved to offer three state-defined routes to becoming a teacher: one is for paraeducators; the second is for career changers and recent graduates; the third is for "early-entry" candidates hired as teachers of record prior to full certification. The APT program offers a two-week summer institute to prepare a cohort comprising candidates from all three routes. From there, course work continues online and is designed to supplement the clinical experience in the classroom.

Because of the unbalanced ratio of pre-service coursework to clinical or practice-based experience, the "apprenticeship of observation" (Lortie, 1975) appears to hold stronger sway than either the online coursework or preservice summer institute. Teacher candidates' constructed experiences of teaching rely heavily upon their mentor teachers' approaches and schoolwide approaches to classroom management. This is particularly pronounced for paraeducators, whose previous teaching experience constructs and shapes their assumptions about teaching. Those candidates who complete a year-long unpaid internship, in general, tend to ground their vision of teaching in their own K–12 and postsecondary experiences. Candidates operating on conditional teaching contracts with a school district are similar to those who complete the unpaid internship, except their interest in summer institute and coursework throughout the year tends to be narrowly confined to teaching techniques that will help them on day one rather than the larger sociocultural contexts of schooling and understanding of the ways in which schools serve to replicate inequities, including discussions around the school-to-prison pipeline. For instance, the majority of teacher candidates on conditional contracts this year submitted required coursework late and have shared that, though they recognize this work is required for their certification because it does not directly serve their planning and teaching practice and is not a factor in their evaluation, it is not a high priority. These teacher candidates resort to completing this work during their holiday breaks and over the summer, even though this coursework is integral to their understandings of schooling and society. In fact, proponents of alternative certification programs such as Kate Walsh with the National Council on Teacher Quality and the Chester Finn Jr., of the conservative Thomas B. Fordham Institute, support scaled-back coursework in alternative certification programs, so that it includes only those components deemed relevant to and necessary for new teachers (Walsh and Jacobs, 2007).

To push against the powerful apprenticeship of observation and desire for practical teaching techniques over grappling with critical questions about the role of teachers as change agents, as a teacher educator and director of this program, I frontload key learning experiences around issues of schooling and society, which serve to shape candidate's teaching experience. Prior to the summer institute, candidates are assigned to read two books, a teacher memoir and a text on the social foundations of education. These texts serve as the lens through which students in the cohort are later asked to reflect on the summer institute and their future teaching practice.

To stress that the APT program is a program that strives to prepare teachers for today's schools, but also to prepare teachers as change agents within the school, on the first day of the summer institute, teacher candidates complete an equity audit lab (Skrla, Scheurich, Garcia, and Nolly, 2004). This lab is designed to familiarize students with the existence of inequities in the schools in which they will teach. For example, the lab challenges teacher candidates to identify demographic and socioeconomic (SES) information about the student population in the state and in their placement school district and particular school. Then, teacher candidates locate the student achievement scores in reading, mathematics, and science for students within these demographic groups. Teacher candidates are also asked to identify other characteristics including the graduation rates and dropout rates for different groups at statewide and district levels, those population groups represented in advanced placement and honors classes, and the groups of students receiving special education services. Candidates look at the inequitable distribution of highly qualified, certificated teachers. Most important in relationship to the school-to-prison pipeline is a section of the equity audit where teachers are asked to compare suspension and expulsion rates of different groups of students in their school and district.

The equity audit also illustrates in a clear and direct way that these inequities are not just inequities in other people's schools, but that they exist in the schools where these teacher candidates will be working and that the teacher candidates, as teachers in these schools, have a responsibility to understand and attend to these inequities. After the boot camp, the equity audit stood out as a key learning experience for a number of students. For instance, one teacher writes in her capstone project at the end of the summer institute:

> At first glance, the white, middle-class American reader of *Education and Racism* may feel offended and want to deny [racial inequities in education] and believe [they do] not exist to the extent the Leonardo and Grubb claim. However, it is hard to refute the evidence to the contrary and the statistics that were glaringly relevant to this claim as was seen in the equity audit exercise that was done in class."

Later on during the summer institute, students complete the implicit association test developed by Harvard University. Students reflect on their results as they consider the impact assumptions and biases might have on becoming culturally responsive classroom managers. To an extent then, the summer institute becomes a call for these teacher candidates to become teachers for social justice.

Once students begin their internship and work in the schools, I use observations, readings, and online discussions to push back and challenge the pull to adopt the practices and policies of what are sometimes constituted through stale school cultures or the resigned affectations of mentor teachers. Overall, the teacher memoir and equity audit resonates with students as they complete their internship and provides a lens through which they begin to navigate the tension between coursework and teaching practice. Student reflections suggest that they are using the critical lens established during the summer institute to reflect on the practice of teaching during their internship. For instance, in reflecting on reading Jana Noel's text, *Becoming Multicultural Educators* (2000) one student writes: This [passage in the text] led me to think about the Equity Audit we conducted in class. [. . .] I need to be cognizant about ensuring I provide all my students with the same opportunities and advocate on their behalf when rules and regulations block their way to success."

Despite small successes, preparing teachers to be change agents—especially when one considers the short duration of the summer institute—is difficult work. I often find, especially for early-entry teachers that critically engaging with the systems serving to reinforce the school-to-prison pipeline assumes a lower priority. And, unfortunately, these same students who during the summer institute were energized about designing culturally responsive classrooms find themselves voicing deficit perspectives of their students, the parents of their students, or the culture of the students and their larger community.

The pull of the clinical experience, including the mentor teacher's own ideational perspective, clearly has an impact on students' abilities to learn and reflect on practices that could dismantle the school-to-prison pipeline. For example, one teacher candidate observes a mentor teacher whose classroom management policies are unintentionally excluding students from learning:

> A female student expressed frustration that there have been times when she had turned to a neighbor to clarify what [the teacher] had said, and was told to stop talking and get back to work. She is concerned that her grade is going to suffer in this class because of the language barrier and because she doesn't feel that [the teacher] is flexible or approachable. [. . .] I'm not sure students feel comfortable asking for clarification, and as a result, may have trouble keeping up with this approach.

Another student, a paraeducator, has internalized the beliefs and structures of her school culture and assumes a deficit perspective of her learners, writing: "In the [emotional-behavioral disabilities classroom] we do have students who do not care about school or learning."

My final example illustrates some of the struggles of early-entry teachers to become critical change agents. In short, they struggle to keep up with all that is required and learn alongside of their day-to-day responsibilities. The stress on these teachers no doubt contributes to their survival attitude and creates a barrier to their own ability to push back on a punitive culture of schooling, which contributes to the school-to-prison pipeline. In the case of a student who started her school year completing the unpaid internship alongside a mentor teacher but was then hired one month into her learning experience to teach a math class writes of establishing her classroom culture: "In all of my other classes, I had the students come up with the classroom expectations as a group. This class, however, has so many exceptional behavioral issues that I have had to just give them my rules." Later on in the passage, the student illustrates the incredible stresses early-entry conditionally licensed teachers face to be both good teachers and critical change agents: "Quite honestly, I would characterize my current style as 'Let's see if I can get through the day without crying in front of the students and then spend the entire rest of the day preparing for the next day and maybe squeeze five minutes of assigned reading in before falling asleep on top of the Marzano text.'"

In summary, even with deliberate attempts to provide a critical view of teachers as change agents working to dismantle the structures of schooling that perpetuate the school-to-prison pipeline, during the summer institute and through ensuing coursework, the unbalanced nature of the clinical experience at the expense of sustained pre-service coursework in social foundations poses challenges to prepare teacher candidates who are willing and able to dismantle the school-to-prison pipeline. As alternatively certified teachers disproportionately represent the teachers employed in poor and minority school districts, the ways in which alternatively certified teachers are prepared to dismantle the school-to-prison pipeline should remain a deep concern for teacher educators, practitioners, school administrators, and the communities they serve.

CONCLUSION

Teacher educators must walk a fine line between preparing teachers for today's schools and preparing teachers to envision and work toward schools for tomorrow. Instruction in classroom management and discipline brings this duality into sharp relief. On the one hand, some of the very same policies and practices teacher educators prepare their teacher candidates to employ reinforce the school to prison pipeline. On the other hand, teacher educators who believe that just as much as systems of schooling reinforce societal inequities, schooling (and teachers) can also serve to dismantle them. For these teacher educators, classroom management coursework must move beyond theories of classroom discipline grounded in educational psychology and positivist perspectives of schooling to include a strong grounding in social foundations coursework, community collaboration, and critical interrogation of the role teachers can play (or equally resist) in perpetuating the school-to-prison pipeline. There is much work to do.

NOTE

1. The RELAY Graduate School of Education website advocates the use of Doug Lemov's teaching tips and techniques both on its website. Norm Atkins, RELAY's founding president and also the founder of the Uncommon Schools charter network, penned the forward of Lemov's latest book. Here is the direct link: http://www.relay.edu/blog-entry/teach-champion-20.

Chapter Thirteen

Exiting the Pipeline

The Role of a Digital Literacy Acquisition Program within the Orleans Parish Prison Reentry Process

Gloria E. Jacobs, Elizabeth Withers, and Jill Castek

The majority of the school-to-prison pipeline literature appropriately focuses on youth and the failures within the educational system that place them into the prison system. Much of the juvenile justice advocacy work necessarily is concerned with preventing youth from entering the pipeline (e.g., Cramer, Gonzalez, and Pellegrini-Lafont, 2014), dismantling the pipeline (e.g., Nance, 2015), or resisting the pipeline (e.g., Martin and Beese, 2015). This work is of paramount importance in that recidivism rates upwards of 75% (National Institute of Justice, 2014) indicate that the pipeline is a closed system—once an individual is in the pipeline, the prospects of exiting are low. As such, efforts to dismantle and disrupt the pipeline need to be comple-mented with efforts at getting people who have served time out of the system. In this chapter, we discuss the implementation of a reentry process and digital literacy acquisition program intended to lower recidivism rates and support individuals as they work to exit the pipeline. We have not masked the location of this study because the reentry and digital literacy acquisition programs are public knowledge and have been written about in the popular press. However, the names of the individuals who participated in the research have been changed to protect their anonymity.

In 2011, Orleans Parish Prison (OPP) in New Orleans, Louisiana, began implementing a reentry process that became available to individuals within nine months of their release date. The reentry process provides incarcerated individuals (mostly Black men between the ages of twenty-five and forty-four) with an opportunity to participate in a program designed to assist them in their transition to life outside of prison. The program is voluntary, and participants are selected based on their risk for recidivism as measured by a reentry tool developed at the University of Cincinnati (Latessa, Lemke, Makarios, Smith, and Lowenkamp, 2008); those men at *higher* risk are selected. According to the director of reentry, the intent is to help participants develop the necessary skills to keep themselves out of prison once they have been released—a state called desistence (Maruna, Porter, and Carvalho, 2004).

The digital literacy acquisition program described in this chapter is part of the reentry process, which includes work on anger management, addiction counseling, problem solving, interpersonal communication, resume writing and job interviewing, money management, and digital literacy. The digital literacy program at OPP came about through the efforts of the director of the reentry program who works for the Orleans Parish Sheriff's office, which manages OPP. The program was also supported by a number of partners who provided equipment and funding. According to the director of reentry, the guiding philosophy has to do with reconnecting the men with their own humanity and centers on instilling a strong sense of self-worth while fostering supportive community connections. The director and program designers believe that by developing the men's confidence in their ability to do what is necessary to stay out of prison and facilitating an open line of communication with their support networks, they will have a better chance at successfully reintegrating into society. Consistent with this humanizing perspective, in this chapter we refer to the men in the program as learners, mentors, or participants rather than inmates, offenders, or prisoners.

This work is part of a larger project exploring how underserved adult learners acquire digital literacy. The larger project included over 12,000 adult learners and 500 tutors and involved community-based organizations such as libraries, workforce centers, and adult education centers across the country. The digital literacy acquisition program at OPP served 1,150 individuals during the 3-year time span we collected data. The larger study also included over 100 interviews conducted with learners, tutors (called mentors in the corrections setting), and key stakeholders who served as program designers and implementation directors.

The sampling process for learners and mentors within the corrections setting was purposive, and participants were chosen for interviews by a lab coordinator, who was hired to oversee implementation of the digital literacy program, and the reentry program director. These individuals were selected for interviews after carefully considering their life circumstances and personal situations. Interviews were conducted with four individuals: two who were currently incarcerated, one of whom was a learner and one of whom was a mentor. The other two interviews were conducted with men who had been recently released, one of whom was a learner, and one who had worked as a mentor. A series of interviews were also conducted with the program director, who worked directly with the sheriff and the lab coordinator, and one interview was conducted with an administrative director who worked for the state and provided funding for the program.

We used a grounded theory approach in our analyses of interview data, which allowed findings to emerge inductively. Although we did not initially set out to conduct a case study of a correctional setting as part of our larger research project, as we iteratively examined the data and looked at the social reality of what it means to be incarcerated and what it means to be facing release in an information-based, technology-dependent world, we realized we had to turn our attention to this particular case. More specifically, the experience of learners in the corrections setting emerged as what we have come to understand as a telling case (Mitchell, 1984). As we approached the data, we posed the focus question: what does the digital literacy acquisition process look like for learners moving through the reentry process within the correctional facility at OPP?

After two research team members separately re-analyzed the interview data from the OPP digital literacy program with the new research question in mind, both independently arrived at similar conclusions; the experience was about identity construction. However, within the correctional setting and with respect to exiting the school-to-prison pipeline, identity construction was understood to have implications and ramifications that go far beyond those seen in the other settings where digital literacy programs took place (e.g., libraries, workforce centers, and community-based organizations). These findings were supported by the literature, and in particular, Holland, Lachicotte, Skinner, and Cain's (2001) concepts of figured worlds and identities in practice, and Barton, Ivanic, Appleby, Hodge, and Tusting's (2007) concept of imagined futures. Both sets of concepts resonated with what we were seeing emerge from the data. Other members of the research team who analyzed the broader set of data confirmed these interpretations.

According to Holland et al. (2001), *figured worlds* are "a socially and culturally constructed realm of interpretation in which particular characters and actors are recognized, significance is assigned to certain acts, and particular outcomes are valued over others" (p. 52), and *identities in practice* are how individuals create a self in response to what is made possible within their figured world. When considered within the context of literacy development, adult basic education, and correctional education, the process of identity shifts being predicated by a learning experience can be further understood through Barton et al.'s (2007) four-part framework of the adult learning life: individuals' histories, current identities, present circumstances, and imagined futures. Due to the confines of data collection, we do not know these individuals' life histories, though it is tempting to make conjectures based on the fact that they were incarcerated. We also lack adequate understanding of participants' current identities. We do, however, know the official story about their present conditions, and the data do provide insights into how the participants began to see their imagined futures. Thus, when considering the experiences of the study participants, we grounded our analysis in the context of the prison and the reentry process and the possibilities open to them after they left the correctional setting.

THE FIGURED WORLD OF THE ORLEANS PARISH PRISON SETTING

We found OPP to be an especially powerful context for considering issues of incarceration, reentry, and recidivism, which exist as a possible point of exit from the school-to-prison pipeline. Louisiana's prison system is privatized and imprisons more people than any nation in the world (Carson, 2015). After Hurricane Katrina, OPP found itself under scrutiny as a result of the suffering experienced by inmates during the flooding (Neyfakh, 2015). In response to the problems in OPP and the Louisiana prison system in general, a number of changes have been made, one of which is the effort being made to address recidivism. Programs designed to support individuals as they make the transition back to civilian life facilitate the reintegration of once incarcerated individuals with a focus on community safety (Caporizzo, 2011).

The reentry program at OPP is part of larger efforts in correctional education. Correctional education has been deemed an essential part of the correctional setting because a majority of the approximately 2 million prisoners in the United States come from high-poverty backgrounds and frequently lack the math, literacy, and problem-solving skills needed to succeed in today's economy. In other words, correctional education is meant to fill the gaps left by an educational system that places the individual in prison rather than addressing needs earlier in life. As such, correctional education includes GED preparation, literacy and numeracy remediation, adult basic education, vocational training, tutoring, and job readiness programs. Additional programs such as creative writing also take place in prison settings (e.g., Appleman, 2013), but programs such as Appleman's are not intended to prepare individuals for life outside prison as much as they are intended to help individuals deal with being in prison.

Although there has been a great deal of research into correctional education, few studies have investigated digital literacy acquisition or Internet use among an incarcerated population. This paucity of research is due in part to laws limiting access to computer technology and the Internet within the prison setting. Prisons may have a highly monitored form of email or electronic messaging available to inmates, and may offer access to computers that are not connected to the Internet for GED courses or similar purposes

(Prisoners, 2015). How much access is allowed is determined on a state-by-state basis, but in general, access to the wide-open Internet is highly restricted. As such, the digital literacy program at OPP is unique. In fact, when we present our research at conferences, individuals working in correctional settings are interested but invariably walk away, saying such a program is not possible in their setting because of the lack of Internet access and the challenges associated with offering it.

THE DIGITAL LITERACY ACQUISITION PROGRAM

The digital literacy acquisition program is labeled as extracurricular and takes place in a converted garage across the alley from the prison. To take part in the program, the learners are shackled and walk from the prison to the computer lab under the supervision of correctional guards. These logistics are necessary because of the laws prohibiting Internet access to incarcerated individuals.

The men spend one week in the lab (about forty hours of work time), although some may be offered less time and others a little more. When the learners complete the digital literacy program, they earn a certificate, and when they complete the reentry program they celebrate their accomplishment at a graduation ceremony to which family is invited. According to the reentry director, the certificate and graduation may be a participant's first positive encounter with an educational program.

While working in the computer lab, the men are unshackled, and the guards remain in the room. There are 14 computers in the lab as well as a desk for the lab coordinator. The lab coordinator can easily see of all the computer screens in the lab in order to both support learners and monitor their use. Two guards are also present in the room. Although these individuals serve as surveillance, the program director stresses that they also serve as additional support for learning. The prison technology support staff also examines each computer once a quarter to investigate whether any misconduct has occurred. There have been few instances of misconduct, and those cases that did occur were addressed within the legal system.

The program director claims that one reason for the small number of misconduct cases is because the men see participation in the program as desirable. Furthermore, an underlying purpose of the program is to instill a sense of responsibility and the skill of self-discipline among the participants. The digital literacy component of the reentry program provides a valuable opportunity for working on the development of these traits because the learners are given a degree of freedom when working online. Additionally, the lab environment is designed to be as humanizing as possible through small acts such as the daily ritual of being offered and poured a cup of coffee by a mentor or the lab coordinator. Within this environment, the learners are able to see themselves as worthy of respect and responsibility and act accordingly.

The learning model. The learning model is self-paced and offers tutor-facilitated support. The online learning system, designed for adult learners, offers goal-directed and learner-driven content that includes links to online and offline resources. The self-paced instructional model allows learners to work independently and spend the time they have productively engaged in learning the content important to them. They can also review what they have learned as needed before moving on to new content. The tutor-facilitated aspect of the program provides learners with support when they need it; during lab time, mentors circulate to check-in, guide, and encourage learners. They answer questions and provide examples as needed. Learners are also seated in ways to prompt informal peer assistance.

Mentors. Originally, tutoring in the digital literacy acquisition program was to be done by volunteers from outside the prison, but the logistics of bringing volunteers into the prison was a barrier. Digital literacy mentors, therefore, were recruited from the existing reentry mentorship program. The mentor program was designed as a means of breaking down the barriers between the men by fostering a sense of community and responsibility. The digital literacy mentor role is filled by individuals identified as having the personal skills, technology skills, and dispositions to work cooperatively with others within the lab setting.

IDENTITIES IN PRACTICE AND IMAGINED FUTURES WITHIN THE REENTRY PROGRAM

The figured world of a corrections setting contains shackles and chains, surveillance, bars and locked doors, and regimented blocks of time. This creates a figured world in which only certain ways of being are made possible. The identities in practice are that of inmate, prisoner, and offender. The reentry process and the digital literacy acquisition program brought the inmates into a different figured world. Although they were surveilled, they were unshackled, treated to coffee, and empowered to make choices about what they wanted to learn and how much time to spend on specific content. Additionally, the program director made the point that the surveillance served more as a tool to provide learning support rather than to control behaviors. Moreover, the participants became mentors and learners, and through those new roles, had the opportunity to form a new identity in which a different future was imagined to be possible.

Many of the program participants had little or no experience with computers or the Internet, especially those who had been incarcerated in the last decade, when digital technologies have fundamentally transformed the ways we access information and interact socially, civically, and in the workplace. The digital literacy curriculum consisted of learning (a) how computers work, (b) basic mouse and keyboarding skills, (c) how the Internet works, (d) how to search for information online, (e) how to use email, (f) how to stay safe online, and (g) social networking. Additional learning plans were available in broadband consumer education and career pathways. The learners indicated they knew how important these skills would be in their life outside the prison. As one mentor said,

> They [program participants] know in today's society technology is just getting better. . . . Without a computer it's really hard, cause that how you really get jobs nowadays. Cause you can't go the old fashioned way and fill out a little form. You gotta do it on the computer now. (Tyson)

Tyson also recognized that not only were digital skills necessary for job applications, they were necessary to be recognized as a viable member of the workforce. He said,

> Without knowing how to get on and access a computer, we are pretty much lost. *We of [sic] no value* [italics added] in a lot of jobs because a lot of jobs require you to use to be able to access computers. (Tyson)

Tyson's comment "we of no value" is especially poignant within the context of the school-to-prison pipeline where students are given similar messages. As Pane and Rocco (2014) noted, the school-to-prison pipeline consists of an iterative process of punishment, exclusion, and ultimately failure. As the participants transition to leaving the prison, they were facing a return to a world that had offered them little opportunity for success.

The digital literacy acquisition program, however, is part of the overall efforts to work against the sense of exclusion. After the positive experience of learning basic computer and Internet skills, the next step for participants was to see how these skills might be useful in their post-release lives. Some of the most significant ways this occurs is through the process of working on a resume and learning how to complete online job applications. Through the act of preparing for employment using the most up-to-date approaches available, participants began to see themselves as people who have new possibilities available. For example, when asked about his plans after release, Travis, a learner, said,

> Definitely going to check out Goodwill [digital literacy acquisition program location] so I can continue to learn about these computers. [I want to go to] School [to be a] substance abuse counselor. It's my first choice. . . . I know I'm going to get it, but just don't know how long it's going to take. (Travis)

In addition to job preparation, participants also begin building or rebuilding a place within their families, and learning digital literacy skills contributes to the shift from being a burden to being a contributing member of the family. For example, Morris, a learner, described how he would be going home to a family with two teenaged children plus two foster children. He was particularly happy to know that he would be able to show his children he could keep learning and "show off a little bit." The program director reinforced this idea when he explained how learners would talk to their children about things like what type of mouse they were using in the computer lab. This conversation, he said, was about more than the technology—it was about the learner and his child having a common experience to bond over.

The two mentors we interviewed experienced dramatic shifts in how they saw themselves. Mentors gained hands-on experience in working productively with other people, and they were able to see themselves as positive contributors with valuable skills, abilities, and attributes. These included learning how to work with a variety of people and coming to see themselves as competent and trustworthy. When asked to share some of the things he learned from being a mentor, Reggie said,

> You can't speak to everybody in the same way. It [being a mentor] gave me insight on how to deal with different people. . . . Dealing with all these different attitudes in a short period of time. (Reggie)

Tyson also experienced a shifting sense of self that extended to his growing realization that he was capable of more than he thought possible and that he was able to have a relationship with people built on trust. He said,

> I never really thought I could interact with a lot of people . . . different people, personalities and all that. So it's really good for people to listen to me and trust my word on the computer . . . so it's nice for people to look up to me. And they trust my word and I'm telling them the right thing. (Tyson)

This shift also helped Tyson see himself as someone capable of bringing pride to his family. He said, "I feel like if my people know, like my mother or somebody, that'll really make her proud because I'm helping people."

Although the learners and mentors interviewed may not be representative of all the individuals who participated in the digital literacy acquisition program, their comments helped us to see the potential of a program such as the digital literacy acquisition program and mentorship for challenging the messages these men had been receiving about who they are and how they fit into the world. The school-to-prison pipeline serves to slot individuals into a particular figured world and identity in practice. The experiences of the men within the reentry process and the digital literacy acquisition program challenged the identities that had been ascribed to them and allowed them to write a new possible future.

IMAGINING A WORLD BEYOND THE PIPELINE

The reentry program and digital literacy acquisition program described in this chapter provides hope for education as a way to exit the pipeline. According to the literature, the concrete reason for correctional education and reentry programs is improving post-release employment rates and reducing recidivism (Davis et al., 2013). However, our analysis suggests that the creation, implementation, and evaluation of programs such as the one described in this case study also offer a powerful way to push back against the school-to-prison pipeline.

Desistence requires that an individual take on new ways of being in the world. We suggest that the identity changes learners and mentors experienced throughout their participation in the digital literacy acquisition program and the reentry process may contribute to changing behaviors post-release. The new identities in practice and imagined futures that the participants begin to build through participation during the reentry process and in digital literacy acquisition program are in direct opposition to the identities ascribed to the individuals by the punitive school policies that moved the individuals into the prison system. The participants are able to move out of a system that has positioned them in one way, and as our model (Figure 13.1) shows, they moved into a process that allows them to position themselves in another way.

It is important to remember that what we have described in this chapter happened within a larger system of corrections, correctional education, and a reentry process. We are not claiming that any changes experienced by the participants solely were due to the digital literacy program. Instead, we suggest that providing digital literacy skills as part of the larger system can be instrumental in helping incarcerated individuals see themselves in a new light and thus come back into the world in a way different than they were before.

The barrier to achieving lasting changes in recidivism rates and moving people out of the school-to-prison pipeline depends on a commitment to policy changes. Current policy prohibits access to the Internet within a correctional setting. This policy, while ostensibly intended to protect society at large, is not helpful for those individuals who are close to the end of their time served in a corrections facility and who are preparing to reenter society. Instead, the policy serves to reinforce the revolving door that feeds people back into the prison system. As Fasching-Varner, Mitchell, Martin, and Bennett-Haron (2014) argued, the school-to-prison pipeline serves its intended purpose: to disenfranchise one group and privilege another. Similarly, pre-

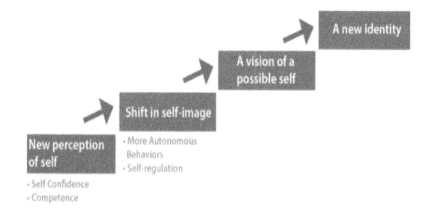

Figure 13.1. Movement toward new imagined futures.

venting individuals from learning how to use digital tools necessary for meaningful engagement in social, civic, and economic worlds ensures that they will, in all likelihood, return to prison.

We argue that policy makers should consider allowing access to the world of digital technology to those individuals who have demonstrated readiness to learn so that they can develop the skills and responsibility that accompanies access to the digital world. Curricula designed to offer adults the skills needed to accomplish even basic life tasks should include support for learning how to operate a computer or smartphone and instruction on how to navigate the Internet and access online information. While we believe the pipeline must be dismantled altogether, we also believe that there must be an exit strategy for those who are already stuck in the revolving door that feeds people back into the prison system. We argue that a successful exit strategy should include access to digital information and communication technologies.

AUTHOR NOTE

The research reported in this piece was made possible in part by the Institute of Museum and Library Services National Leadership Grant # LG-06–11–0340–11. The research was designed and implemented by members of the Literacy, Language and Technology Research Group at Portland State University. Principle Investigator was Jill Castek and other members include Gloria Jacobs, Kimberly Pendell, Drew Pizzolato, Stephen Reder, and Elizabeth Withers. Further information about the full study can be found at http://pdxscholar.library.pdx.edu/digital_literacy_acquisition.

Chapter Fourteen

Punishing Trauma

*How Schools Contribute to the Carceral Continuum
through Its Response to Traumatic Experiences*

Devon Tyrone Wade and Kasim S. Ortiz

Over the past couple of decades there has been a marked transformation of America's schools and their approach to managing student behavior, namely in urban schools of color. In that, many schools have moved from structures that had traditionally viewed the managing of adolescent behavior as in-house response, to one that now uses the intervention of outside control measures that abdicate responsibility to various agencies that make up the criminal justice system (i.e., police officers, social workers, parole officers, juvenile court). As a result, we have seen a tremendous increase in the number of school resource officers (SROs) on secondary campuses across America. In 2009, 69 percent of America's public schools had security guards present in them (Dinkes, Kemp, and Baum, 2009). Moreover, this growth has persisted despite nationwide downward trends in crime (Snyder, 2012), juvenile arrests (Puzzanchera, 2014), and decreases in school infractions (Fuentes, 2013; U.S. Department of Education, 2014). Even more, while there has been a steady decline, or stagnation, in the rates of crime both on and off school campuses, there has been a steady flow of police presence in schools (Morgan, Musu-Gillette, Robers, and Zhang, 2015).

Important to note also, is that a closer assessment of the increased reliance on police enforcement within schools typically reveals a concentration of police presence and reported school infractions in urban schools of color (Shedd, 2015; Skiba and Sprague, 2008). As such, racial disparities in the doling out of school punishment continue to exist, albeit scholars have shown that the disparities seen in punishment are not consistent with the rates of offenses for Black and white children. For example, Welch and Payne (2010) found that predominantly white schools in their study had higher rates of school infractions in comparison to the schools with majority minority students, yet had harsher punitive sanctions. This facilitates the criminalization of youth, wherein youth of color are disproportionately impacted by punitive policies. In addition to the punitive aspect of criminalization, it has also been noted that policies around educational reform that have categorized urban schools as failing have also relied on carceral-like punitive tactics to "fix failure" (Hirschfield and Celinska, 2011).

Such findings reveal a stratifying nature of schools along racial lines. Moreover, they highlight the raced organizational structuring of schools and its implications for how schools think and respond to student behavior. There exists enormous pressure in these environments for schools to instinctively react punitively as a corrective to student behavior that stands out as disruptive. The criminalization of schools of color that has structured them as punitive and reactionary environments points to the paradoxical sorting, labeling, and processing of nature schools. However, in addition to the above noted ways in which the criminalization of schools sorts and stratifies children, there exists another dangerous ramification—the inadvertent punishment of trauma or mental health issues children may deal with while at school.

Punishment and mental health in the schools is a matter that has received very little if any attention in the social stratification literature. This is not surprising however, given that in most institutions that revolve around punishment or coercive control (i.e., courts, corrections, probation), mental health concerns take the back seat to reactionary punishment (Birmingham, Mason, and Grubin, 1996; Briggs et al., 2013; Kupers, 1999). Moreover, providing that there exist huge racial disparities in these punitive institutions as well as other non-punitive institutions, it wouldn't be a stretch to argue that dialogues around the intersection of race, punishment, and mental health services in these institutions are even more rare to find. The carceral-like structures of schools have significant implications for mental health service offered as well as the way in which behaviors of students suffering from traumatic experiences are interpreted and responded to. Under such context, the most vulnerable youth become subjected to punitive and unempathic responses to the traumas they face which could lead to alienation and further traumatization at the hand of the school.

American schools have increasingly been identified as sites of inequality, as exhibited by their disparities in organizational structures and disproportionality in school discipline rates and disparate punitive punishment experienced by racial/ethnic minority youth (Irwin, Davidson, and Hall-Sanchez, 2012; Kalogrides and Loeb, 2013; Kupchik and Ward, 2014; Wakefield and Uggen, 2010). These all work in tandem to contribute to traumatic experiences being reproduced in school settings facilitating further stratification of youth. Throughout this chapter we apply a critical race lens insofar that we elucidate the importance of race in not only determining and establishing why schools seek to exploit punitive punishments, but also to highlight possible solutions for interrupting school-to-prison pipelines. In order to thwart continued growing incidence of trauma it is necessary to consider structural mechanisms from which trauma occurs and manifests. Particularly we are interested in how schools can serve as such spaces to decrease incidence of trauma, while we also recognize that currently schools may serve as sites replicating traumatic experiences. For example, Shedd (2015) discusses the universal carceral apparatus where she expounds:

> A carceral apparatus consisting of securing guards, cameras, and metal detectors may be deemed out of place in a [some] schools, where educational pursuits are foregrounded and violent crime is a rare phenomenon. . . . The universal carceral apparatus does not need to be "activated" in [some] spaces. (p. 95)

Rather the universal carceral apparatus conveys to students passively that a "disciplinary superstructure" is necessary to thwart any potential student misbehavior, even when students might not directly represent any physical threats. Similarly we are invested in expounding upon how these "universal carceral apparatuses" work collectively in a punitive manner to enact trauma or negate it all together, which has been an overlooked area of research until recently.

This book chapter is organized in the following manner. First we highlight the organizational structuring of schools and their reliance on carceral apparatuses. In doing so, we discuss schools and their stratifying processes rooted in punitive punishment regimes. Then we provokingly inquire about an often-missing piece of consideration, mental health of youth and the traumas in which they face outside school settings that can impact student behavior and perceived student misbehavior, schools and their stratifying processes. Lastly, we discuss how schools' over-reliance on punitive punishment regimes leads to a cyclical process wherein trauma is re-traumatized and is a plausible turn for interventions in disrupting school-to-prison pipelines. Lastly, in the conclusion we discuss the vital importance of increasing school mental health services for identifying trauma appropriately in order to facilitate greater fidelity in altering punitive punishment regimes.

ORGANIZATIONAL STRUCTURING OF
SCHOOLS AND CARCERAL APPARATUSES

Schools and the Stratifying Process

Schools can be a mechanism by which reductions in inequality and social stratification occur. However, more and more research has ushered in discourse around the ways in which schools stratify as well. Attention to the ways in which schools stratify points to how schools internally stratify (i.e., testing, special education classifications, tracking, and punitive practices) and are implicit and take part in external stratification (social class and race biases, school and neighborhood demographics). Until relatively recently, the focus remained predominantly on internal mechanisms to which schools stratify, however, presently the conversation has taken a turn to more exogenous mechanisms.

Within sociological discourse, it is now widely argued that disparities in children's social lives outside of schools exacerbate poor academic performance and school disparities. As Condron (2009) puts it, "regardless of what occurs at schools the broader structure of social stratification produces class and racial disparities in learning; and school reforms cannot eliminate achievement gaps as long as that stratification is left intact" (p. 684). Another group of scholars argue that it is primarily non-school-related factors that infiltrate and are brought into the institution that serve as the main driving force of inequality (Downey, Hippel, and Broh, 2004). Both of these schools of thought have found, within specific disciplinary-oriented studies, that achievement disparities grew during the summer months when students were not in school, thus concluding that non-school social and factors are highly determinative in explaining inequalities in academic performance. However, there exist a conundrum with work surrounding schools and the stratification process in that they have primarily all been quite linear in proposing a binary lens, wherein either school or non-school factors are identified as drivers in school performance. Particularly Downey and colleagues who go further and posit that their findings of growth differential between school year and summer demonstrate schools serve as an important equalizer. This assertion of the school as an equalizer and their study does not take into account the interaction that race and socioeconomic factors have on school structures that run counter to schools being equalizers. In fact, their study holds true for class and race with the exception of the black/white disparity gap. As we go along, we hope to provide one possible explanation for what this conundrum may mean for conspicuous racial exception Downey and colleagues argue and the context of school structure. We posit that it is both the interaction of race and class on traumatic experiences as well as the interaction of race and class on school structure that set up for the stratifying nature of schools with children experiencing trauma.

A school not equipped to handle the needs of children who experience traumatic events outside of its walls stands to be implicit in the stratification of children along certain identity lines, chiefly race and class. Poor urban African American and Latino children are most likely to live in traumatizing environments that increase their risk of experiencing PTSD (Zyromski, 2007). The infrastructure and organization of poor urban schools of color impact the ways in which services are provided and illuminate how schools operate differently and deploy services and responses differently than schools that are not majority students of color.

Schools and Punishment

Sociologist Carla Shedd (2015) argues that the modern public high school is the extension of our larger "disciplinary society," wherein there is a coercive punitive apparatus she terms as a school disciplinary superstructure (p. 81). Or in other words, an extension of what Michel Foucault (1977) termed as the carceral continuum—a system of surveillance and punishment that extends from maximum prisons to police and authority figures, to institutions like schools and our everyday life. Discipline in our societal context operates as an exclusionary approach with the preeminent desire being to exclude or remove individuals considered a problem. Suspension is the most commonly used form of exclusionary discipline used in school today (Skiba and Sprague, 2008) in an effort to facilitate a more productive learning environment.

The spout of the digital age and viral video shares on social media in recent years has ushered in a frequent witnessing of videos and headlines of black youths' violent or aggressive interactions with school authority figures and police. Although such moments are now viewable by millions online, these instances are not new strategies within urban education settings. While corrective punishment exists in some form or fashion in all schools, regardless of race and class factors, there still exist disparities in rates of punishment (Gregory, Skiba, and Noguera, 2010; Skiba, Eaton, and Sotoo, 2004; Skiba and Peterson, 1999; Welch and Payne, 2010), even after controlling for students' behavior (Skiba and Sprague, 2008). The uneven application of school punishment is influenced not only by student behavior and characteristics, but also by school factors such as the quality of governance, demographics, and staff attitudes. Suspension and other exclusionary methods (i.e., expulsion and detention) are 1) more often employed by urban schools rather than rural schools (Skiba et al., 2004); 2) they are more likely to be used in charter schools, which serve predominantly urban minority students of color (Frankenberg, Siegel-Hawley, and Wang, 2010), versus traditional public school (Shedd, 2015); and 3) African American students are punished more severely for less serious and more subjective infractions than their white counterparts (Morris and Perry, 2016; Skiba, Michael, Nardo, and Peterson, 2002; Welch and Payne, 2010). These have resounding impacts on the ability of schools to produce racialized stratifying processes, whether directly or indirectly, fueling school-to-prison pipelines.

WHAT ABOUT MENTAL HEALTH AND CHILDHOOD TRAUMA?

Numerous studies on childhood exposure to traumatic stressors and the subsequent responses have oriented discussion toward post-traumatic stress disorder (PTSD) as the most common source of reaction after an adverse experience (Alat, 2002; Cabrera, Hoge, Bliese, Castro, and Messer, 2007; Clements and Burgess, 2002; Copeland, Keeler, Angold, and Costello, 2007; Margolin and Gordis, 2000; Zyromski, 2007). Children experiencing highly criminalized school environments are also more likely to respond with feeling of shame and guilt that induced higher levels of depression and stress (Deblinger and Runyon, 2005; Feiring, Miller-Johnson, and Cleland, 2007; Ferguson, 2005). Internalizing experiences have been shown to increase the engagement in self-harming practices as well (Dube et al., 2001; Rogosch and Cicchetti, 2005). For example, Dube and colleagues (2001) found that a child with adverse childhood experiences (ACEs), risk of attempted suicide increased two- to five-fold than in a child who had not. Additionally, the cumulative effect of multiple traumatic experiences has significant implications. The more traumatic experiences a child undergoes during youth and adolescence, the more heightened their chances are of developing social and health disorders over their life course (Cabrera et al., 2007). One concern that arises for children that experience multiple early-life adversities is that they are more likely to develop path dependency (Schafer, Ferraro, and Mustillo, 2011). That is, they are less likely to alter or revise their expectations for themselves and their life trajectories or goals.

An assortment of research in the area of childhood development and traumatic experiences reveal detrimental and lasting neurobiological and psychobiological effects for children (Ayoub et al., 2006; Copeland et al., 2007; Dube et al., 2003; Porche, Fortuna, Lin, and Alegria, 2011; Porter, Lawson, and Bigler, 2005; Savitz, van der Merwe, Stein, Solms, and Ramesar, 2007; Siegel et al., 1992). For example, Savitz and colleagues (2007) found that sexual abuse severity in children was associated with lower memory performance. Additionally, Cabrera and colleagues (2007) found that military troops who experienced multiple adverse childhood experiences had a significantly increased likelihood of screening positive for depression and PTSD during later stages of their lives. The affects and responses that children have after these traumatic events have important consequences for school performance and behavior and often perceived "student misbehavior."

Impact of Trauma on Academic Trajectories

An examination of the adverse childhood experience (ACE) literature exploring the various kinds of traumatic experiences children face outside the school and their responses elaborated on above brings forth context and understanding to the types of experiences and subsequent reactions to trauma children are bringing into schools. These experiences have significant implications for performance and behavior in school environments.

While empirical research examining behavioral and psychological effects of ACEs allude to the implications that these experiences have for school performance like higher depression and shame (Stuewig and McCloskey, 2005), dissociative coping styles (H. J. Irwin, 1996), aggression and violence (Zyromski, 2007), substance abuse, internalization, and withdrawal, very few studies point out the explicit implications for ACEs or traumatic experiences on school or academic performance. However, from this small empirical literature we know that children have harder times concentrating on work (Porter et al., 2005), and that severe physical abuse has the potential to create emotional overloads impacting a child's ability to be attentive (Pine et al., 2005). Additionally, Slade and Wissow (2007) found that more severe forms of abuse that occurred prior to a child beginning the sixth grade were strongly associated with lower GPAs and difficulties completing homework assignments. Ayoub and colleagues (2006) found that interpersonal trauma in abused children created barriers and obstacles to problem solving when compared to their non-abused peers. Furthermore, Porche and colleagues (2011) found that childhood substance abuse and conduct disorders mediated the relationship between trauma and high school dropout. The researchers found that the likelihood of dropping out was increased for African American and Latino students compared to non-Latino Whites as a function of psychiatric disorders and trauma.

Clear here is that the experiences that children bring with them from the home and other external environments into the school has significant effects on their experiences in the school, interpersonal interactions, academic and cognitive performance, and their perception of support. Disruptions to learning and academic performance are significant in understanding early childhood traumatic experiences and their impacts on psychological and social development. Schools not structured to adequately to handle the deep emotional and physical trauma that students carry with them to school as a consequence of traumatic experiences are placing vulnerable students at greater risk for outcomes and responses that could have substantial implications for life trajectories.

PUNISHING TRAUMA: EXAMINING MENTAL HEALTH IN
RELATION TO SCHOOL DISCIPLINE STRATEGIES

The danger that lies in schools organized heavily around carceral-like techniques to respond to students' behavior is that the reception and translation of traumatic experiences and the behaviors resulting from them can be perceived wrongly in a such punitive context. Simkins and Katz's (2002) study on the criminalization of girls provides some context to this hazard. They find that the justice system routinely criminalizes young girls via the behavior that directly relates to the trauma and neglect they have experienced as well as a lack of interventions or treatment that relates to the crime they are charged for. Failing to encompass an understanding of why girls use force prompts a system which inadequately addresses the needs and concerns of young girls. In much of the same ways the courts routinely criminalize young girls who are victims of abuse, the school does the same thing for youth experiencing trauma who exhibit symptoms of aggression and other externalizing behaviors associated with trauma when they punish youth without attention to understanding the trauma that may have caused such reactions. For example, Porche and colleagues' (2011) study argues that behavior resulting from trauma can often times be interpreted as disruptive to the classroom by teachers. Post-traumatic stress disorder can be a far more frequent occurrence among inner-city African American and Latino youth than in white youth (Zyromski, 2007).

Educators and school professionals are the best positioned to recognized these trauma indicators, however, if the instinctual mode of recognition and response manifests itself through a punitive lens, it becomes extremely problematic and concerning for students experiencing trauma in punitive school environments. This places them at higher risk of suspension, tarnished teacher relationships, expulsion, detention, and other punitive tactics that could lead to withdrawal in school or dropping out. Punishment, in these types of reactionary environments, is often used as a gap-stop measure when administrations need to respond to a behavioral situation, but do not quite know how to directly confront root causes in such behaviors, behaviors which may be largely shaped by structural impediments in contexts outside of schools (Skiba and Sprague, 2008).

The structuring of school as punitive also has implications for the perceived availability of emotional and mental health support. Irwin (1996) notes, "Traumatized students differ in the extent to which their social environments promote a healthy resolution of experience of trauma" (p. 701). He found that emotional support served as a mediator for dissociative coping styles. Punitive school environments perceived as not caring about mental health can be deterring and detrimental for students. Counselors and psychologists seen as not emotionally there, or unavailable, could lead to further concealment and internalizing of the pain attached to dissociative symptoms resulting from trauma. These punishment-heavy environments do very little to signal to students the availability of emotional and psychological support. For those in these environments, predominantly African American and Latino, the first line of response is punishment. Reactionary punishment takes precedent over investigating why certain actions occur that may impact academic performance, school behavior, and perception of support, which further stratifies schools for these children.

It must be noted however, that there has been a recent movement in many schools across the country to eschew exclusionary punishments, like suspensions and expulsions, in favor of the move toward in-school interventions for behavior (Bradshaw, Koth, Bevans, Ialongo, and Leaf, 2008; Bradshaw, Koth, Thornton, and Leaf, 2008; Bradshaw, Mitchell, and Leaf, 2010; Domitrovich et al., 2008; Reinke, Splett, Robeson, and Offutt, 2009). Much of these responses center around the theoretical work of Positive Behavior Intervention and Support (PBIS) research. This literature encourages strategies to reduce punitive outcomes through incentivizing positive behavior. While PBIS-based interventions in schools have had some success in moderately curbing number of school suspension in urban public schools, these interventions still fail to address racial disparities in mental health issues rooted in trauma (Keane, 2012). Thus, the promise of PBIS to reduce racial disparities in the over-reliance on punitive punishment can be quite limiting (Greflund, McIntosh, Mercer, and May, 2014; D. Losen, 2011; D. J. Losen, 2013; Skiba, Arredondo, and Rausch, 2014). Moreover PBIS research also falls short of assessing the impact of restrictive environments, those rooted in carceral apparatuses, on student behavior (Mathur and Nelson, 2013). PBIS research has a large focus on rewarding positive behavior as a means of curbing recurring problematic outburst. There is however, some promising work being done in the area of restorative justice in schools that does take into consideration mental health as a means to provide a thriving healing space for academic productivity in the classroom and school. For example, Maisha Winn's (2013) work uses an approach called Restorative English Education that calls for the use of literature and writing in class to seek justice and embrace a discourse of restoration that creates "radical healing" through resisting zero-tolerance policies that sort, label, and eventually isolate particular groups of youths. The promise of such interventions and programs that invite an analysis of mental health and trauma instead of negating them can be key to dismantling the carceral-like apparatuses of urban schools of color and the unintended consequences of ushering kids into the prison pipeline.

CONCLUSION

A depth of literature exists relative to integration of school mental health services (SMHS) that is useful and accessible for both academic researchers and practitioners alike. Hoagwood et al. (1996) produced a conceptual framework for guidance in implementation of SMHS, in which emphasis is supplied to environmental influences and system influences. These two areas present a clear distinctive framework that can be utilized in considering how schools/school districts may produce universal carceral apparatuses, which have implications for trauma. Another area of consideration for practitioners who are considering the uptake of SMHS is work considering successful implementation of evidence-based practices (EBPs; Domitrovich et al., 2008; Domitrovich and Greenberg, 2000). Lastly, lots of work has highlighted the public health significance of expanded SMHS, particularly increasing the availability of SMHS and sociopolitical challenges in the uptake of SMHS.

Apparent throughout this chapter is children's experiences with trauma are a vital component in the understanding of school experiences and performances. Important also is the organizational structure of the schools; schools' current over-reliance on disciplinary superstructures have implications for social stratifying processes with life-course implications for youth. Schools which are not organizationally structured to redress traumatic experiences of their students, matched with over-reliance on disciplinary superstructures, run the risk of re-traumatizing their students. Such cyclical stratifying processes have meaningful impacts on explaining understudied areas contributing to racial disparities in academic achievement and overall educational gaps. While there exists much ambiguity in the research and literature surrounding what qualifies as traumatic for children and its related effects, what remains evident is that social contextual factors affecting mental health and stability of children that occur outside the school infiltrate and create barriers for learning and thriving inside the school. Moreover, this stratification intensifies when considering the punitive structuring for urban predominately minority schools whereby behavioral and psychological changes due to trauma run the risk of being interpreted as delinquent or responded to within a punitive apparatus. Schools that rely on these models of zero-tolerance and exclusionary punishments face a high possibility of altering students' trajectory by expelling them for behavioral non-compliance caused by events that follow them into the school doors.

Broader implications exist here for sociological discourse regarding the role of institutions in structuring outcomes, trajectories, and life-chances for individuals. Future work should examine more closely the implicit ways that schools contribute to stratification processes. For example, assessing whether schools are implicit participants in creating re-traumatizing environments through carceral-like apparatuses. Another area of focus might consider whether schools ignore or do very little to mitigate the trauma students bring to school with them. Regardless, the consequences for students facing mental health needs stand to be grave for their trajectory and performance in school and beyond and thus warrant greater attentiveness. Further, through such criminalizing and exclusionary punitive apparatuses, schools stand the risk of facilitating the transition of some of their most vulnerable students into the school-to-prison-pipeline pathway. The convergence of school psychological services, school structure, and social/racial factors is therefore critical and necessary for the exploration and understanding of not only the educational gap and stratification. This ultimately has implications for expounding upon links between prisons and schools that eerily haunts the American educational system.

Chapter Fifteen

Still Gifted

*Understanding the Role of Racialized Dis/ability in the
School-to-Prison Pipeline*

Kelsey M. Jones

The school-to-prison pipeline describes a process of exclusion and criminalization that pushes Black and Brown children out of schools and into detention centers, jails, and prisons. One of the most disturbing challenges of the school-to-prison pipeline is that it is simply the most current form of racism that is used to keep Black and Brown children out of traditional educational spaces, the newest text on the palimpsest of a racial history overwhelmed with hierarchy and oppression. The school-to-prison pipeline is not an exceptional phenomenon, but the current iteration of the many pipelines and policies that have marginalized and disenfranchised Black and Brown communities; it is one piece of a much larger system of pipelines, a network with a storied history reaching all the way back to the enslavement of Black and Brown folks in the United States and stretching, unrestricted, into a future that seems intent upon policing and isolating these communities until they are once again completely enslaved. Although we use the phrase to describe present-day challenges for Black and Brown youth and their educational experiences, we must be sure to acknowledge the multifaceted history of the school-to-prison pipeline in order to dismantle it, create sustainable change, and see these youth as capable and gifted.

The school-to-prison pipeline is supported by a number of formidable societal structures; most (if not all) of these structures are thinly veiled forms of racism. Dis/ability (Baglieri, 2008) is perhaps the most widely legitimized structure supporting the school-to-prison pipeline; it is the use of racialized dis/ability narratives that allows schools and racially illiterate educators (Stevenson, 2014) to systematically push generations of Black and Brown children out of schools and into incarceration.

An understanding of dis/ability, broadly, can be useful for families who want to advocate for children and for schools invested in providing free and appropriate educational services for all children. However, the assignment of dis/abilities for Black and Brown children is deeply complicated by the unacknowledged relationship between dis/ability and race. Historically, dis/ability theories and race studies have not been considered together, critically, in research (Ejiogu and Ware, 2008; Erevelles, 2014). Though newer research is starting to address the relationship between race and dis/ability (Erevelles, 2011, 2014; Bialka, 2012; Ben-Moshe, 2014), there is still much work to be done in examining racialized dis/abled people, especially those who are funneled into the school-to-prison pipeline (Erevelles, 2014).

In the same way that we must understand mass incarceration as inherently racialized (Alexander, 2012), we must also acknowledge the effects of racial thinking and racist ideologies in the history of dis/ability and the relationship of that history to the school-to-prison pipeline. As "bodies at the intersections of multiple difference" (Erevelles, 2014, p. 85), Black and Brown youth with classifications of dis/ability represent the peculiarity of racialized dis/ability. Erevelles (2014) insists that we must critically examine

> the simultaneous process of "becoming black" and "becoming disabled" recognizing the complex intersectional politics of race, class, and disability that is used in the incarceration of "outlaw" bodies that eventually become profitable commodities in the neoliberal prison-industrial complex . . . the historical continuities between Jim Crow, the ugly laws, and the contemporary context of mass incarceration mirror in many ways eugenic ideologies that imagined a uniquely modern utopian fantasy of a future world uncontaminated by defective bodies—either disabled, racialized, or both at the same time. (p. 89)

Erevelles also tracks this project through the "(post) modern version of the Middle Passage/Jim Crow," a devastating journey for Black and Brown children from self-contained classrooms and special education (where they are overwhelmingly and cruelly over-represented in comparison to their peers) to alternative and disciplinary schools to prison—at times the only option made available to Black and Brown children who have been labeled with a dis/ability and tagged "superpredators" (p. 95).

The work of the school-to-prison pipeline translates over-representation in special education spaces to over-representation in the prison-industrial complex. Thus, dis/ability becomes a tool not of service and advocacy, but one of deficit-thinking. Although they are oftentimes theorized in separate academic fields, the relationship between dis/ability and race reaches as far back as the Spanish Inquisition and the development of race thinking, or the belief that the people of the world can be separated into different groups or races (Silverblatt, 2004). Therefore, even as discourses of race and dis/ability are separated, they continue to work together to support dominant hegemonies of ability and superiority. The concept of race thinking is now not only applicable to what is considered "biological race," or difference that can be identified by skin color and other phenotypes. Classifications of ability can be understood as ability "races" that operate to advance and oppress groups of people based on biased definitions of intelligence and competency (i.e., deeply subjective classifications of mental retardation, emotional disturbance, and other health impairment). Furthermore, these definitions of dis/ability and intelligence are created by a White and "abled" population and therefore support its beliefs about intelligence and group hierarchies; this makes it almost impossible to examine ability without considering race and vice-versa. Just as we can use historical references to trace concepts of race, we can easily trace concepts of dis/ability *embedded* within race thinking, as well. Building upon arguments from Alexander's (2012) discussion of the continued control of African American communities in poverty, Erevelles (2014) fully acknowledges that these groups are "legally subject to an explicit system of control and social and political exclusion, even among incredulous assertions that the United States is now a postracial society" (p. 86). Erevelles (2014) rightly argues that a racial read of the situation is not enough:

> I argue that this group is defined at the crucial intersection of race, class, and disability . . . disability as deviant pathology [was] utilized to assign African slaves a degraded self-worth. This unawareness results in [the] nonrecognition of the constitutive relationship of race and disability where racialized bodies became disabled and disabled bodies became racialized. . . . (p. 86)

These understandings of racialized dis/ability are particularly useful in creating a space for understanding dis/ability as it works outside of the thirteen categories outlined by the Individuals with Disabilities Education Act (IDEA) (NICHCY, 2012). We see the deep and permanent relationship between dis/ability and race and the power of the inextricability of these two constructs. Over time, the relationship has become stronger and more nuanced, resulting in narratives such as the model of "cultural difference," perpetuating problematic generalizations of children and families of color, and promoting stereotypes that would see these communities as inherently deficient (Valencia, 2010). Thus, in the field of education, specifically, there is a particular urgency to uncover these tools of oppression in ways that will inform pedagogical practices and have an immediate impact on the ways we educate and support other people's children—an issue that is both theoretical and practical. I believe there is a deep need to understand the extent to which many marginalized, dis/abled, and raced communities can understand their emotional experiences as important and their social experiences as violently interrupted, if not through the language of dis/ability, then through the process of a social dis/ablement (Jones, 2015). The school-to-prison pipeline is a tool of this dis/ablement; we must acknowledge that Black and Brown children are forced into a state of dis/ability through special education tracking and deficit-thinking narratives. Understanding the process of racialized dis/ablement reminds us to move the control away from a belief in individual deficits and toward controlling and dis/abling institutions. Racialized dis/ablement is an entirely external process that *actively creates* very real difficulties for individuals within the boundaries of an oppressive society. In order to dismantle the school-to-prison pipeline, we must immediately acknowledge the need for activism that will correct the dis/abling of a multitude of Black and Brown communities and their children.

Despite these deficit-oriented narratives surrounding and imprisoning our Black and Brown children, we must be mindful of the many ways in which we can resist racialized dis/ability frames and remind our communities of the many ways in which we are gifted. Though the most traditional definitions of giftedness are represented in statements put forth by the federal government, these ideas of "gifted" are still rife with racialized and racist notions of what it means to be brilliant and exceptional. The history of giftedness, like the history of dis/ability, reflects a series of temporal changes in a society constantly looking to recreate hierarchies of intelligence. The building of contemporary theories of giftedness has been committed to creating more appropriate and inclusive definitions of giftedness, turning to focus on a more generalized understanding of intelligence rather than specific signs of giftedness. Kaufman (2013) reminds us that

> The most controversial aspect of [contemporary] theory . . . was [the] . . . proposed goal of gifted education: "increasing the number of individuals who make pathbreaking, field-altering discoveries and creative contribution by their products, innovations, and performances." The implication here is that at some point in development, giftedness becomes what you do, not who you are. This means, of course, that people can flow in and out of giftedness throughout the course of their lives. (Kaufman, 2013, p. 79)

This is a crucial point to remember when thinking about racialized dis/ability and how deficit-thinking affects the lives of Black and Brown youth. Because the actions of Black and Brown youth are under constant scrutiny and, specifically, under the lens of the youth control complex (Rios, 2011), it is impossible to separate the ways that the behaviors and humanity of Black and Brown youth are (mis)interpreted by a world convinced of their criminality, dis/abled simply because of the color of their skin. And so, even as contemporary giftedness theorists provide us with frameworks that expand our thinking around *who* is gifted, one of the goals of our work must be to unpack constructions that confine Black and Brown youth and (mis)label their actions. Recognizing dis/ability and giftedness as labels that have been forced upon our children and/or withheld from them may do this. Labels of dis/ability and giftedness are thus not actual indicators of the value of the minds and bodies of our youth, but rather tools of an oppressive system that feed and fuel the narratives legitimizing and extending the reach of the school-to-prison pipeline.

The racial palimpsest upon which we write is full of challenges *and also* the triumphs and resilience that mark Black and Brown histories. In order to dismantle the school-to-prison pipeline we must first do away with the belief that there is something "wrong" with our beautiful and brilliant Black and Brown children. Then, we can start to understand the complexities of racial-ized dis/ability and deficit-thinking and their roles in the maintenance of the school-to-prison pipeline. Our children have *always* been gifted and they are *still* gifted in this very moment. As we begin the tough work of dismantling the school-to-prison pipeline, we must remind ourselves of this fact and begin deconstruction through a language of resistance and pride in our Black and Brown youth.

Chapter Sixteen

The Fight to Be Free

Exclusionary Discipline Practices and the School-to-Prison Pipeline

Runell King

A young African American sixth grade boy is extremely excited as he dials almost every number in his mother's phonebook to inform family and friends that he had just been admitted into one of the most academically challenging middle schools in the state of Louisiana. This young man has been a scholar his entire life, and had great plans to excel at his new school. As a product of two parents, both of whom are highly educated, he was pressured to achieve at high levels, all while balancing a demanding school curriculum, extra-curricular activities, and maintaining acceptable behavior in the classroom. Although the student performed well academically, there were often instances where he would receive negative repercussions for what the school deemed *minor offenses*. At his previous school, he was allowed the autonomy to freely express himself in an acceptable manner, such as: openly communicating with classroom peers, debating and facilitating classroom discussion, free movement throughout the classroom, and the option to wear unique clothing. After approximately three months into the new school year, this student realizes that this may not be the best fit. Within only six months of attending his new school, he was suspended multiple times for simple violation of the dress code and talking out of turn during classroom discussions; which ultimately violated the zero-tolerance policy. While the school had an amazing academic reputation, this student's parents decided to withdraw him, and proceed with homeschooling for the remainder of the year. Over the past five years, this student had become accustom to rules and guidelines that did not restrict his creative expression. However, after speaking with the principal of the school, his parents decided that this particular school, despite their prominent accolades and achievements, mirrored that of a prison system.

Television has provided society with images of what discipline should look like in today's school system. For many decades, schools have used various forms of discipline to regulate student behavior (detention, in-school-suspension, out-of-school suspension, expulsion, etc.) both inside and outside of the classroom. The counternarrative presented above represents my lived experience while attending a prestigious middle school located in South Louisiana. Solórzano and Yosso (2002) introduce counternarrative as a useful approach to educational research. Counternarrative is a method of telling the stories of people who are often overlooked in the literature, and as a means by which to examine, critique, and counter majoritarian stories composed about people of color (Harper and Davis, 2012). In elementary and secondary institutions, it is not uncommon for African American students to be disproportionally targeted, and funneled into the "school-to-prison" pipeline (Douglas, Lewis, Douglas, Scott, and Garrison, 2008). Systemic racism and being targeted as a *student of concern* is what I experienced from sixth grade continuing throughout my high school career. In this chapter, I will expose existing exclusionary discipline policies implemented in Louisiana public schools that disproportionately impact African American students. This analysis will include an assessment of zero-tolerance policies and its role as a catalyst that fuels the school-to-prison pipeline.

SCHOOL-TO-PRISON PIPELINE

The school-to-prison pipeline is the result of several formal policies implemented through legislation, namely the abuse of zero-tolerance policies under the No Child Left Behind Act (NCLB). Since the implementation of NCLB, zero-tolerance policies are used to enforce out-of-school suspensions and expulsions for nonviolent offenses such as truancy and willful disobedience. Students habitually suspended and expelled are forced to enroll in alternative schools or remain absent from school for long periods of time, eventually causing students to drop out of school. Out-of-school youth often commit crimes that navigate them to the juvenile justice system and eventually the criminal justice system. Minorities make up the primary population of individuals who fall victim to the school-to-prison pipeline, as a result of policies enforced under NCLB (Juvenile Law Center, 2011).

In Louisiana, school systems receive federal funding through grant projects to employ school resource officers or law enforcement officers. While the presence of these officers may serve as a benefit to eliminate school violence, school administrators misuse their presence by referring students for minor infractions. For example, a federal civil rights lawsuit was filed against officials in Meridian, Mississippi, by the U.S. Department of Justice for systematically violating the due process rights of children (Equal Justice Initiative, 2012). Practices like this are not isolated to small cities like Meridian. These incidents occur in most minority communities across the country; all in an effort to divide the lines of societal existence to exclude and oppress. This further supports that exclusionary discipline policies serve as a mechanism to imprison minority students, reinforce the school-to-prison pipeline, and aid in the dilemma of mass incarceration. Further, the education system upholds policies that deliberately persecute minority students and enforce practices that render children incapable of learning in an environment that induces progressive growth and development. Consequently, the government has successfully used public policy to reinforce a racial caste social system with a primacy to enforce guidelines that strengthen the school-to-prison pipeline (Alexander, 2010). The public education system is void of any diversion to employ a restorative justice system that eliminates exclusionary policies and racial disparities among minority students.

SCHOOL-TO-PRISON PIPELINE: STATE OF LOUISIANA

The State of Louisiana is infamously known as the "Prison Capitol of the World" (The Institute for Southern Studies, 2012). Statistics show Louisiana ranks highest in incarceration in triple digits among countries like Iran and China; and lowest in education (The Institute for Southern Studies, 2012). Louisiana's expulsion rate is five times the national average and twice the national average for suspension (Gonzalez, 2011). The ambiguity in the state's law has contributed to the overuse of suspension and expulsion. An inconsistency lies between the state and local school boards in aligning policy with the goal of Louisiana's Constitution that pledges to provide an environment that will breed excellence and offered to all persons residing in the state (The Louisiana Justice Institute, 2011). According to the Louisiana Revised Statute (R.S. 17:416.15), the adoption of zero-tolerance policies is optional by any city, parish, or other local public school board. Therefore, the state does not mandate that such a policy exist. Correspondingly, in the Louisiana Revised Statute (R.S. 40:2402(3)), the presence of law enforcement is again optional by local jurisdiction and not a mandate by state policy.

Given the absence of a legal mandate at the state level to enforce exclusionary disciplinary practices, the state leaves a loophole for school boards to implement disciplinary strategies that prevent funneling students of color into the school-to-prison pipeline. To date, the school board has not implemented any alternatives to deter implicating minorities in public schools. In 2011, Families and Friends of Louisiana's Incarcerated Children lobbied to advocate for SB67, which supported the revision of the Louisiana Revised Statute (R.S. 17:416), which would require districts to create alternative solutions to aid in the reduction of suspension and expulsion (Louisiana Justice Institute, 2011). The governor of Louisiana vetoed the policy that would eliminate punitive discipline practices for minor infractions, sustaining the bill would limit the power school administration and teachers can access in the classroom (Louisiana Justice Institute, 2011).

Exclusionary discipline practices serve as the primary source in alienating and removing minority students from public schools throughout Louisiana, causing a disproportionate impact among black males in particular. In 2007–2008, the State of Louisiana Department of Education reported the highest rate of in/out-of-school suspensions and out-of-school expulsions within the last five years (Louisiana State Department of Education, 2014). By 2011–2012, there was a slight decline in out-of-school expulsions. However, the rate of in school expulsions was highest in all five years for the years 2011–2012 (Louisiana State Department of Education, 2014).

Overall, the research suggests black students are disproportionally impacted among any other race or ethnic group as it relates to exclusionary discipline practices, linking poor behavior to low socioeconomic status (SES). According to American Psychological Association (APA), SES is defined as the combination of education, income, and occupation (American Psychological Association, 2014). Low SES affects society as a whole and attributes to higher levels of aggression, hostility, perceived threat, and perceived discrimination for youth (American Psychological Association, 2014). Consequently, Louisiana is ranked second highest in the nation for highest poverty level, with 21.1 percent of its population living below the poverty line (Adelson, 2012). Therefore, Louisiana is well known for its poor rankings in education.

As of February 2014, the Office of Juvenile Justice Youth Services reports, black males ages thirteen to seventeen dominate the population of youth in custody and under supervision status (Louisiana State Department of Office of Juvenile Justice, 2014). Additionally, black males ages thirteen to seventeen make up more than 50 percent of the total population of youth housed in secure care facilities, under supervision, and sanctioned to probation and parole (Louisiana State Department of Office of Juvenile Justice, 2014). This, again, depicts an over-representation of minorities in Louisiana's juvenile justice system.

ZERO-TOLERANCE POLICY

The exploitation of a zero-tolerance policy is parallel to the same barriers imposed during the civil rights movement used to hinder integration in public schools. The existence of policies like NCLB, that are created for the sole purpose of separating one race from the other is evidence that racism is still dominant in America. Welch and Payne (2010) establish the racial threat imposed in school discipline. In a study that supports the previous assertions, sanctions issued to black students are more rigid and punitive than those issued of white students. These practices are most prevalent in urban schools where strict security and surveillance are imposed to restrict and confine students in an environment that mirrors that of a prison (Welch and Payne, 2010). A trend is identified among students who are subject to such punitive discipline; 90 percent are ethnic minority, poor, and most likely male (Welch and Payne, 2010).

Michelle Alexander, author of *The New Jim Crow: Mass Incarceration in the Age of Colorblindness* provides a detailed narrative providing evidence to the current state of minorities in the criminal justice system (Alexander, 2010). Alexander's theory associates laws created to limit the advancement and freedom (socially, economically, and politically) of people of color (Alexander, 2010). The dialogue cites the deception of public policies, like the War on Drugs Act of 1986, that promote institutional racism (Alexander, 2010). These policies contribute to the current mass incarceration and racial segregation through the disproportionate imprisonment of minorities for non-violent crimes that require rehabilitation instead of the harsh disparate sentences imposed (Alexander, 2010). Likewise, zero-tolerance policy has been aligned with crime-related politics where exclusionary discipline is considered a just consequence for misbehavior, yet these practices are considered ineffective as a corrective measure (Gonzalez, 2011). The results of exclusionary discipline policies place minority students in a vulnerable state, subjected to traditions of racial disparity, neglect, and exploitation (Gonzalez, 2011).

The Advancement Project confirms that zero-tolerance policies are a definite link to the school-to-prison pipeline (The Advancement Project, 2005). Research supports that involving police in suspension and expulsion for minor violations likely leads students to the juvenile justice system and eventually to the criminal justice system (The Advancement Project, 2005). The report sustains that zero-tolerance policy is overused and abused by school administrators and indicates the lasting implications and harm it has on students. A student who commits a minor offense should not be categorized with students who commit more serious offenses (The Advancement Project, 2005). These measures likely place students at a greater risk for entry to the criminal justice system by over-exposure to police involvement and resulting desensitization. The study further gives evidence that black students are more likely to be arrested than white students by at least 30 percent, giving credit to discriminatory practices as designed by zero-tolerance policy (The Advancement Project, 2005).

The American Psychological Association (APA) Zero Tolerance Task Force conducted a comprehensive study that examines the effectiveness of zero-tolerance policies in public schools; its findings indicate that the policy invokes a negative effect and serves to contradict the original intent of school safety (American Psychological Association, 2008). As it relates to racial disparity, the article denotes the consistency in zero-tolerance policies and the disproportionate discipline of black students where students are not engaged in the classroom due to lack of teacher preparation and classroom management, lack of training in cultural competency, or racial stereotypes (American Psychological Association, 2008). The findings on the relationship between education and the juvenile justice system indicate that zero-tolerance policies are vague and ambiguous and indicate no clear boundaries to decipher serious offenses as opposed to minor violations (American Psychological Association, 2008). Consequently, students labeled as habitual offenders are likely suspended long-term or expelled, which often leads toward the juvenile justice system, furthering the school-to-prison pipeline (American Psychological Association, 2008).

CONCLUDING THOUGHTS

Information presented in this summary proves the education system is failing minority students with its lack of structure and support for positive academic outcomes. The long-term effects of the current model yield socioeconomic demise, illiteracy, and delinquency. More than 50 years have passed since the Civil Rights Act was implemented, and black students are still fighting for equality in public schools. According to the constitution, education is a fundamental right of each citizen to be distributed equally in every public institution (U.S. Department of Education Office of Civil Rights, 2012). Further, several studies indicate the disproportionate numbers of black students implicated for offenses under exclusionary discipline policies are often guaranteed a life of incarceration. Sadly, educating students has become secondary to discipline practices by enforcing harsh punitive consequences that force students out of public schools and into state prisons.

Louisiana's current education system lacks the ability to create an environment that promotes positive development. The state lacks a formal structure for restorative justice leaving minority students adversely affected and disenfranchised. The system lacks a discipline policy to implement guidelines that may be applicable in distinct situations. Discipline policies should not be restricted to a "one size fits all" model used as a uniform solution to address disciplinary misconduct in every aspect. Instead of utilizing strategies that divert an absence from school, administrators often implement sanctions to students without the consideration of factors beyond the student's control (Southern Law and Poverty Center, 2009). The outcomes most usually indicate the discipline is not comparable to the offense and places the student at risk of falling prey to the pipeline and rules out the possibility to pursue educational achievements (Southern Law and Poverty Center, 2009).

Lastly, statistics in this report ascertain that students who are subjected to punitive disciplinary policies eventually enter the criminal justice system. Further, the research examines the link between exclusionary discipline practices and minority students, and meets the criteria that define the school-to-prison pipeline. Experts perceive that early involvement in the criminal justice system normalizes the prison experience, thereby increasing the expectancy of future involvement (Blake et al., 2010). From adolescence to adulthood, at-risk youth will bear the brunt of practices that assure involvement in the criminal justice system. Racial disparity in public school disciplinary policies will continue until there is proactive change in public policy that mandates alternatives that diminish the probability of students being pushed out of the classroom and into prisons.

Chapter Seventeen

The Criminalization of Blackness and the School-to-Prison Pipeline

Jahaan Chandler

In the fall of 2015, a video showing a white school police officer grabbing a black teenage student by the neck, flipping her out of her desk, and then dragging her across the classroom went viral (Fausset and Southall, 2015). The video drew outrage and condemnation from social activists across the United States who presented it as a clear, visual, illustration of the school-to-prison pipeline in action (Fausset and Southall, 2015). A number of political commentators, quasi-social activists, and news pundits commented on the incident yet, it was Victoria Middleton, the executive director of the South Carolina branch of the American Civil Liberties Union, who truly captured the essence of the pattern of racial discrimination revealed by the incident. Middleton said, "We must take action to address the criminalization of children in South Carolina, especially at school" (Fausset and Southall, 2015).

Middleton correctly pointed to "criminalization," as the primary cause for the abuse observed in the video, and while Middleton attached the term, perhaps for political reasons, specifically to children in South Carolina, it is the "criminalization of blackness" that best explains why the events event took place and the various ways in which the video was indicative of a much larger problem that has plagued the United States for centuries.

The "criminalization of blackness" is a process by which people of color are unjustly viewed and treated as criminals by the institutions that govern them and the society they inhabit. Regardless of its title, the criminalization of blackness is not solely related to the persecution of the black race. The criminalization of blackness is a phenomenon that is used to justify oppression by perceiving the oppressed as individuals deserving of punishment, and the processes and components that comprise it can be applied to the persecution of any oppressed group. Indeed, the term could just as easily been titled the criminalization of "brownness" or "redness." While the "criminalization of blackness," is not something used to refer to exclusively black issues, it is a multifaceted phenomenon that is intimately connected to *race* related issues.

The criminalization of blackness has many functions; however, the function to which this chapter places its focus is primarily psychological. The criminalization of blackness operates in service of the oppressor; its processes and components help to lessen the cognitive dissonance often associated with the act of oppression (Freire, 1970). The processes that constitute the criminalization of blackness operate in concert to present the oppressed as deserving of their oppression thus alleviating the oppressor of the cognitive dissonance that is associated with the act of oppression. The oppressor disconnects from the oppressed either through segregation or "othering," providing the oppressor with the space or means to de-humanize the oppressed. The consequent *degradation* experienced by the oppressed resulting from their *de-humanization* subsequently contributes to the oppressed group's reproduction of the negative attributes projected upon them by their oppressors. This reinforces the validity of the disconnection and de-humanization performed by the oppressors, which in turn, aids in the alleviation of the cognitive dissonance they experience and perpetuates the oppressors' further de-humanization of the oppressed.

The example in the paragraph above is but one way in which the processes that constitute the criminalization of blackness can function to help ease the cognitive dissonance of the oppressor. In reality, there are a myriad of ways in which each of the processes that constitute the criminalization of blackness can contribute to the perpetuation of the other, in the next section of this chapter, I will describe in detail the three processes that constitute the criminalization of blackness.

DISCONNECTION, DE-HUMANIZATION, AND DEGRADATION

Three processes provide the framework for the criminalization of blackness; they are disconnection, de-humanization, and degradation. These processes contribute to the perpetuation of the school-to-prison pipeline, the mass and disproportionate incarceration of black and brown men and women, the discriminatory racial profiling performed by law enforcement, and the overall structural racism that serves as one of the defining characteristics of American society. Disconnection, de-humanization, and degradation function in an interdependent manner each process working to support the other. The operation of these processes are not cyclical in the sense that there is an observably ordered and causal manner in which they interact; their interaction is interdependent only in sense that the products of one process contribute to the perpetuation of other processes. The gravitational pull of earth, for example, causes an object such as an apple to fall if not acted upon by another force such as the ground. Without the gravitational pull of earth, the apple would not fall, because the gravitational pull of earth causes the apple to fall.

Unlike the effect that gravity has upon a falling apple, the three processes that provide the framework for the "criminalization of blackness," do not always operate in such an ordered causal manner. Disconnection, for example, does not necessarily cause de-humanization to occur. The causal properties ascribed to the process of disconnection in reference to the process of de-humanization are dependent upon the form in which the process of disconnection occurs. In order to better explicate the reasoning behind this assertion we must first explore the inner workings of each of the processes that constitute the criminalization of blackness.

Degradation is the process within the criminalization of blackness that is most closely associated with oppression. Oppression, however, is but one component of the process of degradation. The process of degradation also involves the physical and psychological harm that can result when an individual or group experiences oppression. The physical and psychological harm that derives from oppression can then lead to the oppressed group's reproduction of the negative attributes projected upon them by their oppressors. For example, a study by Steele and Aronson has shown that controlling for preliminary differences on SAT scores, black students perform worse than white students on a test when the study participants are led to believe that the test measures intellectual ability (Steele and Aronson, 1995). However, when the same test is not described to the students as being an examination of intellectual ability, blacks score as well as whites (Steele and Aronson, 1995). This research demonstrates how degradation operates, the black students exhibit scores that are similar to their white counterparts when they are unaware that the test measures intellectual ability. When the black students are informed that the test measures intellectual ability they demonstrate the effect of degradation by not scoring as well as their white counterparts, effectively reproducing the common stereotype that black youth are intellectually inferior.

The causal properties ascribed to the process of degradation in reference to any other process within the criminalization of blackness are dependent upon the form in which the process of degradation occurs. The process of degradation only operates in an ordered causal manner in relation to the other processes within the criminalization of blackness when it occurs in the form of "othering." The recognition for coining the term "othering" is often accredited to Spivak who provided a systematic outline of the term in an essay entitled "The Rani of Sirmur: An Essay in Reading the Archives." In the essay, Spivak describes three dimensions of "othering"; the first involves those with power constructing the subordinate as the other, the second dimension is related to constructions of the other as inherently inferior, and the third dimension details how knowledge and technology are the property of the powerful and not the subordinate other (Spivak, 1985). The renowned work of postcolonial theorist Edward Said discussed how western entities have constructed "the Orient" as an exoticized other (Said, 1995). Said's work demonstrates that "othering" can involve situating the subordinate in a negative or relatively positive context, the key factor involved in othering however is the disassociation of the powerful from the subordinate who experiences the "othering." For our purposes then, "othering" is an internal process in which a powerful individual or group disassociates itself from other less powerful individuals or groups by projecting negative or positive attributes onto those individuals or groups.

With this understanding of "othering" in mind we find that when the process of degradation occurs in the form of "othering" it is usually coupled with the processes of de-humanization and disconnection in an ordered causal manner. The three-fifths compromise that transpired during the United States Constitutional Convention in 1787, in which African slaves were counted as only three-fifths of a person, provides a clear example of how the processes of disconnection, de-humanization, and degradation operate in an ordered causal manner when they operate within the form of "othering." The dominant society in the United States disconnected itself from African slaves by projecting a negative attribute (de-humanization) onto them which, in effect, served to actively oppress (degradation) them. In fact, the actual language used to describe African slaves within the three-fifths compromise is "other people."

When the process of degradation occurs outside of "othering" however, it does not operate in an ordered manner, its products can contribute to the other processes within the criminalization of blackness, but they do not necessarily cause them. This is not to say that when the process of degradation operates outside of "othering" it does not contribute to de-humanization or disconnection. The point here is that when the process of degradation operates within the criminalization of blackness outside of "othering," it does not cause the other processes within the criminalization of blackness to occur in the same way that the gravitational pull of earth causes an apple to fall if not acted upon by another force. An examination of the degradation that black and brown students experience within the school-to-prison pipeline illustrates the numerous ways in which the process of degradation can help to facilitate the operation of the other processes within the criminalization of blackness without necessarily causing them to occur.

The degradation of students of color that happens in American schools is well-documented, more than three decades of academic research has acknowledged the over-representation of black students in exclusionary disciplinary practices such as suspension and expulsion (Fenning and Rose, 2007, p. 536; Skiba, Michael, Nardo, and Peterson, 2003; Children's Defense Fund, 1975). Black students are more likely to be exposed to harsher disciplinary practices, such as corporal punishment (Irwin, Davidson, and Hall-Sanchez, 2013; Gregory J. F., 1996; Shaw and Braden, 1990), and are less likely than other students to receive more lenient disciplinary alternatives when referred for a violation (Irwin, Davidson, and Hall-Sanchez, 2013) (McFadden, Marsh, Price, and Hwang, 1992). Even after researchers control for socioeconomic status, black students are still more likely to incur harsher disciplinary penalties for their behavior than their white counterparts (Skiba, Michael, Nardo, and Peterson, 2003). In addition, black students are more likely to receive disciplinary action for infractions that are subjective in nature such as excessive noise or disrespect, contradicting claims that the disparity in the punishments endured by students of color and their white counterparts is due to differences in the severity of the infractions that both groups commit (Fenning and Rose, 2007; Skiba and Peterson, 1999).

As mentioned earlier, the process of degradation can help to facilitate and perpetuate the other processes within the criminalization of blackness in a non-causal manner. This widespread, targeted, degradation of black and brown students can help to facilitate their disconnection from the academic institution. Gregory, Skiba, and Noguera concur, writing, "Suspended students may become less bonded to school, less invested in school rules and course work, and subsequently, less motivated to achieve academic success" (Gregory, Skiba, and Noguera, 2010). The degradation of black and brown students can also contribute to black and brown students reproducing the negative attributes that are ascribed to them, which in turn, encourages the further de-humanization of those students. Research shows that being in school is a protective factor against delinquent conduct (U.S. Department of Health and Human Services, 2001) and that suspension from school increases the risk of antisocial and delinquent behaviors (Teske, 2011). It is clear then, that outside of "othering" the process of degradation operates in a manner that contributes to the other processes within the criminalization of blackness without necessarily causing them.

De-humanization is the process within the criminalization of blackness that is most closely associated with "othering." Again, "othering" is an internal process in which a powerful individual or group disassociates itself from less powerful individuals by projecting a negative or positive attribute onto those individuals. Although de-humanization and "othering" are related, they are not the same concept, as we have discussed earlier, the key factor involved in "othering" is disassociation, the process of de-humanization however, is primarily involved with the projection of unwarranted negative attributes onto an individual or group. A gifted student, for example, can experience "othering" without suffering de-humanization. A teacher, peer, parent, etc., can disassociate him or herself from the gifted student by projecting a positive attribute onto the student, the gifted student may be constructed as an intellectual savant by his or her peer group, a label that engenders adulation or praise. The student, according to the conceptualization of de-humanization described here, has experienced "othering," but not been de-humanized because the attribute projected upon the student resulted in positive not negative support. The distinction between the process of de-humanization and "othering" is subtle but important to remember.

Like degradation, the process of de-humanization can help to facilitate and perpetuate the other processes within the criminalization of blackness in an unordered, non-causal manner. Once again, the school-to-prison pipeline provides a clear demonstration of the numerous ways in which the process of de-humanization can function. The process of de-humanization can contribute to both the processes of degradation and disconnection. The de-humanization of students by teachers, for example, can facilitate their subsequent degradation. Raible and Irizarry underscore this contention, writing:

> When unchallenged, these dominant "good" identities allow teachers to continue to see themselves as the norm and construct student diversity as a problem (Achinstein and Barrett, 2004), thus resulting in the hyper-surveillance of poor, deviant students of colour that can lead to school exclusion, and, as data have demonstrated, set them on the pathway to prison (Raible and Irizarry, 2010, p. 1200).

The de-humanization of students by teachers can also contribute to the disconnection of those students from the academic institutions that they inhabit. Research has shown that one of the factors that contributes to a student expressing a lower level of connectedness with the school that he or she attends is a having a poor relationship with a teacher (Wilson, 2004). Research also highlights the connection between a student's relationship with teachers and student dropout rates (Wilson, 2004). The experiences of minority students within the American educational system illustrate how the process of de-humanization can contribute to both the processes of degradation and disconnection without necessarily causing them. I shall discuss the reasoning behind my emphasis of this aspect of the criminalization of blackness during my outline of the process of disconnection.

Disconnection is a broad multifaceted concept that can be interpreted in a variety of ways. For our purposes, we shall only examine the process of disconnection when it occurs in the form of "othering" and the form of "segregation." As with de-humanization and degradation, the disconnection that occurs in the form of "othering" is an internal process in which the individual disassociates itself from other individuals by projecting a negative attribute onto those individuals; when disconnection occurs in the form of "othering" it is usually connected to de-humanization and degradation in an ordered causal manner.

In contrast to the way in which disconnection works when it operates in the form of "othering" when the process of disconnection operates in the form of segregation, its relationship to the other processes that constitute the criminalization of blackness is not causal nor is it ordered. Within the school-to-prison pipeline, for example, segregation contributes to the de-humanization of black and brown students while not necessarily causing it. Many of the pre-service teachers that serve black and brown students originate from upper- and-middle class backgrounds that are entirely different from the poor and working-class environments that their students experience (Raible and Irizarry, 2010). The segregated living environments of pre-service teachers and the students they serve can contribute to the de-humanization of those students because it allows space for misguided stereotypes perpetuated in general societal discourse regarding underprivileged students to go un-checked. Raible and Irizarry argue that teachers' struggles in class manage-ment, the perceived need to gain classroom control, and the hyper-surveil-lance of poor students of color that can lead to school exclusion, may all be connected to the acceptance, by disconnected teachers, of negative stereo types ascribed to underprivileged urban students of color (Raible and Irizar-ry, 2010). Segregation can also contribute to the degradation of black and brown students. When separate but equal policies were codified laws during the Jim Crow era in the United States the segregation that resulted directly contributed to the degradation of black and brown students without a need for any de-humanization to occur. This is not to say that students of color were not subject to de-humanization during this period, but rather that the segregation caused by separate but equal policies contributed directly to the unequal distribution of resources, which enhanced their oppression (degrada-tion).

Throughout this chapter, I have emphasized the importance of under-standing the differences between the causal manner in which the processes of disconnection, dehumanization, and degradation operate in the form of "othering" and the non-causal manner in which these processes operate out-side of "othering." Understanding this important difference can help to ex-plain how the criminalization of blackness has evolved over history. During slavery, the criminalization of blackness operated primarily through "other-ing." The projection of the slave identity onto black individuals disconnected whites from blacks during that period while simultaneously dehumanizing and degrading blacks. The "othering" of blacks perpetrated by whites during slavery was explicit; the "othering" of blacks was openly codified into the laws and policies of the time. After Reconstruction, during the Jim Crow era, the "othering" of blacks became less explicit at least in comparison to the "othering" blacks experienced during slavery. Blacks were no longer relegated to the role of "slave," at least not by most codified laws.

During the Jim Crow era, the criminalization of blackness transformed from a phenomenon that operated primarily through a form of explicit codified "othering" into a phenomenon that operates through the three processes described throughout this chapter. To be clear, "othering" was very prominent during Jim Crow, however it operated and was codified in a less explicit form. After the ratification of the Fourteenth Amendment, equal protection under the law was guaranteed to all citizens. This constrained the explicit "othering" of blacks that occurred during slavery. Separate but equal, the legal policy in the United States constitutional law that justified and permitted racial segregation, represented a transformation in the criminalization of blackness. Separate but equal policies served as a less explicit means of "othering" blacks than that used before the ratification of the Fourteenth Amendment. These policies disguised themselves under a mask of equality. In effect, the "othering" of people of color during Jim Crow became implicit while segregation became explicit codified law, consequently, increasing the segregation of the races.

The criminalization of blackness historically, then, has not diminished but rather has changed forms. As the criminalization of blackness in the form of explicit "othering" became less tenable for institutions in the United States to perpetuate, the processes that undergirded the phenomenon modified into implicit forms that were couched under explicit, government-sponsored segregation. This illustrates the elasticity and flexibility of the criminalization of blackness, it is not a static, non-reactionary, phenomena, it is a phenomenon that evolves and changes in reaction to the environment that it inhabits. Even after the explicit segregation policies of the Jim Crow era were defeated by the passage of the civil rights legislations of the 1960s the criminalization of blackness remained, the form in which its processes operated simply evolved to adapt to the new circumstances they incurred. In today's alleged, post-racial society, the criminalization of blackness has evolved to operate within the very fabric of America's governing institutions.

In this chapter, I have used aspects of the school-to-prison pipeline to illustrate how the criminalization of blackness functions in contemporary society, but as I have reiterated throughout this chapter, the scope of the criminalization of blackness goes far beyond its function within the school-to-prison pipeline. In *The New Jim Crow: Mass Incarceration in the Age of Colorblindness*, Michelle Alexander argues that the modern mass incarceration system in the United States is but another iteration of social control that is tantamount to the oppressive policies of the Jim Crow era (Alexander, 2010). Alexander points to the redlining policies that keep people of color in specific neighborhoods, the misleading image of black communities presented in the media, and the degradation of the black community brought about by the manufactured "war on drugs" as features of what she calls "The New Jim Crow," a modern system of social control (Alexander, 2010). Through a critical analysis of America's far from laudable economic history, Alexander underscores the financial motivations behind the "The New Jim Crow," a task that, unfortunately, was beyond the scope of the analysis of the criminalization of blackness performed in this chapter.

Although our terminology differs, the elements that support the mass incarceration system that Alexander describes, such as segregation (disconnection), the media's misrepresentation of the black community (de-humanization), and the manufactured "war on drugs" (degradation), are similar to the processes that undergird the criminalization of blackness. This is no accident, as I have repeated throughout this chapter the criminalization of blackness is a phenomenon whose operation can be observed in a variety of forms. In short, the processes and patterns that undergird the criminalization of blackness are the fundamental processes and patterns that support and perpetuate oppressive behavior.

CONFRONTING THE CRIMINALIZATION

Unfortunately, there is no easy or simple way to rectify the social ills and racial oppression that result from the criminalization of blackness. The criminalization of blackness evolves and reacts to new circumstances; its processes work in concert to perpetuate their own existence, stifling efforts to eradicate them completely. Engendering a broad-based societal awareness of the criminalization of blackness and its effects may be the first step to effectively confronting the oppressive phenomenon. This is a task that is easier said than done; although we have progressed somewhat in this area, many in our society claim not to "see" race and are reluctant to entertain the idea that structural racism continues to exist. Nevertheless, society must do away with this, "colorblind" narrative that discounts the structural racism that pervades it if any chance at minimalizing the effects of the criminalization of blackness is to be had.

Chapter Eighteen

Growing Teachers, Not Prisoners

The Potential for Grow Your Own Teacher Preparation
Programs to Disrupt the School-to-Prison Pipeline

George Sirrakos Jr. and Tabetha Bernstein-Danis

The School-to-Prison Pipeline (STPP) is a complex phenomenon that dispro-portionately targets students of color, particularly in urban communities (Elias, 2013). In this chapter, we identify *grow your own* (GYO) teacher preparation programs as one possible tool to assist in dismantling the STPP and share our experiences with a GYO program in an urban school in south-eastern Pennsylvania. Toshalis (2014, p. 217) describes GYO programs as being "designed to recruit, support, and prepare educators to return to teach in the communities from which they spring."

According to Hussar and Bailey (2013), it is estimated that by 2022 nearly 55 percent of our nation's school-aged children will be students of color. However, the increase in diversity in the student population has not translated to an increase in diversity in the teacher force, where nearly 86 percent of all elementary and secondary teachers are White (Toshalis, 2014). The disparity between the racial and ethnic makeup of the students and their teachers is even greater in large, urban school districts (Madkins, 2011). As a result, there are heightened possibilities for cultural mismatches and mis-understandings between students of color and their teachers that can result in "fear, apprehension, and overreaction among many teachers and school ad-ministrators" (Irvine, 1990, p. 27) based on the language, dress, and ways of interacting among students of color, with the unintended (or perhaps in-tended) consequence of contributing to and maintaining the STPP.

Some GYO programs function to encourage students of color to pursue careers in education and assist them in overcoming the academic, financial, and social support barriers that have traditionally prevented students of color from pursuing and achieving successful teaching careers (Madda and Schultz, 2009). Taking the time to nurture and develop students of color as teachers can assist in diversifying the teacher force and narrowing the existing racial and ethnic diversity gap between students and their teachers. Further, the strength of GYO teacher preparation programs is that they produce culturally responsive and multiculturally aware teachers (Toshalis, 2014), who, according to Ladson-Billings (2000), are likely to be more effective and engaging teachers. Teachers who share a common cultural and ethnic heritage with students bring their insider knowledge to the educational context and tend to create classrooms that support, value, and foster student's funds of knowledge and cultural experiences (Villegas and Irvine, 2010). Developing a more diverse pool of teachers will enrich the current landscape of predominantly white and middle-class teachers who often lack connection to underserved urban communities and have generally been acculturated to maintain identities that reproduce hegemonic structures and fail to challenge injustice and oppression.

The school-to-prison phenomenon currently plaguing schools most frequently attended by Black and Brown youth provides contemporary researchers with fertile ground for the interrogation of the impact of GYO programs. Thus, this chapter is organized around two questions:

1. What school and classroom practices foster the STPP's propagation in schools?
2. What do our experiences with a secondary GYO teacher preparation program suggest about the program's ability to disrupt the STPP?

We approach these questions using a critical pedagogy framework; that is, we make the assumption, and subsequent affirmation, of the existence of inequities in education regarding the treatment of students of color, which contribute to the STPP (Giroux, 2011). Bourdieu's (1977) concept of doxa, described as individuals' beliefs and attitudes about themselves rooted in socially constructed misconceptions, elaborates the need to examine nontraditional approaches, in this case GYO teacher preparation programs, to address inequities in education. Thus, in lieu of perpetuating the notion that students of color have an intellectual deficiency or that they possess school-resistant dispositions, the dual lens of critical pedagogy and doxa provides the framework necessary to understand the power of GYO programs in disrupting the STPP.

THE SCHOOL-TO-PRISON PIPELINE AND URBAN SCHOOLS

The 1990s and early 2000s saw a sharp increase in zero-tolerance policies, largely spurred in response to the anti-drug and -weapons rhetoric of the 1980s and the specter of school shootings in the 1990s concomitant with the public perception that school violence was on the rise, despite data that demonstrate actual drops in school violence since the early 1990s (Triplett, Allen, and Lewis, 2014). Although conceived in response to objective offenses (e.g., use of a weapon, physical violence) perpetrated by mostly White rural and suburban students, zero-tolerance policies have come to dominate mostly urban schools, where the majority of students are of color. These policies are often applied to less serious and highly subjective behaviors such as *disrespect* and *insubordination*—behaviors that are largely based on the judgments of teachers and administrators (Triplett et al., 2014).

Zero-tolerance policies are typically tied to exclusionary punishments such as suspensions and expulsions rather than restorative justice procedures (Triplett et al., 2014). The resulting portrait is one that sees students of color in urban schools frequently excluded from the educational setting, and in many cases put directly into contact with law enforcement, for offenses that are based on an educator's perception of a student's behavior and which do not pose a threat to safety. In short, policies born of fear over relatively uncommon acts of White suburban school violence have evolved into policies that directly contribute to the STPP for students of color by depriving them of their education, coding them as offenders, and leaving them vulnerable to entry into the criminal justice system. With the knowledge that school suspensions and expulsions are largely ineffective and provide few benefits in regard to improved behavior or safety along with the consequential grievous damage to the lives of students who are subjected to such practices, schools have a responsibility to explore more supportive and effective options for empowering students of color and preventing their entry into the STPP.

WHEN POLICING SUPPLANTS EDUCATING

Recent years have seen a significant increase in the presence of school safety agents in public schools, increasing the chances that students will come into direct police contact and face consequences which may include arrest over relatively minor infractions (Ward and Delessert, 2014). Reductions in school budgets that cover educational and counseling services paired with a steady flow of funding for safety-related measures in the wake of highly visible and politicized acts of school violence (e.g., Sandy Hook school shooting) place priority on "guns and guards" (Schept, Wall, and Brisman,

2015, p. 104) and inscribe students as potentially violent *problems* that must be monitored and policed rather than individuals with rights to intellectual and social-emotional growth. Thus, the role of the school becomes less focused on the preparation of Black and Brown students as agency-bearing participants in a democracy and contributing citizens who are able to attain meaningful professional goals and shifts instead to policing and containment. The problem is compounded by the fact that school safety agents may not be trained to handle student behaviors in positive ways and may not be well versed in approaches other than arrest for addressing the behavioral needs of students in the schools where they work (Ward and Delessert, 2014).

Although the issues around the positioning of school safety agents as primary authority figures in schools is pressing, significant concerns also emerge regarding the role teachers may play in policing students. The majority-White faculties typical of many urban schools may have more training than their school safety counterparts in regard to teaching and learning, but they do not necessarily have superior knowledge in how to meet the needs of students of color in culturally responsive ways. In fact, many White teachers resist discussions on race, favoring instead a *colorblind* approach through which they "not only exonerate themselves in the maintenance of racial hegemony, but also miss out on understanding how social and institutional racism pervade the lived experiences of students of color" (Allen and White-Smith, 2014, p. 448). As a result, White teachers may primarily rely on their own personal views of students of color, and can miss how those views are frequently rooted in stereotypes and deficit perspectives that blame individuals for problems that are actually products of systemic issues mired in a web of privilege and disenfranchisement.

The result is an emerging pattern of educators in urban schools that construct gatekeeping roles for themselves. They assume the responsibility of conducting surveillance on and ensuring compliance among students to enforce a set of community standards that are often inconsistent with those set by members of the community. In this dynamic, students are positioned as prisoners who are tasked with demonstrating obedience and compliance. Such identities—gatekeeper and prisoner—seem woefully incompatible with the development of teacher identities as caregivers, intellectual facilitators, and role models and student identities as critical thinkers, learners, and independent agents in control of their own future.

DISRUPTING THE SCHOOL-TO-PRISON PIPELINE WITH TEACHER DIVERSITY

Several factors are positioned in a reciprocal relationship with the lack of teacher diversity; these are problems that both contribute to and are perpetuated by the diversity gap between teachers and students in urban schools. Figure 18.1 identifies these factors and illustrates the relationships that contribute to the current dearth of racially, ethnically, linguistically, and culturally diverse teachers. Teacher diversity thus emerges as one of the core issues at the heart of the STPP and is a problem that can be directly addressed through GYO programs.

GYO programs have the potential to dismantle the STPP by decreasing the prevalence of culturally mismatched classrooms, where the STPP is often said to begin (Elias, 2013) and to change teacher perspectives on students of color by increasing their *intercultural connectedness* (Raible and Irizarry, 2010). As a result, teachers who are both visibly similar to students and share their lived experiences can serve as very powerful role models for students. While teachers do not need to share their students' background to be effective and just sharing a common racial, socioeconomic, or cultural background does not automatically lead to effectiveness, middle school math teacher Josè Vilson (2015) captures the power and potential that comes with teachers and students sharing a common ground:

> I'm black and Latino. I'm a guy who grew up in public housing on the Lower East Side of Manhattan. You may or may not share any of these characteristics, and whether you share all of them, some of them, or none of them, you may or may not agree with me. No one group of people—people of color included—is monolithic in their thinking or experience. And just because

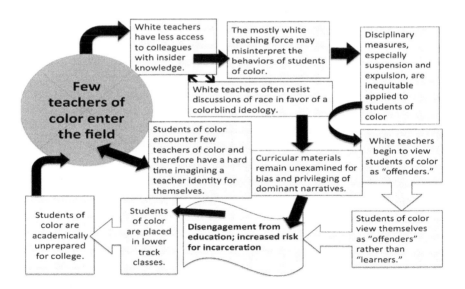

Figure 18.1.   Intersecting Factors Limiting Entry of Students of Color into the Teaching Profession.

someone is a person of color does not mean he or she grew up poor. But based
on my experiences as someone who came of age in a pretty tough neighborhood, and then shocked everyone, including myself, by becoming a middle
school teacher I have some insights into schools and teaching as both a student
and an educator of color. (p. 28)

Vilson's focus on *insights* is crucial for establishing the value of lived experience, building capacity within a school for culturally appropriate interpretations of student behaviors, and providing role models that allow the teacher
identity to be one students of color can imagine adopting for themselves. As
the public school student population becomes increasingly diverse, several
programs have been developed in recent years to cultivate teachers with
insider knowledge of students and their communities.

WORKING WITH A GROW YOUR OWN TEACHER PREPARATION PROGRAM

Toshalis (2014, p. 218) explains, "Because GYO programs' structures and
processes differ depending on the school, district, state, and the nature of
partnerships with institutions of higher education, there is no single standardized version to which we might refer here." As a result of the lack of stan-
dardization in available GYO programs and initiatives, it becomes difficult
for those who are not directly involved with the program to understand its
structures. Therefore, any examination of our work with the GYO must begin
with an understanding of the characteristics specific to this GYO, the setting,
and our role as mentors.

Our GYO program, like many others, has two key goals. First, the program focuses on attracting and recruiting dynamic middle and high school
aged urban youth who have an interest and desire to become educators. The
program's second goal is to assist those students in accessing accurate information about the teaching profession and overcoming the obstacles associated with entrance into formal teacher preparation programs. The GYO was
conceived by university faculty as an attempt to strengthen the relationship
between the university's teacher preparation program and neighboring urban
schools, for the purpose of increasing the diversity of student enrollment.
The initiating faculty also considered the potential of the GYO as a mechanism that could drive conversations regarding social justice issues plaguing
the school and surrounding community and the impact of those issues on
students' identities.

The primary site of this work is an urban public school located in a
densely populated city in southeastern Pennsylvania. The school serves a
student population of about 2,300 students spanning grades 8 and 9. The
student population is 82 percent Hispanic (any race), 10 percent Black (not

Hispanic), 6 percent White (not Hispanic), and 2 percent multiracial or other. Further, the school is a Title I school, and all enrolled students are considered economically disadvantaged and qualify for free or reduced-cost lunch, indicating that they come from socioeconomic backgrounds indicative of traditionally marginalized students.

Unlike other types of GYOs that function as part of a dedicated academy and are integrated within the school day, our GYO operated as an after school program where two university-based faculty members, a school-based teacher advisor, and twelve students met weekly for approximately eighty minutes. The program advisors produced a curriculum driven by the GYO's mission and planned and facilitated activities derived from that curriculum. Some examples of lessons and activities included volunteering to assist teachers, working with counselors to research teacher preparation programs, organizing and participating in community service projects, discussing and debating various educational issues, meeting university students, interacting with guest speakers from the community, and attending multicultural seminars.

THE CONVERSATIONS WE HAD

At first glance, the characteristics and activities associated with our GYO may seem less intensive than GYOs that are integrated within the school day (Sleeter and Milner, 2011) and perhaps ineffective in disrupting the STPP. However, it was the student-driven questions and subsequent conversations and stories that came about as a result of students' involvement with the GYO that are significant. Questions such as: Why are there so few teachers of color in our building? Can I ever become a teacher? Why do we have so many school safety agents in our school? Will I ever be able to get into college? Why is there so much poverty in our community? Do we have the best teachers? How can we better help our community?

A recurring theme among the students in our program was that they found few teaching role models in their community and even fewer in their school. Discussions regarding this issue were often met with the question, "But why do none of my teachers look like me?" The school-based teacher advisor was the exception; a woman of color who graduated from the school district where she taught. Our initial meetings with students provided the teacher advisor with opportunities to share her own stories of hardship in trying to become a teacher, not finding role models in her school, and being initially rejected when she applied for a job after graduating from college. Her perseverance and desire to work within her home community valorized the students' desire to become teachers, and her connection with her students was clear from the beginning. However, the fact that she represented the exception rather than the norm in the school (and, more broadly, in the district) caused students to question the broader social constructs and injustices that created the lack of teacher diversity. Our students therefore grappled with a series of contradictions, first of which was the idea that racism and classism might prevent them from reaching their goals even if they followed the purported pathway to success—graduating from high school, graduating from college, and obtaining teacher certification. Secondly, understanding the trajectory of their teacher advisor's career reinforced that even if they were to reach their goals and become teachers, they might be some of the only teachers of color from their home community in their schools, leading them to believe that as individuals they did not possess the ability to become change agents. These stifling contradictions created the space for students to understand that beyond their development of teacher identities, they would have to develop a sense that they could become teachers who could serve as powerful role models with the power to effect change in their schools.

The conversations had during GYO meetings were *real*, meaning that they dealt with issues relevant to students without trying to make it seem that everything was simply going to be okay. The scope and intensity of these conversations varied, ranging from conversations about the daily activities of a teacher and college entry requirements to more difficult conversations regarding the increased police presence in their school, poverty in the community, the rise of gang violence, segregation of school districts, insufficient academic preparation, the increase in police-related shootings of people of color, and the criminalization of youth. The *realness* of the discussions created a camaraderie between the students with the words "We got your back" rising as the mantra of the GYO. Knowing that the proverbial "deck of cards" was already stacked against them, students understood that navigating the difficulties on the road to achieving their goals would require the support of other like-minded individuals. The following two vignettes describe interactions that highlight the camaraderie developed between students in the GYO.

Vignette 1

Teacher: Where is Maria?

Student 1: Miss, you didn't hear? Some girls were picking on her in the cafeteria. She tried to walk away but when she did they attacked her from behind. She was in the nurse's office but then I think her mom came to pick her up. I heard the security guards say that she was going to get suspended for fighting.

Student 2: That's not even fair. She didn't do anything. Miss, what are we going to do?

Teacher: I will talk to the principal to find out what happened.

Student 1: But we need to let Maria know that we got her back!

Teacher: So what do you suggest?

Student 2: Yeah, Maria is part of our group. She can't just be getting suspended for something she didn't do. All of us need to go and talk to the principal and let him know that her getting suspended isn't fair.

Vignette 2

Student 1: My teacher said if I don't get it together soon, I'm going to fail English.

Teacher: That's crazy! Why did he say that?

Student 1: I don't know. I do most of the work but the class is just so boring.

Teacher: What is so boring about it?

Student 1: I don't know. Some of the stuff I just don't get and other stuff just isn't interesting, so I end up goofing off sometimes.

Student 2: C'mon man! You got this! Show him that you could do the work and that you aren't as dumb as he might think. I can try to help you with whatever you don't understand.

In a school plagued by gang violence and with scant opportunities to develop a sense of belonging, consistent participation in the GYO provided students with opportunities to develop deep connections with each other, their supervising teacher, university supervisors, and community members. Students told stories about their own experiences, listened to others, posed questions, and sought answers. GYO meetings, where many of these conversations were had, brought students closer together and provided them with a sense of belonging. This camaraderie confirmed that students did not have to navigate through their school experiences alone, but rather could rely on their peer network to assist them in a variety of situations, whether that meant advocating for each other during times of need or motivating each other to ensure academic success.

CONCLUSION

The intersecting challenges of few teachers of color to serve as role models, use of curricular materials and instructional approaches that are not relatable to students of color, and the proliferation of zero-tolerance policies that inequitably lead to exclusion from school for students of color combine to create a cycle that often prevents their pursuing teaching careers. When combined with a lack of cultural insiders who can identify students' strengths and interpret their behaviors in culturally relevant ways, one can see how the STPP continues to be not only maintained but proliferated in the schools and communities serving Black and Brown youth. Fortunately, GYO programs are a promising direction in the fight against the STPP as they are "built on a solid foundation of lived commitments to culturally responsive teaching, underserved students, and locally accountable school reform (Toshalis, 2014, p. 232). The potential for GYO programs to recruit more students of color into the teaching profession offers great promise for shifting the diversity of the teacher force. Consequently, these newly recruited and trained teachers can return to their communities and work within the very schools from which they came, in an effort to ameliorate the factors that contribute to the STPP. Further, as demonstrated in the conversations had during our meetings, GYOs can empower students to seek change, develop positive identities, and foster meaningful relationships by offering opportunities to dissect and better understand issues that directly affect them and which they are unlikely to encounter in their traditional school curriculum.

In addition to GYO teacher preparation programs, there are several other organizations across the United States whose work aligns with the ultimate goal of GYOs: assist students in making good choices for the purpose of bettering themselves and their communities. We describe the work of these programs because it is imperative to understand that, while GYO programs offer great promise, there is no *silver bullet* that will magically dismantle the STPP. The STPP is a complex structure whose dismantling requires multiple modes of attack. One such program is the BUILD program (build.org) that aims to curb unemployment and incarceration rates by targeting youth in under-resourced communities who are at risk for dropping out of school. By providing these students with entrepreneurial and experiential learning opportunities, the BUILD approach to pedagogy improves student engagement and leads to greater numbers of high school completers, who are known to enter the STPP at rates much less than students who drop out of high school. Another program, the Hip Hop Chess Federation (HHCF) (hiphopchess.com) uses a combination of chess, hip hop, and martial arts to build academic achievement and community consciousness within participants.

HHCF has spent many years deepening the valuable relationship it has forged with local schools and various community based organizations by being able to provide life-enriching programming in a safe setting to youth who otherwise have limited access to high quality alternative learning, culture and arts experiences. The HHCF uses its unique program as a platform to promote the idea that every young person is High In Potential and has the capacity to Help Other People (HIP-HOP framed differently). (Hip Hop Chess, n.d., http://www.hiphopchess.com/#!mission-and-vision/cdqz)

The Fresh Lifelines for Youth (FLY) (flyprogram.org) program in California works with high school-aged youth who are either in or at risk of entering the juvenile justice system. The FLY program states its mission and vision as follows:

FLY's mission is to prevent juvenile crime and incarceration through legal education, leadership training, and one-on-one mentoring. At FLY we believe all our children deserve a chance to become more than their past mistakes. FLY's vision is that our most at-risk and disadvantaged youth will transform from juvenile delinquents into positive community leaders, a community of people will support them in that process and our local juvenile justice systems will provide more effective and humane services. (Fresh Lifelines for Youth, n.d., http://flyprogram.org/about/what-we-do/mission-history/)

GYO programs and others like the ones described above serve as school- and community-based interventions for students' entry into the STPP. With a growing body of data supporting the ineffectiveness of zero-tolerance policies in making schools safer, the widening gap in suspension and expulsion rates between White and Black/Brown youth, and the growing rate of entry of Black and Brown students into the juvenile justice system, it is imperative that programs such as these continue to grow and become embedded within schools and communities serving youth who are most at risk of entering the STPP.

Bibliography

Abdul-Adil, J. K., and Farmer, A. D. (2006). Inner-city African American parental involvement in elementary schools: Getting beyond urban legends of apathy. *School Psychology Quarterly, 21*(1), 1–12.

Abrams, L. (2004). *Teachers' views on high-stakes testing: Implications for the classroom.* Education Policy Research Unit, (EPSL-0401-104-EPRU).

Acosta, J., Chinman, M., Engberg, J., and Augustine, C. (2015). Rethinking student discipline and zero tolerance. *Education Week, 35*(8), 24.

Adelson, J. (2012, September 12) Louisiana ranks poorly on latest income, health insurance statistics. *The Times Picayune.* Retrieved from: http://www.nola.com.

Adams, D. W. (1995). *Education for extinction: American Indians and the boarding school experience.* Lawrence, KS: University Press of Kansas.

Advancement Project/Civil Rights Project. (2000, February). *Opportunities suspended: The devastating consequences of zero tolerance and school discipline.* Cambridge, MA: Author.

Advancement Project. (2005, March). *Education on lockdown: The schoolhouse to jailhouse track.* Retrieved from: http://b.3cdn.net.

Advancement Project. (2010). *Test, punish, and push out: How "zero tolerance" and high-stakes testing funnel youth into the school-to-prison pipeline.* Retrieved from http://www.educationjustice.org.

Advancement Project, Education Law Center, Fair Test, The Forum for Education and Democracy, Juvenile Law Center, NAACP Legal Defense and Educational Fund, Inc. (2011). *Federal policy, ESEA reauthorization, and the school-to-prison pipeline.* Retrieved from http://qqq/naacpldf.org.

Agarwal, R., Epstein, S., Oppenheim, R., Oyler, C., and Sonu, D. (2010). From ideal to practice and back again: Beginning teachers for social justice. *Journal of Teacher Education, 61*(3), 237–247.

Alat, K. (2002). Traumatic events and children: How early childhood educators can help. *Childhood Education, 79*(1), 2–8.

Alberto, P. A., and Troutman, A. C. (2003). *Applied behavior analysis for teachers.* Upper Saddle River, NJ: Merrill/Prentice Hall.

Allen, Q. and White-Smith, K. A. (2014). Just as bad as prisons: The challenge of dismantling the school-to-prison pipeline through teacher and community education. *Equity and Excellence in Education, 47,* 445–460.

Alexander, M. (2010). *The New Jim Crow.* New York, NY: New Press.

Alexander, M., and West. C. (2012). *The new Jim Crow: Mass incarceration in the age of colorblindness.* New York, NY: New Press.

Alexander, S. N. (2009). *Intersectionality and its impact on the school experiences of African-American females.* (Doctoral dissertation) (UMI 3412021).

Anderson, J. (1988). *The education of blacks in the south 1860–1935.* Chapel Hill, NC: University of North Carolina Press.

American Association of School Administrators and The Children's Defense Fund. (2014). *School discipline in the eyes of school superintendents.* Alexandria, VA: Author. Retrieved from http://www.aasa.org.

American Civil Liberties Union. (2008). *Locating the school-to-prison pipeline.* Retrieved from http://www.aclu.org.

American Civil Liberties Union of Nevada (2012). *Minority students in Nevada public schools overrepresented in discipline, underrepresented in advanced math and science courses.* Retrieved from http://aclunv.org.

American Civil Liberties Union of Florida, Advancement Project, Florida State Conference of the NAACP. (2011). *Still haven't shut off the school-to-prison pipeline: Evaluating the impact of Florida's new zero tolerance law.* Retrieved from http://www.advancementproject.org.

America's cradle to prison pipeline. (2007). Retrieved from http://cdf.childrensdefense.org.

American Educator, Winter 2015–6. Retrieved from: http://www.aft.org.

American Psychological Association Zero Tolerance Task Force (2008). Are zero tolerance policies effective in the schools? An evidentiary review and recommendations. *American Psychologist, 63*(9), 852–62.

American Psychological Association (2014). *Children, youth and families and socioeconomic status.* Retrieved from: http://www.apa.org.

American School Counselor Association. (ASCA). (2012). *ASCA national model: A framework for school counseling programs* (3rd ed.). Alexandria, VA: Author.

Anyon, J. (1997). *Ghetto schooling: A political economy of urban educational reform.* New York, NY: Teachers College Press.

Aos, S., Phillips, P., Barnoski, R., and Lieb, R. (2001). *The comparative costs and benefits of programs to reduce crime.* Olympia, WA: Washington State Institute of Public Policy.

Apple, M. W. (1992). Educational reform and educational crisis. *Journal of Research in Science Teaching,* 29, 779–789.

Apple, M. (1996). *Cultural politcs and education.* New York, NY: Teachers College Press.

Appleman, D. (2013). Teaching in the dark: The promise and pedagogy of creative writing in prison. *English Journal, 102*(4), 24–30.

Archer, D. N. (2009). Introduction: Challenging the school-to-prison pipeline. *New York Law School Law Review,* 54, 867.

Arcia, E. (2006). Achievement and enrollment status of suspended students. *Education and Urban Society, 38,* 359–369.

Argyris, C. (1990). *Overcoming organizational defenses.* Upper Saddle River, NJ: Prentice Hall.

Astramovich, R. L., and Harris, K. R. (2007). Promoting self-advocacy among minority students in school counseling. *Journal of Counseling and Development, 85,* 269–276.

Aull, E. H. (2012). Zero tolerance, frivolous juvenile court referrals, and the school-to-prison pipeline: Using arbitration as a screening-out method to help plug the pipeline. *Ohio State Journal on Dispute Resolution, 27*(1), 179–206.

Austin, J., Clear, T., Duster, T., Greenberg, D. F., Irwin, J., McCoy, C., Mobley, A., Owen, B., and Page, J. (2007). *Unlocking America: Why and how to reduce America's prison population.* Washington, DC: JFA Institute.

Avraham, S. (2005). Seeing things differently: Restorative justice and school discipline. *Education and the Law, 17*(3), 87–104.

Ayers, R., and Ayers, W. (2015). Breathe: Notes on White Supremacy and the Fierce Urgency of Now. In K. Fasching-Varner, N. D. Hartlep, L. L. Martin, C. Hayes, R. Mitchell, and C. M. Allen-Mitchell (Eds.), *The Assault on Communities of Color* (pp. xi–xvii). Lanham, MD: Rowman and Littlefield.

Ayers, W. (2014, July 13). *The myth of military might.* Retrieved from http://billayers.org.

Ayoub, C. C., O'Connor, E., Rappolt-Schlichtmann, G., Fischer, K. W., Rogosch, F. A., Toth, S. L., and Cicchetti, D. (2006). Cognitive and emotional differences in young maltreated children: A translational application of dynamic skill theory. *Development and Psychopathology, 18*(3), 679–706.

Baer, J., and Chambliss, W. (1997). Generating fear: The politics of crime reporting. *Crime, Law and Social Change, 27*(2), 87–107.

Baglieri, S., Valle, J. W., Connor, D. J., and Gallagher, D. J. (2010). Disability studies in education: The need for a plurality of perspectives on disability. *Remedial and Special Education.*

Balfanz, R., Spiridakis, K., Neild, R. C., and Legters, N. (2003). High poverty secondary schools and the juvenile justice system. In J. Wald and D. J. Losen (Eds.), *Deconstructing the school to prison pipeline* (pp. 77–78). San Francisco, CA: Jossey-Bass.

Balfanz, R., Byrnes, V., and Fox, J. (2015). Sent home and put off-track: The antecedents, disproportionalities, and consequences of being suspended in the ninth grade. In D. J. Losen (Ed.), *Closing the school discipline gap: Equitable remedies for excessive exclusion* (pp. 17–30). New York: Teachers College Press.

Bandura, A. (1977). Self-efficacy: Toward a unifying theory of behavioral change. *Psychological Review, 84*(2), 191–215.

Bandura, A. (1994). Self-efficacy. In V. S. Ramachaudran (Ed.), *Encyclopedia of human behavior* (pp. 71–81). New York, NY: Academic Press.

Banks, J. A., and Banks, C. A. (2012). *Multicultural Education: Issues and Perspectives.* Hoboken, NJ: Wiley.

Banks, J. A. (2000). *Multicultural education: Issues and perspectives* (4th ed.). Hoboken, NJ: Wiley.

Banks, J. A. (2013). The construction and Historical Development of Multicultural Education 1962–2012. *Theory Into Practice, 52*(1), 73–82.

Baroque, L. (1981). Applied research in the 1970s: Can anything be learned about children? *Annals of the American Academy of Political and Social Science, 32*–42.

Barton, P. E., and Coley, R. J. (2009). *Parsing the achievement gap II.* https://www.ets.org.

Barton, D., Ivanič, R., Appleby, Y., Hodge, R., and Tusting, K. (2007). *Literacy, lives and learning.* London, UK: Routledge.

Bauer, R., and Bauer, A. (1942). Day to day resistance to slavery. *The Journal of Negro History, 27*(4), 388–419.

Bauman, Z. (2009). *Wasted Lives: Modernity and its outcasts.* Cambridge, MA: Polity Press.

Baszile, D. T. (2008). Beyond all reason indeed: The pedagogical promise of critical race testimony. *Race Ethnicity and Education, 11*(3), 251–265.

Bell, D. A. (1992a). *Faces at the bottom of the well: The permanence of racism.* New York, NY: Basic Books.

Bell, D. (1992b). Racial Realism. *Connecticut Law Review ,* 363–379.

Ben-Moshe, L., Chapman, C., and Carey, A. (Eds.). (2014). *Disability incarcerated: Imprisonment and disability in the United States and Canada.* New York, NY: Springer.

Bialka, C. S. (2012). *Taking the" dis" out of disability: Attending to pre-service teacher dispositions related to students with special needs.* Philadelphia, PA: UPenn Repository.

Birmingham, L., Mason, D., and Grubin, D. (1996). Prevalence of mental disorder in remand prisoners: Consecutive case study. *BMJ, 313*(7071), 1521–1524.

Blake, J., Darensbourg, A., and Perez, E., (2010). Overrepresentation of African American males in exclusionary discipline: The role of school based mental health professionals in dismantling the school to prison pipeline. *Journal of African American Males in Education, 1*(3).

Bemak, F., and Chung, R. Y. (2005). Advocacy as a critical role for urban school counselor: Working towards equity and social justice. *Professional School Counseling, 8,* 196–202.

Bemak, F., and Chung, R. C. (2008). New professional roles and advocacy strategies for school counselors: A multicultural/social justice perspective to move beyond the nice counselor syndrome. *Journal of Counseling and Development, 86,* 372–381.

Bennett, W., Dilulio, J. and Walters, J. (1996). *Body count: Moral poverty—and how to win America's war against crime and drugs.* New York, NY: Simon and Schuster.

Bergin, C. A., and Bergin, D. A. (2009). Attachment in the classroom. *Educational Psychology Review, 21*, 141–170.

Berliner, D. C., and Biddle, B. J. (1995). *The manufactured crisis: Myths, fraud, and the attack on America's public schools.* New York, NY: Addison-Wesley.

Berlowitz, M. J., Frye, R., and Jette, K. M. (2015). Bullying and zero-tolerance policies: The school to prison pipeline, 1–19.

Bertrand, M., and Mullainathan, S. (2004). Are Emily and Greg more employable than Lakisha and Jamal? A field experiment on labor market discrimination. *American Economic Review*, 991–1013.

Blake, J. J., Butler, B. A., Lewis, C. L., and Darensbourg, A. (2011). Unmasking the inequitable discipline experiences of urban Black girls: Implications for urban stakeholders. *Urban Review, 43*, 90–106.

Bloom, B. S. (Ed.). (1984). *Taxonomy of educational objectives book 1: Cognitive domain.* New York, NY: Pearson, Allyn and Bacon.

Blumstein, A. (1982). On the Racial Disproportionality of United States' Prison Populations. *Journal of Criminal Law and Criminology, 73*(3), 1259–1281.

Bondy, E., Ross, D. D., Gallingane, C., and Hambacher, E. (2007). Creating environments of success and resilience: Culturally responsive classroom management and more. *Urban Education, 42*(4), 326–48.

Bonilla-Silva, E. (2001). *White supremacy and racism in the post-civil rights era.* New York, NY: Lynne Rienner Publishers.

Bonilla-Silva, E. (2006). *Racism without racists: Color-blind racism and the persistence of racial inequality in America.* Lanham, MD: Rowman and Littlefield.

Bonilla-Silva, E. (2013). *Racism without racists: Color-blind racism and the persistence of racial inequality in America.* Lanham, MD: Rowman and Littlefield.

Bonn, S. A. (2010). *Mass deception: Moral panic and the US war on Iraq.* Rutgers, NJ: Rutgers University Press.

Bourdieu, P. (1977). Cultural reproduction and social reproduction. In J. Karabel and A. H. Hasley (Eds.), *Power and ideology in education* (pp. 487–511). New York, NY: Oxford University Press.

Bourdieu, P. (1997). *Pascalian meditations.* Stanford, CA: Stanford University Press.

Bowditch, C. (1993). Getting rid of troublemakers: High school disciplinary procedures and the production of dropouts. *S o c ial Probl e ms, 40*, 493–507.

Bowles, S., and Gintis, H. (1976). Schooling in capitalist America: Educational reform and the contradictions of economic life. New York, NY: Basic.

Boykin, A. W. (1994). Afrocultural expression and its implications for schooling. In E. R. Hollins, J. E. King, and W. C. Hayman (Eds.), *Teaching diverse populations: Formulating a knowledge base* (pp. 243–274). Albany, NY: SUNY Press.

Bradshaw, C. P., Koth, C. W., Bevans, K. B., Ialongo, N., and Leaf, P. J. (2008). The impact of school-wide positive behavioral interventions and supports (PBIS) on the organizational health of elementary schools. *School Psychology Quarterly, 23*(4), 462–473.

Bradshaw, C. P., Mitchell, M. M., O'Brennan, L. M., and Leaf, P. J. (2010). Multilevel exploration of factors contributing to the overrepresentation of black students in office disciplinary referrals. *Journal of Educational Psychology, 102*(2), 508–520.

Bradshaw, C. P., Mitchell, M. M., and Leaf, P. J. (2010). Examining the effects of schoolwide positive behavioral interventions and supports on student outcomes: Results from a randomized controlled effectiveness trial in elementary schools. *Journal of Positive Behavior Interventions, 12*(3), 133–148.

Brand, S., Felner, R. D., Shim, M., Seitsinger, A., and Dumas, T. (2003). Middle school improvement and reform: Development and validation of a school-level assessment of climate, cultural pluralism and school safety. *Journal of Educational Psychology, 95*, 570–588.

Brewer, R. M., and Heitzeg, N. A. (2008). The racialization of crime and punishment criminal justice, color-blind racism, and the political economy of the prison industrial complex. *American Behavioral Scientist, 51*, 625–644.

Britzman, D. (2003). *Practice makes practice: A critical study of learning to teach.* Albany, NY: State University of New York Press.

Bronfenbrenner, U. (1992). *Ecological systems theory.* London, UK: Jessica Kingsley Publishers.

Brookover, W., and Erickson, E. (1969). *The trouble with Black boys: The role and influence of environmental and cultural factors on the academic performance of African American males.* East Lansing, MI: Michigan State University Press.

Brookover, W. (1985). Can we make schools effective for minority students? *The Journal of Negro Education, 54,* 257–268.

Brooks, G. (1956). *Bronzeville boys and girls.* New York, NY: Harper and Row.

Brooks, K., Schiraldi, V., and Ziedenberg, J. (1999). *School house hype: Two years later.* San Francisco, CA: Center on Juvenile and Criminal Justice. Retrieved from http://www.cjcj.org.

Brophy, J. E. (1988). Research linking teacher behavior to student achievement: Potential implications for instruction of Chapter 1 students. *Educational Psychologist, 23,* 235–286.http://dx.doi.org.

Brown v. Board of Education., 347 U.S. 483 (1954).

Brown, D. F. (2004). Urban teachers' professed classroom management strategies: Reflections of culturally responsive teaching. *Urban Education, 39*(3), 266–289.

Brown, E. R. (2003). Freedom for some, discipline for 'Others:' The structure of inequity in education. In K. J. Saltman and D. A. Gabbard (Eds.), *Education as enforcement: The militarization and corporatization of schools* (pp. 127–152). New York, NY: Routledge Falmer Press.

Brown Foundation for Educational Equity, Excellence and Research. (2004). Retrieved from http://brownvboard.org.

Buras, K. (2011). Race, charter schools, and conscious capitalism: On the spatial politics of whiteness as property (and the unconscionable assault on black New Orleans). *Harvard Educational Review,* 296–330.

Burke, J. D., Loeber, R., and Birmaher, B. (2002). Oppositional defiant and conduct disorder: A review of the past 10 years, part II. *Journal of American Academic Psychiatry, 41,* 1275–1293.

Burris, M. W. (2012). *Mississippi and the school-to-prison pipeline.* Retrieved from http://blogs.law.widener.edu

Burris, C. C., and Welner, K. G. (2005). Closing the achievement gap by detracking. *Phi Delta Kappan,* 594–598.

Byrd, C. M., and Chavous, T. (2011). Racial identity, school racial climate, and school intrinsic motivation among African American youth: The importance of Person–Context congruence. *Journal of Research on Adolescence, 21*(4), 849–860.

Cabrera, O. A., Hoge, C. W., Bliese, P. D., Castro, C. A., and Messer, S. C. (2007). Childhood adversity and combat as predictors of depression and post-traumatic stress in deployed troops. *American Journal of Preventive Medicine, 33*(2), 77–82.

Caporizzo, C. (2011). *Prison reentry programs: Ensuring a safe and successful return to the community.* Retrieved from https://www.whitehouse.gov.

Carroll, L. (1871). *Through the Looking Glass, and What Alice Found There.* London: Macmillan.

Carson, E. A. (2015). *Prisoners in 2014.* Washington, DC: Bureau of Justice Statistics. Retrieved from http://www.bjs.gov.

Carbonaro, W. (2005). Tracking student effort and academic achievement. *Sociology of Education,* 27–49.

Carmichael, D., Booth, E., and Patnaik, A. (2010). *Addressing disproportionate minority contact in the Texas juvenile justice system: Causes and solutions from the community perspective.* College Station: Texas AandM University, Public Policy Research Institute.

Casella, R. (2003). Zero tolerance policy in schools: Rationale, consequences, and alternatives. *Teachers College Record,* 105(5), 872–893.

Castillo, J. (2013). Tolerance in schools for Latino students: Dismantling the school-to-prison pipeline. *Harvard Journal of Hispanic Policy, 26*(43), 43–58.

Center for Civil Rights Remedies. (2012). [Data file]. Retrieved from: http://www.schooldisciplinedata.org.

Center for Labor Market Studies. (2009). *Left behind in America: The nation's dropout crisis.* Chicago: Northeastern University, Center for Labor Market Studies.

Chang, F. H., and Thompkins, D. E. (2002). Corporations go to prisons: The expansion of corporate power in the correctional industry. *Arbor Studies Journal, 27*(1), 45–69.

Charles, C. (2003). The Dynamics of Racial Residential Segregation. *Annual Review of Sociology, 167–207.*

Charles, C. M. (2013). *Building classroom discipline.* Pearson: Boston, MA.

Christle, C. A., Jolivette, K., and Nelson, C.M. (2005). Breaking the school to prison pipeline: Identifying school risk and protective factors for youth delinquency. *Exceptionality, 13,* 69–88.

Clandinin, D. J., and Connelly, F. M. (1986). Rhythms in teaching: The narrative study of teachers' personal practical knowledge of classrooms. *Teaching and teacher education, 2*(4), 377–387.

Clandinin, D. J., and Connelly, F. M. (1994). Personal experience methods. In N. Denzin and Y. Lincoln (Eds.), *Collecting and interpreting qualitative materials* (pp. 413–427). London, England: Sage.

Clandinin, D.J. and Connelly, F. M. (2000). *Narrative inquiry: Experience and story in qualitative research.* San Francisco, CA: Jossey-Bass.

Clark, C. (2012). School-to-prison pipeline. In J. A. Banks (Ed.), *Encyclopedia of diversity in education: Volume 4* (pp. 1894–1897). Thousand Oaks, CA: Sage Publications.

Clark, C. (2011). *Dismantling the school-to-prison pipeline : Black male students, white female teachers: Urban educational research in the public interest* (Unpublished Powerpoint presentation). University of Nevada, Las Vegas.

Clarke, A., and Erickson, G. (2004). Self-study: The fifth commonplace. *Australian Journal of Education, 48.*

Clear, T. (2009). *Imprisoning communities: How mass incarceration makes disadvantaged neighborhoods worse.* New York, NY: Oxford University Pres.

Clements, P. T., and Burgess, A. W. (2002). Children's responses to family member homicide. *Family and Community Health, 25*(1), 32–42.

Cleaver, F. (2005). The inequality of social capital and the reproduction of chronic poverty. *World Development, 33,* 893–906.

Coates, T. (2015). *Between the world and me.* New York, NY: Spiegel and Grau.

Cole, H. A., and Heilig, J. V. (2011). Developing a school-based youth court: A potential alternative to the school to prison pipeline. *Journal of Law and Education, 40*(2), 305.

Condron, D. J. (2009). Social Class, School and Non-School Environments, and Black/White Inequalities in Children's Learning. *American Sociological Review, 74*(5), 685–708.

Cooc, N., Currie-Rubin, R., Kuttner, P., and Ng, M. (2012). *Disrupting the school-to-prison pipeline.* Boston, MA: Harvard Education.

Copeland, W. E., Keeler, G., Angold, A., and Costello, E. J. (2007). Traumatic events and posttraumatic stress in childhood. *Archives of General Psychiatry, 64*(5), 577–584.

Cornelius-White, J. (2007). Learner-centered teacher-student relationships are effective: A meta-analysis. *Review of Educational Research, 77,* 113–143.

Costenbader, V., and Markson, S. (1998). School suspension: A study with secondary school students. *Journal of School Psychology, 36*(1), 59–82.

Counsel for Accreditation of Counseling and Related Educational Programs. (CACREP). (2016). *2016 standards for accreditation.* Alexandria, VA: Author.

Cramer, E. D., Gonzalez, L., and Pellegrini-Lafont, C. (2014). From classmates to inmates: An integrated approach to break the school-to-prison pipeline. *Equity and Excellence in Education, 47*(4), 461–475.

Craven, J. (2015). The girl who was assaulted by a cop on camera at Spring Valley high is now facing charges. Retrieved from http://www.huffingtonpost.com.

Crawford, C., Chiricos, T., and Kleck, G. (1998). Race, racial threat, and sentencing of habitual offenders. *Criminology, 36,* 481–511.

Crenshaw, K. W. (2003). Demarginalizing the intersection of race and sex. In A. K. Wing (Ed.), *Critical race feminism: A reader* (second edition) (pp. 23–33). New York, NY: New York University Press.

Crenshaw, K. W., Ocen, P., and Nanda, J. (2015). *Black girls matter: Pushed out, overpoliced, and underprotected.* Center for Intersectionality and Social Policy Studies and African American Policy Forum. Retrieved from: http://www.law.columbia.edu.

Crenshaw, K. W., Ocen, P., and Nanda, J. (2015). *Black girls matter: Pushed out, overpoliced, and underprotected.* NY, Columbia Law School: Center for Intersectionality and Social Policy Studies.

Cross, W. E., Jr., and Vandiver, B. J. (2001). Nigrescence theory and measurement: Introducing the cross racial identity scale. In J. Ponterotto, J. M. Casas, L. A. Suzuki, and C. M. Alexander (Eds.), *Handbook of multicultural counseling* (pp. 371–393). Thousand Oaks, CA: Sage.

Curry, T. (2008). Saved by the bell: Derrick Bell's racial realism as pedagogy. *Ohio Valley Philosophy of Education Society, 39,* 35–46.

Dancy, T. E. II (2014). (Un)Doing Hegemony in Education: Disrupting School-to-Prison Pipelines for Black Males. *Equity and Excellence in Education, 47*(4), 476–493.

Darling-Hammond, L. (2010). *The flat world and education: How America's commitment to equity will determine our future.* New York, NY: Teachers College Press.

Darensbourg, A., Perez, E., and Blake, J. (2010). Overrepresentation of African American males in exclusionary discipline: The role of school-based mental health professionals in dismantling the school to prison pipeline. *Journal of African American Males in Education, 1*(3), 196–211.

Davis, L. M., Bozick, R., Steele, J. L., Saunders, J. and Miles, J. N. V. (2013). *Evaluating the effectiveness of correctional education: A meta-analysis of programs that provide education to incarcerated adults.* Santa Monica, CA: RAND Corporation. Retrieved from http://www.rand.org.

Davis, J. E. and Jordan, W. J. (1994). The effects of school context, structure, and experiences on African American males in middle and high schools. *Journal of Negro Education, 63,* 570–587.

Davis, A. (2003). *Are Prisons Obsolete?* New York, NY: Seven Stories Press.

Deblinger, E., and Runyon, M. K. (2005). Understanding and Treating Feelings of Shame in Children Who Have Experienced Maltreatment. *Child Maltreatment, 10*(4), 364–376.

DCSD. (2014). *Cultural diversity competency training for [DCSD] administrators.* Retrieved from: http://tv.ccsd.net

DCSD. (2013). *Final report on overrepresentation by gender, race/ethnicity, or disability in discipline-related actions and/or special education placement.* Retrieved from: http://ccsd.net.

Deci, E. L., and Ryan, R. M. (1985). *Intrinsic motivation and self-determination in human behavior* (perspectives in social psychology). New York, NY: Plenum Press.

Deci, E. L., and Ryan, R. M. (2002). The handbook of self-determination research. Rochester, NY: University of Rochester Press.

Dee, T., and Penner, E. (2016). *The causal effects of cultural relevance: Evidence from an ethnic studies curriculum.* Stanford: Stanford University. Paper presented at the Graduate School of Education.

DeGruy, J. (2005). *Post traumatic slave syndrome: America's legacy of enduring injury and healing.* Portland, OR: Uptone Press.

Delgado, R., and Stefancic, J. (2001). *Critical race theory: An introduction.* New York, NY: New York University Press.

Delgado, R. (2000). Derrick Bell's toolkit: Fit to dismantle that famous house. *New York University Law Review, 75,* 283–307.

Deliovsky, K. (2008). Normative white femininity: Race, gender and the politics of beauty. *Atlantis, 33*(1), 49–59.

Delpit, L. (1995). *Other people's children: Cultural conflict in the classroom.* New York, NY: The New Press.

Delpit, L. D. (1988). The silenced dialogue: Power and pedagogy in educating other people's children. *Harvard Educational Review, 58*(3), 280–98.

Deruy, E. (2013). Student Diversity Is Up But Teachers Are Mostly White. Retrieved January 2, 2016, from https://aacte.org.

Diamond, J. (2012). Accountability policy, school organization, and classroom practice: Partial recoupling and education opportunity. *Education and Urban Society*, 151–182.

DiIulio, J. (1995, December 15). Moral poverty: The coming of the super-predators should scare us into wanting to get to the root causes of crime a lot faster. *Chicago Tribune*, 31.

Dinkes, R., Kemp, J., and Baum, K. (2009). Indicators of School Crime and Safety: 2009. NCES 2010–012/NCJ 228478. *National Center for Education Statistics*. Retrieved from http://eric.ed.gov.

Dixon, A. D., and Rousseau, C. K. (2006). *Critical race theory in education theory: All God's children got a song.* New York, NY: Routledge.

Dixon, A. L., Tucker, C., and Clark, M. A. (2010). Integrating social justice advocacy with national standards of practice: Implications for school counselor education. *Counselor Education and Supervision, 50,* 103–115.

Dolovich, S. (2005). State punishment and private prisons. *Duke Law Journal, 55,* 439–548.

Domitrovich, C. E., Bradshaw, C. P., Poduska, J. M., Hoagwood, K., Buckley, J. A., Olin, S., ... Ialongo, N. S. (2008). Maximizing the Implementation Quality of Evidence-Based Preventive Interventions in Schools: A Conceptual Framework. *Advances in School Mental Health Promotion, 1*(3), 6–28.

Douglass, F. (1845/1995). *The narrative life of Frederick Douglass. An American slave. Written by himself.* New York, NY: Dover Thrift Editions.

Douglas, M. (1966). *Purity and danger.* New York, NY: Routledge.

Douglas, B., Lewis, C. W., Douglas, A., Scott, M. E., and Garrison-Wade, D. (2008). The Impact of White Teachers on the Academic Achievement of Black Students: An Exploratory Qualitative Analysis. *Educational Foundations, 22,* 47–62.

Downey, D. B., Hippel, P. T. von, and Broh, B. A. (2004). Are Schools the Great Equalizer? Cognitive Inequality during the Summer Months and the School Year. *American Sociological Review, 69*(5), 613–635.

Downey, D., and Pribesh, S. (2012). *When race matters: Teachers' evaluation of students' behavior.* New York, NY: Routledge.

Dube, S. R., Anda, R. F., Felitti, V. J., Chapman, D. P., Williamson, D. F., and Giles, W. H. (2001). Childhood abuse, household dysfunction, and the risk of attempted suicide throughout the life span: Findings from the Adverse Childhood Experiences Study. *JAMA, 286*(24), 3089–3096.

Dube, S. R., Felitti, V. J., Dong, M., Chapman, D. P., Giles, W. H., and Anda, R. F. (2003). Childhood abuse, neglect, and household dysfunction and the risk of illicit drug use: The adverse childhood experiences study. *Pediatrics, 111*(3), 564–572.

Duncan-Andrade, J. M. R. (2005). Developing social justice educators. *Educational Leadership, 62*(6), 70–73.

Dweck, C. (2006). *Mindset: The new psychology of success.* New York, NY: Ballantine Books.

Dweck, C. S., and Elliott, E. S. (1988). A social-cognitive approach to motivation and personality. *Psychological Review, 95*(2), 256–273.

Eitle, T. M. N., and Eitle, D. J. (2004). Inequality, segregation, and the overrepresentation of African Americans in school suspensions. *Sociological Perspectives, 47,* 269–287.

Ejiogu, N., and Ware, S. M. (2008). How disability studies stays white, and what kind of white it stays. *Society for Disability Studies.*

Elias, M. (2013). The school-to-prison pipeline: Policies and practices that favor incarceration over education do us all a grave injustice. *Teaching Tolerance, 43,* 39–40.

Elikann, P. T. (2002). *Superpredators: The demonization of our children by the law.* Cambridge, MA: Da Capo Press.

Engels, F. (1843). Outlines of a critique of political exonomy. *DeutschFranzösische Jahrbücher,* 1–6.

Equal Justice Initiative. (November 15, 2012). *Department of Justice Sues Mississippi Officials for Operating School to Prison Pipeline.* Retrieved: http://www.eji.org

Erevelles, N. (2011). Coming out crip in inclusive education. *Teachers College Record, 113*(10), 2155–2185.

Erford, B. T. (2014). *Transforming the school counseling profession.* Boston, MA: Pearson.

Evans, K. R., Lester, J. N., and Anfara, V. A. (2013). Restorative justice in education: What we know so far. *Middle School Journal, 44*(5), 57–63.

Evans, M. P., Zambrano, E., Cook, K., Moyer, M., and Duffey, T. (2011). Enhancing school counselor leadership in multicultural advocacy. *Journal of Professional Counseling: Practice, Theory, and Research, 38,* 52–67.

Fabelo, T., Thompson, M. D., Plotkin, M., Carmichael, D., Marchbanks III, M. P., and Booth, E. A. (2011). *Breaking schools' rules: A statewide study of how school discipline relates to students' success and juvenile justice involvement.* New York, NY: The Council of State Governments Justice Center.

Fajana, F. (2007). The Intersection of Race, Poverty, and Crime. *Clearinghouse Review, 41,* 120–127.

Farmer, S. (2010). Criminality of Black youth in inner-city schools: 'moral panic', moral imagination, and moral formation. *Race Ethnicity and Education, 13*(3), 367–381.

Fasching-Varner, K. (2012). *Working through whiteness: Examining white racial identity and profession with pre-service teachers.* Lanham, MD: Lexington Books.

Fasching-Varner, K., Mitchell, R., Martin, L., and Bennett-Haron, K. (2014). Beyond School-to-Prison Pipeline and Toward an Educational and Penal Realism. *Equity and Excellence in Education, 47*(4), 410–429.

Fasching-Varner, K. J., and Mitchell, R. W. (2013a). Capturing the moment to debunk the crisis. *Journal of Curriculum and Pedagogy, 10,* 124–127.

Fasching-Varner, K. J., and Mitchell, R. (2013b). CRT's challenge to educators' articulation of abstract liberal perspectives of purpose. In A. Dixson and M. Lynn (Eds.), *Handbook of critical race theory in education* (pp. 355–367). New York, NY: Routledge.

Fasching-Varner, K., and Seriki, V. D. (2012). Moving Beyond Seeing with Our Eyes Wide Shut. *Democracy and Education, 20*(1), 1–6.

Fausset, R., and Southall, A. (2015, October 26). *Video Shows Officer Flipping Student in South Carolina, Prompting Inquiry.* Retrieved from www.nytimes.com.

Federal Writers Project. (1941/2007). *South Carolina slave narratives: A folk history of slavery in the United States from interviews with former South Carolina slaves.* Native American Book Publishers.

Feiring, C., Miller-Johnson, S., and Cleland, C. M. (2007). Potential pathways from stigmatization and internalizing symptoms to delinquency in sexually abused youth. *Child Maltreatment, 12*(3), 220–232.

Fenning, P., and Rose, J. (2007). Overrepresentation of African American Students in Exclusionary Discipline. *Urban Education, 42*(6), 536–559.

Ferguson, T. J. (2005). Mapping Shame and Its Functions in Relationships. *Child Maltreatment, 10*(4), 377–386.

Figlio, D. N. (2006). Testing, crime and punishment. *Journal of Public Economics, 90*(4), 837–851.

Focus On Us. (February 2011). *National Education Association.* Retrieved from http://www.nea.org.

Foucault, M. (1977). *Discipline and punish: The birth of the prison.* (A. Sheridan, trans.). New York, NY: Pantheon Books.

Foucault, M. (1995). *Discipline and punish: The birth of the prison.* New York, NY: Vintage Books.

Feagin, J. R. (2013). *The white racial frame: Centuries of racial framing and counter-framing.* New York, NY: Routledge.

Freire, P. (1970). *Pedagogy of the oppressed.* New York, NY: Continuum.

Feierman, J., Levick, M., and Mody, A. (2009). The school-to-prison pipeline . . . and back: Obstacles and remedies for the re-enrollment of adjudicated youth. *New York University Law School Review, 54,* 1115.

Ferguson, A. A. (2001). *Bad boys: Public schools in the making of Black masculinity.* Ann Arbor, MI: University of Michigan Press.

Ferriter, W. M., and Graham, P. (2010). Building a professional learning community at work: A guide to the first year. Bloomington: Solution Tree Press.

Fine, M. (1991). *Framing dropouts: Notes on the politics of an urban high school.* Albany, NY: State University of NY Press.

Finn, J. D., and Servoss, T. J. (2015). Misbehavior, suspensions, and security measures in high school: Racial/ethnic and gender differences. In D. J. Losen (Ed.), *Closing the school discipline gap: Equitable remedies for excessive exclusion* (pp. 45–58). New York: Teachers College Press.

Ford, D. Y. (2010). Reversing underachievement among gifted Black students: *Theory, research, and practice* (2nd ed.). Waco, TX: Prufrock Press.

Ford, D. Y. (2011). *Multicultural gifted education: Rationale, models, strategies, and rescourses* (2nd ed.) Waco, TX: Prufrock Press.

Ford, D. Y. (2011). Conducting research that is culturally responsive. *Gifted Child Today, 34*(3), 25–27.

Ford, D. Y. (2013). Multicultural issues: Gifted underrepresentation and Prejudice—Learning from Allport and Merton. *Gifted Child Today, 36*(1), 62–67.

Ford, D.Y. (2012). Culturally different students in special education: Looking backward to move forward. *Exceptional Children, 78*(4), 391–405.

Ford, D. Y. (2013). *Recruiting and retaining culturally different students in gifted education.* Waco, TX: Prufrock Press.

Ford, D. Y., Grantham, T. C., and Harris III, J. J. (1997). The recruitment and retention of minority teachers in gifted education. *Roeper Review, 19*(4), 213–220.

Ford, D. Y., Grantham, T. C., and Whiting, G. W. (2008). Culturally and linguistically diverse students in gifted education: Recruitment and retention issues. *Exceptional Children, 74*(3), 289–308.

Fordham, S. (1988). Racelessness as a factor in Black students' school success: Pragmatic strategy or pyrrhic victory? *Harvard Educational Review, 58*(1), 54–85.

Fordham, S. (1996). *Blacked out: Dilemmas of race, identity, and success at Capital High.* Chicago, IL: University of Chicago Press.

Fordham, S., and Ogbu, J. U. (1986). Black students' school success: Coping with the "burden of 'acting white.'" *Urban Review, 18*, 176–206.

Foucault, M. (1977). *Discipline and punish: The birth of the prison.* New York, NY: Random House.

Fowler, D. (2011). School discipline feeds the "pipeline to prison." *Phi Delta Kappan, 93*(2), 14–19.

Fowler, D., Lightsey, R., Monger, J., and Aseltine, E. (2010). *Texas' school to prison pipeline: Ticketing, arrest, and use of force at schools: How the myth of the "blackboard jungle" reshaped school disciplinary policy.* Austin: Texas Appleseed. Retrieved from http://www.texasappleseed.net

Frankenberg, E., Siegel-Hawley, G., and Wang, J. (2010). *Choice without Equity: Charter School Segregation and the Need for Civil Rights Standards.* Civil Rights Project / Proyecto Derechos Civiles. Retrieved from http://eric.ed.gov

Freire, P. (2000). *Pedagogy of the oppressed.* New York, NY: Continuum.

Fresh Lifelines for Youth. (n.d.). *Mission and History.* Retrieved from http://flyprogram.org.

Frost, A. (2015, Feb 11). *Study: Black girls are suspended 6 times more often than White girls.* Retrieved from http://college.usatoday.com.

Fryer, R. G. (2006). Acting White. *Education Next, 6*(1), 1. Retrieved from http://educationnext.org.

Fuentes, A. (2013). *Lockdown High: When the Schoolhouse Becomes a Jailhouse* (1 edition). London, UK: Verso.

Gaes, G. G., Camp, S. D., Nelson, J. B., and Saylor, W. G. (2004). *Measuring prison performance: Government privatization and accountability.* Lanham, MD: Altamira Press.

Gamoran, A. (2001). American schooling and educational inequality: Forecast for the 21st century. *Sociology of Education, 34*, 135–153.

Gamoran, A., Secada, W., and Marrett, C. (2000). The organizational context of teaching and learning. In M. Hallinan (Ed.), *Handbook of sociology of education* (pp. 37–63). New York, NY: Kluwer Academic/Plenum Press.

Gause, C. P., Okun, T., Stalnaker, A., Nix-Stevenson, D., and Chapman, D. (2007). The Counterstory and the promise of collaborative compassion in education. *Learning for democracy, 3*(1), 42–51.

Gay, G. (2000). *Culturally responsive teaching: Theory, research and practice.* New York, NY: Teachers College Press.

Gay, G. (2002). Preparing for culturally responsive teaching. *Journal of Teacher Education, 53*(2), 106–116.

Gay, G. (2010). *Culturally responsive teaching: Theory, research, and practice* (2nd ed.). New York, NY: Teachers College.

Gay, G. (2010). Acting on beliefs in teacher education for cultural diversity. *Journal of Teacher Education, 61*(1–2), 143–152.

Gee, J. P. (2014). *An introduction to discourse analysis: Theory and method.* New York, NY: Routledge.

Geller, A. (2013). Paternal incarceration and father-child contact in fragile families. *Journal of Marriage and Family, 75*, 1288–1303.

Gershoff, E., Aber, J., and Raver., C. (2003). School Resources and Environment. In R. Lerner, F. Jacobs, and D. Wertleib, (Eds.), *Handbook of Applied Developmental Science: Promoting Positive Child, Adolescent, and Family Development through Research, Policies, and Programs* (pp. 81–136). Thousand Oaks, CA: Sage.

Gillborn, D. (2008). *Racism and education: Coincidence or conspiracy?* New York, NY: Routledge.

Giroux, H. (1981). *Ideology, culture, and the process of schooling.* Philadelphia, PA: Temple University Press.

Giroux, H. (2001). *Theory and resistance In education: Towards a pedagogy for the opposition* (revised and expanded ed.) Westport, CT: Greenwood.

Giroux, H. (2011). *On critical pedagogy.* New York, NY: The Continuum International Publishing Group.

Giroux, H. A., Lankshear, C., McLaren, P., and Peters, M. (2013). *Counternarratives: Cultural studies and critical pedagogies in postmodern spaces.* New York, NY: Routledge.

Glasser, W. (1997). A new look at school failure and school success. *Phi Delta Kappan, 78*, 596–602.

Goff, P. A., Jackson, M. C., Di Leone, B. L., Culotta, C. M., and DiTomasso, N. A. (2014). The essence of innocence: Consequences of dehumanizing Black children. *Journal of Personality and Social Psychology, 106*(4), 526–545.

Goings, R. B. (2015). The lion tells his side of the (counter)story: A Black male educator's authoethnographic account. *Journal of African American Males in Education, 6*(1), 90–105.

Goings, R. B., Smith, A., Harris, D., Wilson, T., and Lancaster, D. (2015). Countering the narrative: A layered perspective on supporting Black males in education. *Perspectives on Urban Education, 12*(1), 54–63.

Gonzalez, T. (2011). Restoring Justice: Community Organizing to Transform School Discipline Policies. *University of California, Davis Journal of Juvenile Law and Policy, 15*(1).

Gonzalez, T. (2012). Keeping Kids in Schools: Restorative justice, punitive discipline, and the school to prison pipeline. *Journal Of Law and Education*, 41 (2), 281–335.

Gonzalez, T., and Hayes, B. G. (2009). Rap music in school counseling based on Don Elligan's rap therapy. *Journal of Creativity in Mental Health, 4*, 161–172.

Gorski, P. (2011). Unlearning deficit ideology and the scornful gaze: Thoughts on authenticating the class discourse in education. In R. Ahluist, P. Gorski, and T. Montano (Eds.), *Assault on Kids: How Hyper-Accountability, Corporatization, Deficit Ideology, and Ruby Payne are Destroying our Schools* (pp. 152–176). New York, NY: Peter Lang.

Gould, S. J. (1996). *The mismeasure of man.* New York: W. W. Norton and Company.

Grantham, T. (2003) Rocky Jones: *Case study of a high achieving black male's motivation to participate in gifted classes Roeper Review, 26*(4) 208–215

Greenwald, R., and Laine, L. H. (1996). Have times changed? The effect of school resources on student achievement. *American Educational Research Journal*, 361–396.

Greenwood, C. R., Horton, B. T., and Utley, C. A. (2002). Academic engagement: Current perspectives on research and practice. *School Psychology Review, 31*, 328–349.

Greflund, S., McIntosh, K., Mercer, S. H., and May, S. L. (2014). Examining Disproportionality in School Discipline for Aboriginal Students in Schools Implementing PBIS. *Canadian Journal of School Psychology, 29*(3), 213–235.

Gregory, A., and Weinstein, R. S. (2008). The discipline gap and African Americans: Defiance or cooperation in the high school classroom. *Journal of School Psychology, 46*(4), 455–475.

Gregory, A., Skiba, R. J., and Noguera, P. A. (2010). The achievement gap and the discipline gap: Two sides of the same coin? *Educational Researcher, 39*(1), 59–68.

Gregory, A., Bell, J., and Pollack, M. (2014). *How educators can eradicate disparities in school discipline: A briefing paper on school-based interventions.* Bloomington, IN: The Equity Project at Indiana University. Retrieved from www.rtpcollaborative.indiana.edu.

Gregory, A., Cornell, D., and Fan, X. (2005). The relationship of school structure and support to suspension rates for Black and White high school students. *American Educational Research Journal, 48*(4), 904–934.

Gregory, A., Clawson, K., Davis, A., and Gerewiz, J. (2015). The promise of restorative practices to transform teacher-student relationships and achieve equity in school discipline. *Journal of Educational and Psychological Consultation, 25*(1), 1–29.

Griffin, D., and Steen, S. (2011). A social justice approach to school counseling. *Journal for Social Action in Counseling and Psychology, 3,* 74–85.

Grissom, J. and Redding, C. (2016). *Discretion and disproportionality: Explaining the underrepresentation of high-achieving students of color in gifted programs.* Retrieved from http://ero.sagepub.com.

Gutierrez, K., and Rogoff, B. (2003). Cultural ways of learning: Individual traits or repertoires of practice. *Educational Researcher, 32*(5), 19–25.

Gutierrez, R. (2008). A "gap-gazing" fetish in mathematics education? Problematizing research on the achievement gap. *Journal for Research in Mathematics Education,* 357–364.

Hallett, M. A. (2002). Race, crime, and for profit imprisonment Social disorganization as market opportunity. *Punishment and Society, 4,* 369–393.

Hamre, B. K. and Pianta, R. C. (2001). Early teacher-child relationships and the trajectory of children's school outcomes through eighth grade. *Child Development, 72,* 625–638.

Hardt, M., and Negri, A. (2006). *Multitude.* London, UK: Penguin Books.

Harlow, C. W. (2003). *Education and correctional population.* Washington, DC: U.S. Department of Justice Office of Justice Programs, Bureau of Justice Statistics. Retrieved June 24, 2013, from http://www.bjs.gov.

Harper, S. R., and Davis III, C. H. (2012). They (Don't) Care about Education: A Counternarrative on Black Male Students' Responses to Inequitable Schooling. *Educational Foundations, 26,* 103–120.

Harris, A. P. (2003). Race and Essentialism in Feminist Legal Theory. In A. K. Wing (Ed.), *Critical race feminism: A reader (second edition)* (pp. 34–41). New York, NY: New York University Press.

Harry, B., and Klingner, J. (2006). *Why are so many minority students in special education? Understanding race and disability in schools.* New York, NY: Teachers College Press.

Harry, B., and Klingner, J. (2007). Discarding the deficit model. *Improving Instruction for Students with Learning Needs, 64*(5), 16–21.

Hartlep, N. D., and Ball, D. (2014). An Untold Story of Two Races and the Criminal Justice System. In *(Re) Teaching Trayvon* (pp. 143–161). Rotterdam, Netherlands: Sense Publishers.

Hartman, S. V. (1997). *Scenes of subjection: Terror, slavery and self-making in nineteenth century America.* New York, NY: Oxford University Press.

Hattery, A. J., and Smith, E. (2014). Families of incarcerated African American men: The impact on mothers and children. *Journal of Pan African Studies, 7*(6), 128–154.

Hawken, L. S., MacLeod, S. K., and Rawlings, L. (2007). Effects of the behavior education program on office discipline referrals of elementary school students. *Journal of Positive Behavior Interventions, 9*(2), 94–101.

Hawkins, J. D., Guo, J., Hill, K. G., Battin-Pearson, S., and Abbott, R. D. (2001). Long-term effects of the Seattle Social Development intervention on school bonding trajectories. *Applied Developmental Science, 5,* 225–236.

Hayes, C., and Juarez, B. (2012). There is no culturally responsive teaching spoken here: A Critical Race Perspective. *Democracy and Education.*

Hayes, C., Juarez, B., and Escoffery-Runnels, V. (2014). We were there too: Learning from Black male teachers in Mississippi about successful teaching of black students. *Democracy and Education, 22.*

Heaviside, S., Rowand, C., Williams, C., and Farris, E. (1998). *Violence and discipline problems in U.S. Public Schools: 1996–97.* (NCES 98–030). Washington, DC: U.S. Department of Education, National Center for Education Statistics.

Heitzeg, N. A. (2009). Education or Incarceration: Zero Tolerance Policies and the School to Prison Pipeline. *Forum of Public Policy: A Journal of the Oxford Round Table, 2009*(2).

Henderson, A. T., and Mapp, K. L. (2002). *A new wave of evidence: The impact of school, family and community connections on student achievement.* Austin, TX: Southwest Educational Development Laboratory.

Henning, K. (2013). Criminalizing Normal Adolescent Behavior in Communities of Color: The Role of Prosecutors in Juvenile Justice Reform [article]. *Cornell Law Review*, (2), 383.

Henry, A. (2005). Black feminist pedagogy: Critiques and contributions. In W. H. Watkins *Black protest thought and education* (pp. 89–105). New York, NY: Peter Lang.

Higgin, T. (2009). Blackless fantasy: The disappearance of race in massively multiplayer online role-playing games. *Games and Culture*, 4(1), 3–26.

Hill Collins, P. (1997/2007). Pornography and black women's bodies. In L. L. O'Toole, J. R. Schiffman, and M. L. K. Edwards (Eds.), *Gender violence: Interdisciplinary perspectives.* New York, NY: New York University Press.

Hill Collins, P. (2000/2014). *Black feminist thought: Knowledge, consciousness, and the politics of empowerment.* (2nd ed.). New York, NY: Routledge.

Himmelstein, K. E. W., and Bruckner, H. (2011). Criminal-justice and school sanctions against nonheterosexual youth: A national longitudinal study. *Pediatrics.*

Hip Hop Chess Federation. (n.d.). *About HHCF.* Retrieved from http://www.hiphopchess.com.

Hipolito-Delgado, C., and Lee, C. C. (2007). Empowerment theory for the professional school counselor: A manifesto for what really matters. *Professional School Counseling, 10,* 327–332.

Hirschfield, P. J. (2008). Preparing for prison? The criminalization of school discipline in the USA. *Theoretical Criminology, 12*(1), 79–101.

Hirschfield, P. J., and Celinska, K. (2011). Beyond Fear: Sociological Perspectives on the Criminalization of School Discipline. *Sociology Compass, 5*(1), 1–12.

Hoagwood, K., Jensen, P. S., Petti, T., and Burns, B. J. (1996). Outcomes of Mental Health Care for Children and Adolescents: I. A Comprehensive Conceptual Model. *Journal of the American Academy of Child and Adolescent Psychiatry, 35*(8), 1055–1063.

hooks, b. (1994). *Teaching to transgress.* New York, NY: Routledge.

hooks, b. (2004). *We real cool: Black men and masculinity.* New York, NY: Routledge.

hooks, b. (2009). *Teaching critical thinking: Practical wisdom.* New York, NY: Routledge.

Holcomb-McCoy, C. (2004). Assessing the multicultural competence of school counselors: A checklist. *Professional School Counseling, 7,* 178–186.

Holland, D., Lachicotte, W., Skinner, D., and Cain, C. (1998). *Identity and agency in cultural worlds.* Cambridge, MA: Harvard University Press.

Hopkins, B. (2004). *Just schools: A whole school approach to restorative justice.* London, UK: Jessica Kingsley.

Horner, S. B., Fireman, G. D., and Wang, E. W. (2010). The relation of student behavior, peer status, race, and gender to decisions about school discipline using CHAID decision trees and regression modeling. *Journal of School Psychology, 48*(2), 135–161.

House, R. M., and Martin, P. J. (1998). Advocating for better futures for all students: A new vision for school counselors. *Education, 119,* 284–291.

Howard, G. (2006). *We can't teach what we don't know: White teachers, multiracial schools (second edition).* New York, NY: Teachers College Press.

Huber, J., Caine, V., Huber, M., and Steeves, P. (2013). Narrative inquiry as pedagogy in education the extraordinary potential of living, telling, retelling, and reliving stories of experience. *Review of Research in Education, 37*(1), 212–242.

Hudson, P. J. (2014). The geographies of blackness and anti-blackness: An interview with Katherine McKittrick. *The CLR James Journal (20)*1–2, 233–240.

Hughley, M., and Jost, J. (2011). *The Obamas and a (post) racial America? Series in political psychology*. New York, NY: Oxford Press.

Hussar, W. J. and Bailey, T. M. (2013). *Projections of education statistics to 2022* (NCES 2014–051).

Individuals with Disabilities Education Improvement Act. (2004). Public Law 108–446 (20 U.S.C. 1400 et seq.).

Irby, D. (2014).Trouble at School: Understanding School Discipline Systems as Nets of Social Control. *Equity and Excellence in Education, 47*(4), 513–530.

Irizarry, J. (2011a). Buscando la libertad: Latino youths in search of freedom in school. *Democracy and Education, 19*(1), 4.

Irizarry, J. G. (2011b). En la lucha: The struggles and triumphs of Latino/a preservice teachers. *Teachers College Record, 113*(12), 28–34.

Irizarry, J. (2011c). *The Latinization of U.S. schools: Successful teaching and learning in shifting cultural contexts*. Boulder, CO: Paradigm.

Irwin, H. J. (1996). Traumatic childhood events, perceived availability of emotional support, and the development of dissociative tendencies. *Child Abuse and Neglect, 20*(8), 701–707.

Irvine, J. J. (1990). *Black students and school failure: Policies, practices, and prescriptions*. Westwood, CT: Greenwood.

Irwin, K., Davidson, J., and Hall-Sanchez, A. (2012). The Race to Punish in American Schools: Class and Race Predictors of Punitive School-Crime Control. *Critical Criminology, 21*(1), 47–71.

Jain, S., Bassey, H., Brown, M. and Kalra, P. (2014). *Restorative justice in Oakland schools implementation and impacts: An effective strategy to reduce racially disproportionate discipline, suspensions and improve academic outcomes*. Retrieved from http://www.oused.org.

James, B. (2013, July). *School safety and the school to prison pipeline: Fact and fiction*. National School Law Update at the meeting of the National Association of School Resource Officers, Orlando, FL.

Jones, B. (2013, August 11). Back to school means big changes, challenges at LAUSD. *Los Angeles Daily News*. Retrieved from http://www.dailynews.com.

Jones, K. M. (2015). *Never been: An exploration of the influence of dis/ability, giftedness, and incarceration on adolescents in adult correctional facilities*. Philadelphia, PA: UPenn Repository.

Joseph, G. (1988). Black feminist pedagogy in capitalist America. In M. Coles (Ed.), *Bowles and Gintis revisited: Correspondence and contradiction in educational theory* (pp 174–186), London, UK: Falmer

Juvenile Law Center (2011, March). *Federal Policy, ESEA Reauthorization and the School to Prison Pipeline*. Retrieved from: http://www.jlc.org.

Kaba, M., and Meiners, E. R. (February 2, 2014). Arresting the carceral state: Educators must work to end the school to prison pipeline. *Jacobin Mag.com*. Retrieved from https://www.jacobinmag.com.

Kalogrides, D., and Loeb, S. (2013). Different Teachers, Different Peers: The Magnitude of Student Sorting Within Schools. *Educational Researcher, 42*(6), 304–316.

Kaplan, R. H. (2011). *The myth of post-racial America: Searching for equality in the age of materialism*. Lanham, MD: Rowman and Littlefield.

Kapp, D. and Breslin, B. (2001). Restorative Justice in school communities. *Youth and Society, 33*(2), 249–72.

Karpinski, C. F. (2006). Bearing the burden of desegregation: Black principals and Brown. *Urban Education, 41*(3), 237–276.

Kaufman, S. (2013). *Ungifted: Intelligence redefined*. New York, NY: Basic Books.

Keane, M. N. (2012). *A Quantitative Assessment of the Effect of Positive Behavior Intervention and Supports on Math Achievement: A Middle School Analysis*. ProQuest LLC.

Kennedy, R. (1997). *Race, crime, and the law*. New York, NY: Pantheon Books.

Kim, C. Y. (2003). Procedures for public law remediation in school-to-prison pipeline litiga-tion: Lessons learned from *Antoine v. Winner School* District. *New York Law School Law Review, 54*(2009–2010), 955.

Kim, C. Y., Losen, D. J., and Hewitt, D. T. (2010). *The school-to-prison pipeline: Structuring legal reform.* New York, NY: New York University Press.

Kirkham, C. (2012, June 7). Private prisons profit from immigration crackdown: Federal and local law enforcement partnerships. *Huffington Post.*

KLAS-TV (2014). *[Desert] county schools see discipline rise in bullying.* Retrieved from: http://www.8newsnow.com

Koball, H., Dion, R., Gothro, A., and Bardos, M. (2011). *Synthesis of Research and Resources to Support At-Risk Youth.* Washington, DC: Office of Planning, Research and Evaluation, Administration for Children and Families, U.S. Department of Health and Human Services.

Kozol, J. (1991) *Savage inequalities: Children in America's school.* New York, NY: Random House.

Kozol, J. (2005). *The shame of the nation: The restoration of apartheid schooling in America.* New York, NY: Crown Publishers.

Krezmien, M. P., Leone, P. E., and Achilles, G. M. (2006). Suspension, race, and disability: Analysis of state-wide practices and reporting. *Journal of Emotional and Behavioral Disor-ders, 14,* 217–226.

Krueger-Henney, P. (2013). Co-research school spaces of dispossession: A story of survival. *Association of Mexican American Educators, 7*(3), 42–53.

Kunjufu, J. (1985). *Countering the Conspiracy to Destroy Black Boys.* Chicago, IL: African American Images Press.

Kupchik, A., and Ellis, N. (2008). School discipline and security: Fair for all students? *Y outh and So c i e t y, 39,* 549–574.

Kupchik, A., and Ward, G. (2014). Race, poverty, and exclusionary school security: An empiri-cal analysis of U.S. elementary, middle, and high schools. *Youth Violence and Juvenile Justice, 12*(4), 332–354.

Kupers, T. A. (1999). *Prison madness: The mental health crisis behind bars and what we must do about it.* San Francisco, CA: Jossey-Bass.

Ladson-Billings, G. (1994). *The dreamkeepers: Successful teachers of African American stu-dents.* San Francisco, CA: Jossey Bass.

Ladson-Billings, G. (1995). Toward a theory of a culturally relevant pedagogy. *American Educational Research Journal, 35*(4), 248–255.

Ladson-Billings, G. (1998). Preparing teachers for diverse student populations: A critical race perspective. *Review of Research in Education, 24,* 211–247.

Ladson-Billings, G. (2005). Toward a theory of a culturally relevant pedagogy. *American Educational Research Journal, 35*(4), 248–255.

Ladson-Billings, G. (2006). From the achievement gap to the education debt: Understanding achievement in US schools. *Educational Researcher, 35*(7), 3–12.

Ladson-Billings, G. (2007). "It's Not the Culture of Poverty, It's the Poverty of Culture: The Problem with Teacher Education." *Anthropology and Education Quarterly,* 37(2), pp. 104–109.

Ladson-Billings, G. (2009). *The dreamkeepers: Successful teachers of African American chil-dren.* San Francisco: Jossey Bass.

Ladson-Billings, G. (2013). Critical race theory—what it is not! In Lynn, M. and Dixson, A. D. (Eds). *The handbook of critical race theory in education.* London, UK: Routledge.

Ladson-Billings, G. (December 2015). Literate Lives Matter: African Americans Reading, Writing, Speaking, and Listening. Keynote lecture delivered at the Literacy Research Asso-ciation Annual Conference. Carlsbad, CA.

Landsman, J., and Lewis, C. W. (Eds.). (2011). *White teachers/diverse classrooms: Creating inclusive schools, building on students' diversity, and providing true educational equity* (2nd ed.). Sterling, VA: Stylus Publishing. Retrieved from http://www.ebrary.com.

Latessa, E. J., Lemke, R., Makarios, M., Smith. P., and Lowenkamp, C. (2008). The creation and validation of the Ohio Risk Assessment System (ORAS). *Federal Probation, 72*(3),

2–9. Lee, C. C. (1987). Black manhood training: Group counseling for male Blacks in grades 7–12. *The Journal for Specialists in Group Work, 12,* 18–25.

Lee, C. C., and Lindsey, C. R. (1985). Black consciousness development: A group counseling model for Black elementary school students. *Elementary School Guidance and Counseling, 19,* 228–236.

Lee, C. C., and Simmons, S. (1988). A comprehensive life-planning model for Black adolescents. *The School Counselor, 36,* 5–10.

Lee, J. (2002). Racial and ethnic achievement gap trends: Reversing the progress toward equity? *Educational Researcher, 31*(1), 3–12.

Lemov, D. (2010). *Teach like a champion: 49 techniques that put students on the path to college* (1st ed., Jossey-Bass teacher). San Francisco, CA: Jossey-Bass.

Lewin, T. (2012). Black students face more discipline, data suggest. The New York Times , March 6. Accessed at: http://www.nytimes.com.

Lewis, C. W., Butler, B. R., Bonner III, F. A., and Joubert, M. (2010). African American male discipline patterns and school district responses resulting impact on academic achievement: Implications for urban educators and policy makers. *J ournal of Afri c an Am e ri c an M al e s in Edu c ation, 1*(1), 1–19.

Lilienfield, S. O., Lynn, S. J., Ruscio, J., and Beyerstein, B. L. (2010). *50 great myths of popular psychology: Shattering widespread misconceptions about human behavior.* Malden, MA: Wiley-Blackwell, 225.

Lilienfield, S. O. (2005). Scientifically unsupported and supported interventions for childhood psychopathology: A summary. *Pediatrics, 115,* 761–764.

Lipman, P. (2011). *The new political economy of urban education: Neoliberalism, race, and the right to the city.* New York, NY: Taylor and Francis.

Locke, E. A. (1968). Toward a theory of task motivation and incentives. *Organizational Behavior and Human Performance, 3*(2), 157–189.

Logan, J., Stults, B., and Farley, R. (2004). Segregation of minorities in the metropolis: Two decades of change. *Demography, 41*(1), 1–22.

Lorde, A. (1982). *Zami, A new spelling of my name.* New York, NY: Random House LLC.

Lorde, A. (1984). *The master's tools will never dismantle the master's house.* Berkeley, CA: Crossing Press.

Lord Spoda [Screen name]. (2015, October 27). *Both Videos Of Cop Slamming High School Girl... Your Reaction* [Video file].

Lortie, D. (1975). *Schoolteacher: A sociological study.* London: University of Chicago Press.

Losen, D. J., and Gillespie, J. (2012). *Opportunities suspended: The disparate impact of disciplinary exclusion from school.* Los Angeles, CA: The Civil Right Project, The Center for Civil Rights Remedies.

Losen, D. J. (2013). Discipline Policies, Successful Schools, Racial Justice, and the Law. *Family Court Review, 51,* 388–400.

Losen, D., Hodson, C., Keith, M. A., Morrison, K., Belway, S., (2015). *Are we closing the school discipline gap?* Los Angeles: UCLA, The Civil Rights Project.

Losen, D., Hewitt, D., and Toldson, I. (2014). *Eliminating excessive and unfair exclusionary discipline in schools: Policy recommendations for reducing disparities.* Bloomington, IN: The Equity Project at Indiana University. Retrieved from www.rtpcollaborative.indiana.edu.

Louisiana Justice Institute. (2011, July 18). Moving forward with the status quo: A response to Louisiana Governor Bobby Jindal's veto of Senate Bill 67 by families and friends of Louisiana's incarcerated children. *Justice Roars.* Retrieved from: http://louisianajusticeinstitute.blogspot.com.

Louisiana State Department of Education (2014). *District Composite Scores.* Retrieved: http://www.laeducationresults.net.

Louisiana State Department Office of Juvenile Justice. (2014). *Demographic Profiles of the Secure Youth Population.* Youth Services Office of Juvenile Justice. Retrieved from: http://ojj.la.gov.

Louisiana State Legislative Auditor. (2014, February 15). *Office of Juvenile Justice Monitoring of Prevention and Diversion Contract Providers: Performance Audit.* Retrieved from: http://app1.lla.la.gov.

Lusted, D. (1986). Why pedagogy? *Screen, 27*(5), 2–14.

Lynch, M. (2011, December 14). What is culturally responsive pedagogy? *The Huffington Post.* Retrieved from http://www.huffingtonpost.com.

Lynch, J. P., and Sabol, W. J. (2004). Assessing the effects of mass incarceration on informal social control in communities. *Commentary, 3,* 267–294.

Lynn, M., and Parker, L. (2006). Critical race studies in education: Examining a decade of research on US schools. *The Urban Review,* 38(4), 257–290.

Lyons, J. E., and Chestley, J. (2004). 50 years after Brown: The benefits and trade-offs for African American educators and students. *Journal of Negro Education, 73*(3), 298–313.

Lyotard, F. (1984/1979). *The postmodern condition.* Minneapolis, MN: University of Minnesota Press.

Lundy, G. F. (2003). The myths of oppositional culture. *Journal of Black Studies, 33*(4), 450–467.

Madda, C. L., and Schultz, B. D. (2009). (Re)Constructing ideals of multicultural education through grow your own teachers. *Multicultural Perspectives, 11,* 204–207.

Madkins, T. C. (2011). The black teacher shortage: A literature review of historical and contemporary trends. *The Journal of Negro Education, 80,* 417–427.

Malcolm, X., Haley, A., and Handler, M. S. (1992). *The autobiography of Malcolm X.* New York, NY: Ballantine Books.

Mann, H. (1848). *Horace Mann on education and national welfare.* Retrieved from http://www.tncrimlaw.com.

Margolin, G., and Gordis, E. B. (2000). The Effects of Family and Community Violence on Children. *Annual Review of Psychology, 51*(1), 445–479.

Martin, J. L., and Beese, J. A. (2015). Talking back at school: Using the literacy classroom as a site for resistance to the school-to-prison pipeline and recognition of students labeled "at-risk." *Urban Education,* 1–29.

Martin, L. L. (2011). Debt to Society: Asset Poverty and Prisoner Reentry. *The Review of Black Political Economy, 38*(2), 131–143.

Martin, L. L. (2012). Debt to society. *Review of the Black Political Economy, 38,* 131–143.

Martin, L. L. (2013). *Black asset poverty and the enduring racial divide.* Boulder, CO: First Forum Press.

Martin, L. (2015). *Big Box Schools: Race, Education, and the Danger of the Wal-Martization of Public Schools in America.* New York, NY: Lexington Books.

Martin, L., Fasching-Varner, K., Quinn, M., and Jackson, M. (2014). Racism, Rodeos, and the Misery Industries of Louisiana. *The Journal of Pan African Studies, 7*(6), 60–83.

Maruna, S., Porter, L., and Carvalho, I. (2004). The Liverpool desistance study and probation practice: Opening the dialogue. *The Journal of Community and Criminal Justice, 51*(3). 221–232.

Mathur, S. R., and Nelson, C. M. (2013). PBIS as prevention for high-risk youth in restrictive settings: Where do we go from here? *Education and Treatment of Children, 36*(3), 175–181.

Mattison, E., and Aber, M. S. (2007). Closing the achievement gap: The association of racial climate with achievement and behavioral outcomes. *American Journal of Community Psychology, 40*(1), 1–12.

McClelland, D. C. (1978). Managing motivation to expand human freedom. *American Psychologist, 33*(3), 201–210.

McDermott, R. P. (1974). Achieving school failure: An anthropological approach to illiteracy and social stratification. *Education and Cultural Process,* 82–118.

McFadden, A. C., Marsh, G. E., Price, B. J., and Hwang, Y. (1992). A study of race and gender bias in the punishment of school children. *Education and Treatment of Children, 15,* 140–146.

McKernan, S. M., Ratcliffe, C., Steuerle, E., and Zhang, S. (2013). *Less than equal: Racial disparities in wealth accumulation.* New York, NY: Urban Institute.

McMahon, H. G., Mason, E. C. M., Daluga-Guenther, N., and Ruiz, A. (2014). An ecological model of professional school counseling. *Journal of Counseling and Development, 92,* 459–471.

McNeely, C. A., and Falci, C. (2004). School connectedness and the transition into and out of health risk behavior among adolescents: A comparison of social belonging and teacher support. *Journal of School Health, 74,* 284–292.

McNeely, C. A., Nonemaker, J. M., and Blum, R. W. (2002). Promoting student connectedness to school: From the national longitudinal study of adolescent health. *J ournal of S c hool H e alth, 72*(4), 138–147.

Meier, K., Stewart, J., and England, R. (1989). *Race, class and education: The politics of second generation discrimination.* Madison, WI: University of Wisconsin Press.

Meiners, E. R., and Benita Reyes, K. (2008). Re-making the incarceration-nation: Naming the participation of schools in our prison industrial complex. *Perspectives on Urban Education,* (5)2. Retrieved from http://www.urbanedjournal.org.

Meiners, E. R. (2010). *Right to be hostile: Schools, prisons, and the making of public enemies.* New York, NY: Routledge.

Meiners, E. R. (2011). Ending the school-to-prison pipeline/building abolition futures. *U r b a n R e vi e w, 43*(4), 547–565.

Meiners, E. R. (2013). Schooling the carceral state: Challenging the school-to-prison pipeline. In D. Scott (Ed.), *Why prison?* (pp. 261–277). Cambridge, UK: Cambridge University Press.

Mendieta, E. (2004). Plantations, ghettos, prisons: US racial geographies. *Philosophy and Geography, 7*(1), 43–59.

Merton, R. K. (1948) The self-fulfilling prophecy. *The Antioch Review, 8*(2) 193–210.

Metzler, J. (2008). *The construction of rearticulation of race in a post-racial America.* Bloomington, IN: Author House.

Meyers, L. H., and Evans, I. M. (2012). *The school leader's guide to restorative school discipline.* Thousand Oaks, CA: Corwin.

Miller, K. S., Potter, G. W., and Kappeler, V. E. (2006). The myth of the juvenile superpredator. In B. Sims and B. Preston (Eds.), *The handbook of juvenile justice: Theory and practice* (pp. 173–192). Boca Raton, FL: Taylor and Francis.

Milner, H. R. (2010). What does teacher education have to do with teaching? Implications for diversity studies. *Journal of Teacher Education, 61,* 118–131.

Minke, K., and Anderson, K. (2005). Family-school collaboration and positive behavior support. *Journal of Positive Behavior Interventions, 7*(3), 181–5.

Mitcham-Smith, M. (2007). Advocacy-Professional school counselor closing the achievement gap through empowerment: A response to Hipolito-Delgado and Lee. *Professional School Counseling, 10,* 341–343.

Mitchell, C. J. (1984). Typicality and the case study. In P. F. Ellen (Ed.), *Ethnographic research: A guide to general conduct* (pp. 238–241). New York, NY: Academic Press.

Mitchell, R. (2010). The African American church, education and self determination. *Journal of Negro Education, 79,* 202–205.

Moll, L., Amanti, C., Neff, D., and González, N. (1992). Funds of knowledge for teaching: Using a qualitative approach to connect homes and classrooms. *Theory Into Practice, 31*(2), 132–41.

Monroe, C. R. (2006). Understanding the discipline gap through a cultural lens: Implications for the education of African American students. *Intercultural Education, 16*(4), 317–330.

Morgan-D'Atrio, C., Northrup, J., LaFleur, L., and Spera, S. (1996). Toward prescriptive alternatives to suspensions: A preliminary evaluation. *Behavioral Disorders, 21,* 190–200.

Morgan, R., Musu-Gillette, L., Robers, S., and Zhang, A. (2015). Indicators of School Crime and Safety: 2014. Retrieved from http://nces.ed.gov.

Moore, M.G. (1993). *Theory of transactional distance.* In D. Keegan (Ed.), *Theoretical Principles of Distance Education.* New York, NY: Routledge.

Morris, E. W., and Perry, B. L. (2016). The Punishment Gap: School Suspension and Racial Disparities in Achievement. *Social Problems, 63*(1), 68–86.

Morris, E. W. (2007) "Ladies" or "loudies"? Perceptions and experiences of black girls in classrooms. *Y outh and Society, 38*(4): 490–515.

Morris, M. (2012). Race, gender and the school-to-prison pipeline. *African American Forum, 1,* 2–12.

Morrison, B. E. (2002). *Bullying and Victimisation in Schools: A Restorative Justice Approach.* Trends and Issues in Crime and Criminal Justice, # 219 (February). Canberra, AU: Australian Institute of Criminology.

Morrison, B., Blood, P., and Thorsborne, M. (2005). Practicing restorative justice in school communities: Addressing the challenge of culture change. *Public Organization Review, 5*(4), 335–357.

Morrow, R., and Torres, C. (1995). *Social theory and education.* Albany, NY: SUNY Press.

Muschert, G. W. (2007). The Columbine victims and the myth of the juvenile superpredator. *Youth Violence and Juvenile Justice, 5*(4), 351–366.

Muscott, H. S., Mann, E. L., and LeBrun, M. R. (2008). Positive behavioral interventions and supports in New Hampshire: Effects of large-scale implementation of schoolwide positive behavior support on student discipline and academic achievement. *Journal of Positive Behavior Interventions, 10*(3), 190–205.

Museus, S. D., and Jayakumar, U. M. (2012). *Creating campus cultures: Fostering success among racially diverse student populations.* New York, NY: Routledge.

NAACP Legal Defense and Educational Fund, Inc. (2005). *Dismantling the School to Prison Pipeline.* Authors.

Nance, J. P. (2015). Dismantling the school-to-prison pipeline: Tools for change. *Arizona State Law Journal, 16*(?). Retrieved from http://papers.ssrn.com.

National Center for Educational Statistics (NCES). (2013). *School and Staffing Survey (SASS), public school teacher data file 1987–88 through 2011–12.* Retrieved online from https://nces.ed.gov.

National Center for Educational Statistics (NCES). (2015). *The Condition of Education 2015.* Retrieved online from https://nces.ed.gov.

National Institute of Justice. (2014). *Recidivism.* Retrieved from http://www.nij.gov.

Nava Delgado, M. (2014). School climate and the relationship to student learning of Hispanic 10th grade students in Arizona schools. *Journal of Arts and Humanities, 3*(1), 188–221.

Neal, L. V. I., McCray, A. D., Webb-Johnson, G., and Bridgest, S. T. (2003). The effects of African American movement styles on teachers' perceptions and reactions. *The Journal of Special Education, 37*(1), 49–57.

Neyfakh, L. (2015, June). Fewer beds, fewer inmates. *Slate Magazine.* Retrieved from http://www.slate.com/articles/news_and_politics/crime/2015/06/new_orleans_how_hurricane_katrina_helped_reduce_the_population_of_the_orleans.html.

Nichols, J. D. (2004). An exploration of discipline and suspension data. *Journal of Negro Education, 73*, 408–423.

Nicholson-Crotty, S., Birchmeier, Z., and Valentine, D. (2009). Exploring the impact of school discipline on racial disproportion in the juvenile justice system. *Social Science Quarterly, 90*(4), 1003–1018.

Nieto, S., and Bode, P. (2012). *Affirming diversity: The sociopolitical context of multicultural education* (6th ed.). Boston, MA: Pearson.

Noel, J. (2000). *Developing Multicultural Educators.* New York, NY: Longman.

Noguera, P. (2001). Racial politics and the elusive quest for excellence and equity in education. *Education and Urban Society, 34*(1), 18–41.

Noguera, P. A. (2003). Schools, prisons, and social implications of punishment: Rethinking disciplinary practices. *Theory Into Practice, 42*, 341–350.

Noguera, P. A. (2009). *The trouble with black boys: And other reflections on race, equity, and the future of public education.* San Francisco, CA: Jossey-Bass.

Noguera, P., and Wing, J. Y. (2006). *Unfinished business: Closing the racial achievement gap in our schools.* San Francisco, CA: Jossey-Bass.

Noltemeyer, A. L., and Mcloughlin, C. S. (2010). Changes in exclusionary discipline rates and disciplinary disproportionality over time. *International Journal of Special Education, 25*(1), 59–70.

Oakes, J. (1986). Tracking, inequality, and the rhetoric of reform: Why schools don't change. *The Journal of Education, 168*(1), 60–80.

Ogbu, J. U. (1978). *Minority education and caste: The American system in cross-cultural perspective.* New York: Academic Press.

Ogbu, J. U. (1997). Understanding the school performance of urban African-Americans: Some essential background knowledge. In H. Walberg, Reyes, O., and R. Weissberg (Eds.), *Children and youth: Interdisciplinary perspectives* (pp. 190–222). London: Sage.

Oliver, M., and Shapiro, T. (1995). *Black wealth white wealth*. New York, NY: Routledge.

Omolade, B. (1993). A Black feminist pedagogy. *Women's Studies Quarterly 21*, 31–38.

Opportunities Suspended: The Devastating Consequences of Zero Tolerance and School Discipline Policies (Advancement Project and The Civil Rights Project, Cambridge, MA), June 2000, at 7, available at http://b.3cdn.net.

Orivel, F. (1986). Economic crisis and educational crisis: Looking ahead. *Prospects: Quarterly Review of Education, 16*, 197–204.

Osborne, J. W. (1999). Unraveling Underachievement among African American Boys from an Identification with Academics Perspective. *The Journal of Negro Education, 68*(4), 555–565.

Osher, D., Bear, G., Sprague, J., and Doyle, W. (2010). How can we improve school discipline? *Educational Researcher, 39*(1), 48–58.

Osher, D., Woodruff, D., and Sims, A. (2002). Schools make a difference: The relationship between education services for African American children and youth and their overrepresentation in the juvenile justice system. In D. Losen (Ed.), *Minority issues in special education* (pp. 93–116). Cambridge, MA: Harvard Education Publishing Group.

Pager, D., and Quillian, L. (2005). Walking the talk: What employers say versus what they do. *American Sociological Review, 70*(355), 355–380.

Pane, D. M., and Rocco, T. S. (2014). *Transforming the school-to-prison pipeline: Lessons from the classroom* (1st ed.). Rotterdam, NE: Sense Publishers.

Parents Involved in Community Schools. v. Seattle School District No. 1, 127 S. Ct. 2738, 2750 (2007).

Parikh, S. B., Post, P., and Flowers, C. (2011). Relationship between a belief in a just world and social justice advocacy attitudes of school counselors. *Counseling and Values, 56*, 57–72.

Payne, A. A., and Welch, K. (2010). Modeling the effects of racial threat on punitive and restorative school discipline practices. *Criminology, 48*, 1019–1062.

Payne, A. A., and Welch, K. (2015). Restorative Justice in Schools: The Influence of Race on Restorative Discipline. *Youth and Society, 47*(4), 539–564.

Peguero, A. A., and Shekarkhar, Z. (2011). Latino/a student misbehavior and school punishment. *Hispanic Journal of Behavioral Sciences, 33*(1), 54-70.

Pew Charitable Trust. (2010), *Collateral costs: Incarceration's effects on economic mobility*. Washington, DC: Pew Charitable Trusts.

Perry, B. L., and Morris, E. W. (2014). Suspending Progress Collateral Consequences of Exclusionary Punishment in Public Schools. *American Sociological Review*, 1–21.

Perry, T., Steele, C., and Hilliard, A., III (2003). *Young gifted and Black: Promoting high achievement among African American students*. Boston, MA: Beacon Press.

Peter P., et al. v. Compton Unified School District, et al. (2015). S.C. Code Ann. §16–17–420.

Pine, D. S., Mogg, K., Bradley, B. P., Montgomery, L., Monk, C. S., McClure, E., . . . Kaufman, J. (2005). Attention bias to threat in maltreated children: implications for vulnerability to stress-related psychopathology. *The American Journal of Psychiatry, 162*(2), 291–296.

Pinto, L. (2013). *From Discipline to Culturally Responsive Engagement*. Corwin: Thousand Oaks, CA.

Prisoners, parolees, sex offenders, computers, and the internet. (2015). *AELA Monthly Law Journal, 5*, 301–309. Retrieved from http://www.aele.org.

Plato. (1966). *Plato in twelve volumes*, Vol. 1 (H. N. Fowler, Trans.), intro. W. R. M. Lamb. Cambridge, MA: Harvard University Press.

Porche, M. V., Fortuna, L. R., Lin, J., and Alegria, M. (2011). Childhood trauma and psychiatric disorders as correlates of School dropout in a national sample of young Adults. *Child Development, 82*(3), 982–998.

Porter, T. R. (2015). The School-to-Prison Pipeline: The Business Side of Incarcerating, Not Educating, Students in Public Schools. *Arkansas Law Review, 68*(1), 55–81.

Porter, C., Lawson, J. S., and Bigler, E. D. (2005). Neurobehavioral sequelae of child sexual abuse. *Child Neuropsychology: A Journal on Normal and Abnormal Development in Childhood and Adolescence*, *11*(2), 203–220.

Poteat, V. P., Scheer, J. R., and Chong, E. S. (2015). Sexual orientation-based disparities in school and juvenile justice discipline: A multiple group comparison of contributing factors. *Journal of Educational Psychology*, *108*(2), 229–241.

Potts, R. G. (2003). Emancipatory education versus school-based prevention in African American communities. *American Journal of Community Psychology*, *31*, 173–183.

Powell, J. A. (1991). Racial realism or racial despair. *Connecticut Law Review*, *24*, 533–551.

Price, J. and Shildrick, M. (2002). Bodies together: Touch, ethics and disability. In M. Corker and T. Shakespeare (Eds.), *Disability/Postmodernity: Employing disability theory* (pp. 63–75). London, UK: Continuum.

Price, P. (2009). When is a police officer an officer of the law?: The status of police officers in schools. *The Journal of Criminal Law and Criminology*, 541–570.

Pyscher, T. (2015a). *Contradictions and Opportunities: Learning from the Cultural Knowledges of Youth with Histories of Domestic Violence.* Unpublished Dissertation, University of Minnesota.

Pyscher, T. (2015b). Against Rubbish Collecting: Educators and Resistively Ambivalent Youth. *Journal of Educational Controversy*, Special Issue: Challenging the Deficit Model and the Pathologizing of Children. Envisioning Alternative Models.

Pyscher, T. (In Press). Domestic Violence and Reterritorializing Girlhood. *Journal of Cultural Studies-Critical Methodology*, Special issue: From Outer Space: Emerging Girl Subjectivities and Reterritorializing Girlhood.

Pyscher, T. and B. Lozenski. (2014). Throwaway youth: The sociocultural location of resistance to schooling. *Equity and Excellence in Education*, *47*(4), 531–545. Special issue: Breaking the School-to-Prison Pipeline.

Public Agenda. (2004). *Teaching interrupted: Do discipline policies in today's schools foster the common good?* Retrieved from: http://wwwpublicagenda.org.

Puzzanchera, C. (2014). Juvenile arrests 2012. *Washington, DC: US Department of Justice, Office of Justice Programs, Office of Juvenile Justice and Delinquency Prevention*, *3*. Retrieved from http://www.ojjdp.gov.

Ramsey, P.G. (2004). Teaching *and learning in a diverse world: Multicultural education for young children* (3rd ed.). New York, NY: Teachers College Press.

Raffaele Mendez, L. M. (2003). Predictors of suspension and negative school outcomes: A longitudinal investigation. In J. Wald and D. J. Losen (Eds.), *New Directions for Youth Development* (no. 99; Deconstructing the school-to-prison pipeline) (pp. 17–34). San Francisco: Jossey-Bass.

Raffaele Mendez, L. M. and Knoff, H. M. (2003). Who gets suspended from school and why: A demographic analysis of schools and disciplinary infractions in a large school district. *Education and Treatment of Children*, *26*, 30–51.

Raffaele Mendez, L. M., Knoff, H. M., and Ferron, J. F. (2002). School demographic variables and out-of-school suspension rates: A quantitative and qualitative analysis of a large, ethnically diverse school district. *Psychology in the Schools*, *39*, 259–277.

Raible, J. and Irizarry, J. G. (2010). Redirecting the teacher's gaze: Teacher education, youth surveillance, and the school-to-prison pipeline. *Teaching and Teacher Education*, *26*, 1196–1203.

Ratts, M. J. (2011). Multiculturalism and social justice: Two sides of the same coin. *Journal of Multicultural Counseling and Development*, *39*, 24–37.

Ratts, M. J., and Hutchins, A. M. (2009). ACA advocacy competencies: Social justice advocacy at the client/student level. *Journal of Counseling and Development*, *87*, 269–275.

Ratts, M. J., DeKruyf, L., and Chen-Hayes, S. (2007). The advocacy competencies: A social justice advocacy framework for professional school counselors. *Professional School Counseling*, *13*, 90–97.

Rausch, K. M., and Skiba, R. J. (2005, April). *The academic cost of discipline: The contribution of school discipline to achievement.* Paper presented at the Annual Meeting of the American Educational Research Association, Montreal, Canada.

Ravitch, D. (1987). *The schools we deserve: Reflections on the educational crisis of our time.* New York, NY: Basic Books.

Reinke, W. M., Splett, J. D., Robeson, E. N., and Offutt, C. A. (2009). Combining school and family interventions for the prevention and early intervention of disruptive behavior problems in children: A public health perspective. *Psychology in the Schools, 46*(1), 33–43.

Resmovits, J. (October 7, 2013). School safety for America's youngest students means more officers, more guns. *The Huffington Post.* Retrieved from http://www.huffingtonpost.com.

Resnick, M. D., Bearman, P. S., Blum, R. W., Bauman, K. E., Harris, K. M., Jones, J., et al. (1997). Protecting adolescents from harm: Findings from the National Longitudinal Study on Adolescent Health. *Journal of the American Medical Association, 287,* 823–832.

Restifo, S., Roscigno, V., and Qian, Z. (2013). Segmented assimilation, Split labor markets, and racial/ethnic inequality: The case of early-twentieth-century New York. *American Sociological Review, 78*(5), 897–924.

Rhineberger Dunn, G. M. (2013). Myth versus Reality: Comparing the Depiction of Juvenile Delinquency in Metropolitan Newspapers with Arrest Data. *Sociological Inquiry, 83*(3), 473–497.

Rideout, V., Roberts, D. F., and Foehr, U. G. (2005). *Generation M: Media in the lives of 8- to 18-year-olds report* (Program for the Study of Entertainment Media and Health, KFF Publication No. 7251). Menlo Park, CA: Kaiser Family Foundation.

Rios, V. (2011). *Punished: The lives of Black and Latino boys.* New York, NY: New York University Press.

Roberts, D. E. (2004). The Social and Moral Cost of Mass Incarceration in African American Communities. *Stanford Law Review* 56(5), 1271–1305.

Rocque, M. (2010). Office discipline and student behaviors: Does race matter? *American Journal of Education, 116*(4), 557-581.

Rogosch, F. A., and Cicchetti, D. (2005). Child maltreatment, attention networks, and potential precursors to borderline personality disorder. *Development and Psychopathology, 17*(4), 1071–1089.

Roscigno, V. (2000). Family/School Inequality and African American/Hispanic Achievement. *Social Problems,* 266–290.

Rosen, L. (1997). *School discipline: Best practices for administrators.* Thousand Oaks, CA: Corwin Press.

Russakoff, Dale (2015). *The Prize: Who's in Charge of America's Schools?.* Boston: Houghton Mifflin Harcourt.

Sadovnik, A. (2011). Waiting for School Reform: Charter Schools as the Latest Imperfect Panacea. *Teachers College Record,* 1–12.

Said, E. (1995). *Orientalism.* London, UK: Penguin Books.

Samara, T. (2000). Prisons, punishment and profiteers. *Workplace, 6,* 23–53.

Samuels, A. L. (2004). *Is separate unequal? Black colleges and the challenge to desegregation.* Lawrence, KS: University Press of Kansas.

Sarabi, B., and Bender, E. (2000). *The prison payoff: The role of politics and private prisons in the incarceration boom.* A Report of the Western States Center and Western Prison Project.

Savitz, J., van der Merwe, L., Stein, D. J., Solms, M., and Ramesar, R. (2007). Genotype and childhood sexual trauma moderate neurocognitive performance: A possible role for brain-derived neurotrophic factor and apolipoprotein E variants. *Biological Psychiatry, 62*(5), 391–399.

Schafer, M. H., Ferraro, K. F., and Mustillo, S. A. (2011). Children of Misfortune: Early Adversity and Cumulative Inequality in Perceived Life Trajectories. *AJS; American Journal of Sociology, 116*(4), 1053–1091.

Schept, J., Wall, T., and Brisman, A. (2015). Building, staffing, and insulating: An architecture of criminological complicity in the school-to-prison pipeline. *Social Justice, 41,* 96–115.

Schiraldi, V., and Zeidenberg, J. (2001). *Schools and suspensions: Self-reported crime and the growing use of suspensions.* Washington, DC: Justice Policy Institute.

Scott, J. C. (1990). *Domination and the arts of resistance: Hidden transcripts.* New Haven, CT: Yale University Press.

Sedlak, A. J., and McPherson, K. (2010). *Survey of youth in residential placement: Youth's needs and services.* SYRP Report. Rockville, MD: Westat.

Senge, P. M. (1990). *The fifth discipline: The art and practice of the learning organization.* New York, NY: Currency Doubleday.

Sentencing Project, The. (2012). *Parents in prison.* Washington, DC: The Sentencing Project.

Shedd, C. (2015). *Unequal City: Race, Schools, and Perceptions of Injustice.* New York, NY: Russell Sage Foundation.

Shajahan, R. (2013). Coloniality and global testing regime in higher education: Unpacking the OECD's AHELO initiative. *Journal of Education Policy, 28*(5), 676–694.

Sharpley-Whiting, T. D. (2009). *The speech: Race and Barack Obama's "a more perfect union."* New York, NY: Bloomsbury.

Shaw, L. (2014). Suspensions hit minorities, special-ed students hardest, data show. *The Seattle Times.* Retrieved from http://www.seattletimes.com.

Shaw, S. R., and Braden, J. P. (1990). Race and gender bias in the administration of corporal punishment. *School Psychology Review, 19,* 378–383.

Shelby County v. Holder. (2013). 570 U.S.

Sheets, R. H. (1996). Urban classroom conflict: Student-teacher perception: Ethnic integrity, solidarity, and resistance. *The Urban Review, 28,* 165–183.

Shollenberger, T. L. (2015). Racial disparities in school suspension and subsequent outcomes: Evidence from the National Longitudinal Survey of Youth 1997. In D. J. Losen (Ed.), *Closing the school discipline gap: Equitable remedies for excessive exclusion* (pp. 31–43). New York: Teachers College Press.

Siddle-Walker, V. (1996). *Their highest potential: An African American school community in the segregated south.* Chapel Hill, NC: University of North Carolina Press.

Siddle-Walker, V. (2001). African-American teaching in the south: 1940–1960. *American Educational Research Journal, 38,* 751–779.

Siegel, K., Mesagno, F. P., Karus, D., Christ, G., Banks, K., and Moynihan, R. (1992). Psychosocial adjustment of children with a terminally ill parent. *Journal of the American Academy of Child and Adolescent Psychiatry, 31*(2), 327–333.

Silverblatt, I. (2004). *Modern Inquisitions: Peru and the colonial origins of the civilized world.* Raleigh, NC: Duke University Press.

Simkins, S., and Katz, S. (2002). Criminalizing Abused Girls. *Violence Against Women, 8*(12), 1474–1499.

Skiba, R. J., Arredondo, M. I., and Rausch, M. K. (2014). *New and developing research on disparities in discipline.* Bloomington, IN: The Equity Project at Indiana University.

Skiba, R., Eaton, J., and Sotoo, N. (2004). *Factors Associated with State Rates of Out-of-School Suspension and Expulsion.* Children Left Behind Policy Briefs. Supplementary Analysis 2-B.

Skiba, R. J., Horner, R. H., Chung, C.-G., Rausch, M. K., May, S. L., and Tobin, T. (2011). Race is not neutral: A national investigation of African American and Latino disproportionality in school discipline. *School Psychology Review, 40*(1), 85–107.

Skiba, R., and Horner, R. (2011). Race is not neutral: A National investigation of African American and Latino disproportionality in school discipline. *School psychology Review, 40,* 85–107.

Skiba, R. J., and Knesting, K. (2001). Zero tolerance, zero evidence: An analysis of school disciplinary practice. *New directions for youth development, 2001*(92), 17–43.

Skiba, R., Michael, R., Nardo, A., and Peterson, R. (2002). The color of discipline: Sources of racial and gender disproportionality in school punishment. *Urban Review, 34,* 317–342.

Skiba, R., Shure, L., and Williams, N. (2011, September). *What do we know about racial and ethnic disproportionality in school suspension and expulsion?* Paper presented at the Closing the School Discipline Gap Conference, Los Angeles, California.

Skiba, R. J., Simmons, A., Staudinger, L., Rausch, M., Dow, G., and Feggins, R. (2003, May). *Consistent removal: Contributions of school discipline to the school-prison pipeline.* Boston, MA: School to Prison Pipeline Conference.

Skiba, R., and Sprague, J. (2008). Safety Without Suspensions. *Educational Leadership, 66*(1), 38.

Skiba, R. J., Peterson, R. L., and Williams, T. (1997). Office referrals and suspension: Disciplinary intervention in middle schools. *Education and Treatment of Children, 20*(3), 295–316.

Skiba, R., and Peterson, R. (1999). The dark side of zero tolerance can punishment lead to safe schools? *Phi Delta Kappan, 65*(4), 372–82.

Skiba, R. and Peterson, R. (2000). School discipline at a crossroads: From zero tolerance to early response. *Exceptional Children, 66*(3), 335–47.

Skiba, R. J., and Rausch, M. K. (2006). Zero tolerance, suspension, and expulsion: Questions of equity and effectiveness. *Handbook of classroom management: Research, practice, and contemporary issues,* 1063–1089.

Skiba, R., and Reece, P. (2000). School discipline at a crossroads: From zero tolerance to early response. *Exceptional Children, 66*(3), 335–46.

Skinner, B. F. (1953). *Science and human behavior.* New York: Free Press.

Skrla, L., Scheurich, J., Garcia, J., and Nolly, G. (2004). Equity Audits: A Practical Leadership Tool for Developing Equitable and Excellent Schools. *Educational Administration Quarterly, 40*(1), 133–161.

Slade, E. P., and Wissow, L. S. (2007). The influence of childhood maltreatment on adolescents' academic performance. *Economics of Education Review, 26*(5), 604–614.

Sleeter, C. (2001). Preparing teachers for culturally diverse schools: Research and the overwhelming presence of whiteness. *Journal of Teacher of Education, 52*(2), 94–106.

Sleeter, C. E. and Milner, H. R. (2011). Researching successful efforts in teacher education to diversify teachers. In A. F. Ball and C. A. Tyson (Eds.), *Studying diversity in teacher education* (pp. 81–103). Lanham, MD: Rowman and Littlefield.

Smith, C. D. (2009). Deconstructing the pipeline: Evaluating school-to-prison pipeline equal protection cases through a structural racism framework. *Fordham Urban Law Journal, 36*(5), 1009.

Smith, E., and Roberts, D. (2004). The Social and Moral Cost of Mass Incarceration in African-American Communities. *Stanford Law Review, 56,* 1271–1306.

Smith, E. J., and Harper, S. R. (2015). *Disproportionate impact of K-12 school suspension and expulsion on Black students in southern states.* Philadelphia: University of Pennsylvania, Center for the Study of Race and Equity in Education.

Smith, R. (2002). Race, gender, and authority in the workplace: theory and research. *Annual Review of Sociology,* 509–542.

Smith and Angela Hattery. 2007. If We Build It They Will Come: Human Rights Violations and the Prison Industrial Complex. *Societies Without Borders 2* (2): 273-288. Available at: http://scholarlycommons.law.case.edu/swb/vol2/iss2/7

Smith, W. A., Allen, W. R., and Danley, L. L. (2007). "Assume the Position . . . You Fit the Description": Psychosocial Experiences and Racial Battle Fatigue Among African American Male College Students. *American Behavioral Scientist, 51*(4), 551–578.

Snyder, H. (2012). Arrest in the United States, 1990–2010. U.S. Department of Justice.

Solórzano, D. G., and Yosso, T. J. (2002). Critical race methodology: Counter-storytelling as an analytical framework for education research. *Qualitative Inquiry, 8*(1), 23–44.

Southern Law and Poverty Center. (2009). Louisiana School to Prison Reform Coalition: Reducing Student and Teacher Dropout Rates in Louisiana. Retrieved: http://www.splcenter.org.

Spivak, G. C. (1985). The Rani of Sirmur: An Essay in Reading the Archives. *History and Theory,* 247–272.

[State] Department of Education. (2015). *[Let's Go] Innovative Elementary School accountability report.* Retrieved from: [Redacted to maintain data confidentiality].

[State] Department of Education. (2013). *2012–2013 state accountability summary report.* Retrieved from: http://www.nevadareportcard.com.

[State] Department of Education. (2013). *2011–2012 state accountability summary report.* Retrieved from: http://www.nevadareportcard.com.

St. George, D. (2012, December 13). School-to-prison pipeline' hearing puts spotlight on student discipline. *Washington Post.* Retrieved from http://articules.washingtonpost.com.

Stecher, B., Barron, S., Chun, T., and Ross, K. (2000). *The effects of Washington state education reform on schools and classrooms.* Center for the Study of Evaluation Technical Report 525.

Steele, C. (2012). *Whistling Vivaldi and other clues to how stereotype threat affects us.* New York, NY: Norton.

Steele, C., and Aronson, J. (1995). Stereotype threat and the intellectual test performance of African Americans. *Journal of Personality and Social Psychology, 69*(5), 797–811.

Steiker, C. S. (2012). Mass incarceration: Causes, consequences, and exit strategies. *Ohio State Journal of Criminal Law, 9*(1), 1–6.

Steinberg, M. P., Allensworth, E., and Johnson, D. W. (2015). What conditions jeopardize and support safety in urban schools? The influence of community characteristics, school composition and school organizational practices on student and teacher reports of safety in Chicago. In D. J. Losen (Ed.), *Closing the school discipline gap: Equitable remedies for excessive exclusion* (pp. 118–131). New York: Teachers College Press.

Stevenson, J., and Stevenson, H. C. (2013). *Promoting racial literacy in schools: Differences that make a difference.* New York, NY: Teachers College Press.

Stinson, D. W. (2008). Negotiating sociocultural discourses: The counter-storytelling of academically (and mathematically) successful African American male students. *American Educational Research Journal, 45*(4), 975–1010.

Stinson, D. W. (2011). When the "burden of acting White" is not a burden: School success and African American male students. *The Urban Review, 43*(1), 43–65.

Stuewig, J., and McCloskey, L. A. (2005). The relation of child maltreatment to shame and guilt among adolescents: Psychological routes to depression and delinquency. *Child Maltreatment, 10*(4), 324–336.

Sudbury, J. (2004). A world without prisons: Resisting militarism, globalized punishment, and empire. *Social Justice, 31*(1–2), 9–30.

Sue, D. W., Capodilupo, C. M., and Holder, A. (2008). Racial microaggressions in the life experience of Black Americans. *Professional Psychology: Research and Practice, 39*(3), 329–336.

Suh, S., and Suh, J. (2007). Risk factors and levels of risk for high school dropouts. *Professional School Counseling, 10*(3), 297–306.

Sullivan, A. L., and Bal, A. (2013). Disproportionality in special education: Effects of individual and school variables on disability risk. *Exceptional Children, 79*(4), 475–494.

Swain, A., and Noblit, G. (2011). Education in a punitive society: An introduction. [Published online]. *Urban Review-New York*, 43, 465–475.

Swanson, D., Cunningham, M., and Spencer, M.B., (2003). Black males' structural conditions, achievement patterns, normative needs, and "opportunities." *Urban Education Journal, 38*, 608–633.

Tatum, B. D. (2007). *Can we talk about race?* Boston, MA: Beacon Press .

Taubman, P. (2007). *Teaching by the numbers: Deconstructing the discourse of standards and accountability in education.* New York, NY: Routledge Press.

Taylor E. (1998). A primer on critical race theory: Who are the critical race theorists? And what are they saying? *Journal of Blacks in Higher Education, 19*, 122–124.

Taylor, G., Shepard, L., Kinner, F., and Rosenthal, J. (2003). *A survey of teachers' perspectives on high-stakes testing in Colorado: What gets taught, what gets lost.* Center for the Study of Evaluation Technical Report 588.

Teacher's Protection Act of 2015, TX HB868, 84th State Legislature. (2015). Retrieved from: https://legiscan.com.

Teaching Tolerance. Spring 2013. http://www.tolerance.org.

Teske, S. C. (2011). A Study of Zero Tolerance Policies in Schools: A Multi-Intergrated Systems Approach to Improve Outcomes for Adolescents. *Journal of Child and Adolescent Psychiatric Nursing*, 88–97.

Test, Punish, and Push Out: How "Zero Tolerance" and High States Testing Funnel Youth Into the School-To-Prison Pipeline. (January 2010). Paper by *Advancement* Project (Online Data File). Retrieved from: http://www.educationjustice.org.

Theriot, M. (2009). School resource officers and the criminalization of student behavior. *Journal of Criminal Justice, 37*, 7.

Theriot, M. T., and Dupper, D. R. (2010). Student discipline problems and the transition from elementary to middle school. *Education and Urban Society, 42*(2), 205–222.

Thomas, J. M. (2013). Mass incarceration of minority males. *Race, Gender and Class, 20*, 177–190.

Thurau, L. H., and Wald, J. (2009/2010). Controlling partners: When law enforcement meets discipline in public schools. *New York Law School Law Review, 54*, 977–1020.

Tillman, L. C. (2008). The scholarship of Dr. Asa G. Hilliard, III: Implications for Black principal leadership. *Review of Educational Research, 78*(3), 589–607.

Tobin, T., Sugai, G., and Colvin, G. (1996). Patterns in middle school discipline records. *Journal of Emotional and Behavioral Disorders, 4*, 82–94.

Togut, T. D. (2011). The gestalt of the school-to-prison pipeline: The duality of overrepresentation of minorities in special education and racial disparity in school discipline on minorities. *The American University Journal of Gender, Social Policy and the Law, 20*(1), 163.

Toldson, I. A. (2011). *Breaking barriers 2: Plotting the path away from juvenile detention and toward academic success for school-age African American males*. Washington, DC: Congressional Black Caucus Foundation, Inc.

Toldson, I. (2013). *Single Parents Aren't The Problem*. Retrieved January 2, 2016, from http://www.theroot.com.

Toldson, I. A., McGee, T., and Lemmons, B. P. (2015). Reducing suspensions by improving academic engagement among school-age Black males. In D. J. Losen (Ed.), *Closing the school discipline gap: Equitable remedies for excessive exclusion* (pp. 107–117). New York: Teachers College Press.

Tonry, M. (2012). *Punishing Race: A Continuing American Dilemma*. New York, NY: Oxford University Press.

Torres, Z. and Menezes, R. (2015). *Only 35 L.A. public schools get an A in supporting the arts*. Retrieved January 2, 2016, from http://www.latimes.com.

Toshalis, E. (2014). Grow your own teachers for urban education. In H. Richard Milner IV and K. Lomotey (Eds.), *Handbook of urban education* (pp. 217–238). New York, NY: Routledge.

Touré and Dyson, M. E. (2012). *Who's afraid of post-Blackness? What it means to be Black now*. New York, NY: Free Press.

Travis, J. (2005). *But they all come home*. New York, NY: Urban Institute Press.

Triplett, N. P., Allen, A., and Lewis, C. W. (2014). Zero tolerance, school shootings, and the post-Brown quest for equity in discipline policy: An examination of how urban minorities are punished for white suburban violence. *Journal of Negro Education, 83*, 352–370.

Trueba, E. H. T. (1988). Culturally based explanations of minority students' academic achievement. *Anthropology and Education Quarterly, 19*, 270–287.

Trusty, J., and Brown, D. (2005). Advocacy competencies for professional school counselors. *Professional School Counseling, 8*, 259–265.

Tuck, E., and Yang, K. W. (2014). *Youth resistance research and theories of change*. New York, NY: Routledge.

Turner, M., Ross, S., Gaister, G., and Yinger, J. (2002). *Discrimination in Metropolitan Housing Markets: National Results from Phase 1 HDS 2000*. Urban Institute. Washington, DC: Department of Housing and Urban Development.

Turner, M., and Ross, S. (2005). How racial discrimination affects the search for housing . In X. S. Brigs, *The Geography of Opportunity: Race and Housing Choice in Metropolitan America* (pp. 81–100). Washington, DC: Brookings Inst. Press.

Tuzzolo, E., and Hewitt, D. T. (2006). Rebuilding inequity: The re-emergence of the school-to-prison pipeline in New Orleans. *High School Journal, 90*(2), 59–68.

U.S. Census Bureau. (2013a). *Table 1. Median value of assets for households, by type of asset owned and selected characteristics: 2011*. Washington, DC.

U.S. Census Bureau. (2013b). *Table 2. Percent holding assets for households, by type of asset owned and selected characteristics: 2011*. Washington, DC.

U.S. Department of Education, Individuals with Disabilities Act (IDEA) (2004). U.S. Code, Title 20, Chapter 22, Subchapter II, § 1412 (a) (5).

U.S. Department of Education. (2007). *Disproportionality*. Retrieved from http://idea.ed.gov

U.S. Department of Education, Office for Civil Rights. (2010). Free Appropriate Public Education for Students with Disabilities: Requirements Under Section 504 of the Rehabilitation Act of 1973 , Washington, DC.

U.S. Department of Education Office of Civil Rights. (2012). Revealing New Truths About our Nation's Schools. *Civil Rights Data Collection*. Retrieved: http://www2.ed.gov.

U.S. Department of Education, Office of Postsecondary Education. (2013). *Preparing and Credentialing the Nation's Teachers: The secretary's ninth report on teacher quality.* Authors.

U.S. Department of Education Office of Civil Rights. (2014). *Data snapshot: School discipline, Issue brief 1.*

U.S. Department of Education, National Center for Education Statistics (NCES). (2014). *State nonfiscal public elementary/secondary education survey data.*

U.S. Department of Education, National Center for Education Statistics. (2015). *Digest of Education Statistics, 2013* (NCES 2015–011), Introduction and Chapter 2.

Valencia, R. R. (2010). *Dismantling contemporary deficit thinking: Educational thought and practice critical educator.* New York: Taylor and Francis.

Vaandering, D. (2014). Implementing restorative justice practice in schools: What pedagogy reveals. *Journal of Peace Education, 11*(1), 64–80.

Valencia, R. R. (2010). *Dismantling contemporary deficit thinking: Educational thought and practice.* New York, NY: Routledge.

Vanderhaar, J. F., Petrosko, J. M., and Munoz, M. (in press). Reconsidering the alternatives: The relationship between suspension, disciplinary alternative school placement, subsequent juvenile detention, and the salience of race. In D. J. Losen (Ed.), *Closing the school discipline gap: Research for policymakers.* New York, NY: Teachers College Press.

Varenne, H., and McDermott, R. (1998). *Successful failure: The school America builds.* Boulder, CO: Westview.

Vernaza, N. (2012). Teachers' perceptions of high-stakes accountability in Florida's Title I elementary schools. *Current Issues in Education,* 15(1).

Villegas, A. M. and Irvine, J. J. (2010). Diversifying the teaching force: An examination of major arguments. *Urban Review, 42,* 175–192.

Vilson, J. L. (2015). The need for more teachers of color. *American Educator, 39*(4), 27–31.

Wacquant, Loic. 2002. "From Slavery to Mass Incarceration: Rethinking the 'Race Question' in the U.S." *New Left Review, 13,* 41–60.

Wakefield, S., and Uggen, C. (2010). Incarceration and Stratification. *Annual Review of Sociology, 36*(1), 387–406.

Wald, J., and Losen, D. J. (2003). Defining and redirecting a school-to-prison pipeline. *New Directions for Youth Development, 99,* 9–15.

Wallace, J. M., Jr., Goodkind, S., Wallace, C. M., and Bachman, J. G. (2008). Racial, ethnic, and gender differences in school discipline among U.S. high school students: 1991–2005. *The Negro Educational Review, 59*(1–2), 47–62.

Walls, T. (2015). *Personnel survey* (Unpublished raw data). University of Nevada, Las Vegas.

Walsh, V. (2015). *Disparities in Discipline: A Look at School Disciplinary Actions for Utah's American Indian Students.*

Walsh, K. and Jacobs, S. (2007). *Alternative certification isn't alternative.* Thomas B. Fordham Institute.

Wang, M. T., Selman, R. L., Dishion, T. J., and Stormshak, E. A. (2010). A tobit regression analysis of the covariation between middle school students' perceived school climate and behavioral problems. *Journal of Research on Adolescence, 20,* 274–286.

Ward, S. F., and Delessert, E. (2014). Less than zero. *ABA Journal, 100,* 55–61.

Warren, C. A. (2015). Making Relationships Work: Elementary-Age Black Boys and the Schools That Serve Them. In J. L. Harper, Shaun R.; Wood (Ed.), *Advancing Black Male Student Success From Preschool Through Ph.D.* (pp. 21–43). Sterling, VA: Stylus.

Washington, A. R. (2015). Addressing social injustice with urban African American young men through hip-hop: Suggestions for school counselors. *Journal for Social Action in Counseling and Psychology, 7,* 101–121.

Watkins, W. (2001). *The white architects of black education: Ideology and power in America, 1865–1954.* New York, NY: Teachers College Press.

Wayne, A., and Ferrare, J. (2014). Sponsors of Policy: A Network Analysis of Wealthy Elites, their Affiliated Philanthropies, and Charter School Reform in Washington State. *Teachers College Record,* 1–24.

Weatherspoon, F. (2014). *African-American Males and the US Justice System of Marginalization: A National Tragedy.* New York, NY: Palgrave Macmillan.

Weiner, B. (1980) The role of affect in rational (attributional) approaches to human motivation. Educational Researcher, *9*(7), 4–11.

Weinraub, M., Clemens, L. P., Sockloff, A., Ethridge, T., Gracely, E., and Myers, B. (1984). The Development of Sex Role Stereotypes in the Third Year: Relationships to Gender Labeling, Gender Identity, Sex-Types Toy Preference, and Family Characteristics. *Child Development*, 55(4), 1493–1503.

Weinstein, C. S., Tomlinson-Clarke, S., and Curran, M., (2003). Culturally responsive Classroom management: Awareness into action. *Theory Into Practice, 42*(4), 269–76.

Weinstein, C. S., Tomlinson-Clarke, S., and Curran, M., (2004). Toward a conception of culturally responsive classroom management. *Journal of Teacher Education, 55*(1), 25–38.

Welsh, W., Greene, J., and Jenkins, P. (1999). School disorder: The influence of individual, institutional, and community factors. *C riminolog y, 37*(1), 73–115.

Welch, K., and Payne, A. A. (2010). Racial threat and punitive school discipline. *Social Problems, 5,* 25–48.

Weller, C., and Fields, J. (2011). *The Black and White Labor Gap in America: Why African Americans Struggle to Find Jobs and Remain Employed Compared to Whites.* Washington, DC: Center for American Progress.

West, C. (2001) Progressive politics in these times. Mario Savio Annual Lecture Series, Berkeley, CA.

Whiting, G. W. (2006a). Enhancing culturally diverse males' scholar identity: Suggestions for educators of gifted students. *Gifted Child Today, 29*(3), 46–50.

Whiting, G. W. (2006b). From at risk to at promise: Developing scholar identities among Black males. *Journal of Advanced Academics, 17*(4), 222–229.

Whiting, G. W. (2009a). The Scholar Identity Institute: Guiding Darnel and other Black males. *Gifted Child Today, 32*(4), 53–56, 63.

Whiting, G. W. (2009b). Gifted Black males: Understanding and decreasing barriers to achievement and identity. *Roeper Review, 31*(4), 224–233.

Whiting G. W. (2010). Overrepresentation of African American males in special education: A clarion call for action and change. In E. M. Gallaher, and V. C. Polite (Eds.), *The state of the African American male* (pp. 19–44). East Lansing, MI: Michigan State University Press.

Willis, P. (1977). *Learning to labor: How working class kids get working class jobs.* New York, NY: Columbia University Press.

Wilson, D. (2004). The Interface of School Climate and School Connectedness and Relationships with Aggression and Victimization. *Journal of School Health,* 293–299.

Wilson, H. (2014). Turning off the school-to-prison pipeline. *Reclaiming Children and Youth, 23*(1), 49.

Wilson, W. J. (1987). *The Truly Disadvantage: The Innercity, The Underclass, and Public Policy .* Chicago, IL: The University of Chicago Press.

Wilson, W. J. (1996). *When Work Disappears: The World of the New Urban Poor.* New York, NY: Vintage Books.

Wink, J. (2005). *Critical pedagogy: Notes from the real world* (3rd ed.). New York, NY: Pearson.

Winn, M. T. (2011). *Girl time: Literacy, justice, and the school-to-prison pipeline: Teaching for social justice.* New York, NY: Teachers College Press.

Winn, M. T., and Behizadeh, N. (2011). The right to be literate: Literacy, education, and the school-to-prison pipeline. *Review of Research in Education, 35,* 147–173.

Winn, M. T. (2013). Toward a restorative English education. *Research in the Teaching of English*, *48*(1), 126–135.

Wise, T. J. (2010). *Colorblind: The rise of post-racial politics and the retreat from racial equity*. San Francisco, CA: City Light Books.

Witt, H. (2007). School Discipline Tougher on African Americans. *Chicago Tribune*. September 5.

Wood, K. (2014). Restoring Our Children's Future: Ending Disparate School Discipline through Restorative Justice Practices [notes]. *Journal of Dispute Resolution*, (2), 395.

Woodson, C. G. (1933/2013). *The mis-education of the Negro*. Trenton, NJ: Africa World Press.

The World Factbook 2014. Washington, DC: Central Intelligence Agency, 2014.

Wu, S. C., Pink, W. T., Crain, R. L., and Moles, O. (1982). Student suspension: A critical reappraisal. *The Urban Review, 14*, 245–303.

Wun, C. (2014). Unaccounted foundations: Black girls, anti-black racism, and punishment in schools. *Critical Sociology*, 1–14.

Wun, C. (2015). Against captivity: Black girls and school discipline policies in the afterlife of slavery. *Educational Policy*, 1–26.

Yan, H. and Castillo, M. (2015, October 29). *Attorney defends actions of fired school officer as 'justified and lawful.'* Retrieved from http://www.cnn.com.

Yosso, T. J. (2005). Whose culture has capital? *Race, Ethnicity and Education*, *8*(1), 69–91.

Young, V. A. (2007). *Your average nigga: Performing race, literacy, and masculinity*. Detroit, MI: Wayne State University Press.

Young, V. A. (2010). Momma's memories and the new equality. *Present Tense: A Journal of Rhetoric in Society, 1*(1), 6.

Zeichner, K., and Conklin, H. (2005). "Teacher education programs." In M. Cochran-Smith and K. Zeichner (Eds), *Studying teacher education.* (pp. 645–735). New York: Routledge.

Zeichner, K., and Hutchinson, E. (2008). "The development of alternative certification policies and programs in the United States." In P. Grossman and S. Loeb (Eds), *Alternative routes to teaching: Mapping the new landscape of teacher education* (pp. 15–29). Cambridge, MA: Harvard Education Press.

Zimmerman, B., Bandura, A., and Martinez-Pons, M. (1992). Self-motivation for academic attainment: The role of self-efficacy beliefs and personal goal setting. *American Educational Research Journal, 29*(3), 663–676.

Zyromski, B. (2007). African American and Latino Youth and Post-Traumatic Stress Syndrome. *Journal of School Violence*, *6*(1), 121–137.

Index

About the Editors and Contributors

ABOUT THE EDITORS

Kenneth J. Fasching-Varner is the Shirley B. Barton Endowed Associate Professor of Education, director of the Higher Education Administration program at Louisiana State University, and the author or editor of over fifty publications, including articles in leading academic journals. Varner's work centers on systemic and institutional racism, educational equity, and critical race theory. Varner can be reached at varner@lsu.edu.

Lori Latrice Martin is associate professor of sociology and African and African American studies at Louisiana State University. Martin is the author of numerous academic books and articles, and her recent books include *After the Storm: Militarization, Occupation, and Segregation in Post-Katrina America; Big Box Schools: Race, Education, and the Danger of the Wal-Martization of Public Schools in America;* and *White Sports/Black Sports: Racial Disparities in Athletic Programs*. Martin can be reached at lorim@lsu.edu.

Roland Mitchell is the Jo Ellen Levy Yates Endowed Professor and associate dean of research engagement and graduate studies in the College of Human Sciences and Education at Louisiana State University. Mitchell has authored over forty scholarly works that have appeared in leading educational journals and is the co-editor of *The Crisis of Campus Sexual Violence: Critical Perspectives on Prevention and Response* and *The Assault on Communities of Color: Exploring the Realities of Race-Based Violence*. Mitchell can be reached at rwmitch@lsu.edu.

Karen P. Bennett-Haron serves as justice of the peace in Department 7 for the Las Vegas Justice Court, and is past chief justice of the court. Bennett-Haron served as assistant federal public defender for the District of Nevada as well as general counsel for the Las Vegas Housing Authority. Bennett-Haron was appointed, in 2002, to the Las Vegas Justice Court Bench, and became the first African American female ever appointed to the State's justice system at any level.

Arash Daneshzadeh is a faculty member at the University of San Francisco—School of Education, and serves as director of programs for Communities United for Restorative Youth Justice (CURYJ). A co-editor of the *Journal of Peace Studies* and book review editor of *Taboo: The Journal of Culture and Education*, his praxis converges between identity formation, gender studies, carceral studies, and school organizational theory. Daneshzadeh can be reached at adaneshzadeh@curyj.org.

ABOUT THE CONTRIBUTORS

Sheree N. Alexander is an adjunct professor at Rowan University in the Africana Studies Department and K-12 public school administrator. Her research interests include 1) race, class, gender and its impact on schooling experiences of urban students; 2) culturally responsive teaching; and 3) urban school leadership. Her publications include book chapters with Information Age Publishing and Routledge publishers. Alexander can be reached at s.alexander2004@verizon.net.

Mariella I. Arredondo is associate director of the Equity Project at Indiana University. Her research interests include the examination of impediments to educational equity, such as racial/ethnic disparities in exclusionary school discipline, as well as the development, implementation, and assessment of education policies geared toward improving the educational access, survival, and outcomes of under-served students. Arredondo can be reached at marredon@indiana.edu.

Tabetha Bernstein-Danis is a faculty member at Kutztown University. Bernstein-Danis has research interests in the areas of co-teaching in inclusive classrooms, effective approaches to supporting the literacy learning of students with diverse learning needs, and effective approaches for supporting English learners with disabilities. Bernstein-Danis can be reached at rnstein@kutztown.edu.

Jill Castek is associate professor of literacy and technology for bi/multicultural learners and STEM education at the University of Arizona, examining digital literacy and across the lifespan. She co-edits a column in the *Journal of Adolescent and Adult Literacy* (JAAL) focused on digital literacy for disciplinary learning, and is published in the *Educational Forum*, the *Journal of Education*, *Reading and Writing Quarterly*, *Reading Teacher*, and *Journal of Adolescent & Adult Literacy*. Castek can be reached at jcastek@email.arizona.edu.

Jahaan Chandler is a doctoral student in the Department of Sociology at Louisiana State University, focusing on racial justice, sociological theory, and social movements. His publications include a co-authored book chapter in the edited compilation *Assault on Communities of Color: Exploring the Realities of Race Based Violence*. Chandler can be reached at jahaanchandler@yahoo.com.

Christine Clark is professor and senior scholar in multicultural education, and founding vice president for diversity and inclusion in the Department of Teaching and Learning at the University of Nevada, Las Vegas. Clark can be reached at chris.clark.unlv@me.com.

Donna Y. Ford is professor of education and human development at Vanderbilt University. Ford's areas of expertise and interest include gifted education with emphasis on minority children and youth, recruitment and retention of racially different students in gifted education and advanced placement classes/programs, underachievement and closing achievement and opportunity gaps by race and income, equity issues in testing and assessment, multicultural education, issues in urban education, and family involvement. Ford can be reached at donna.ford@vanderbilt.edu.

Ramon B. Goings is assistant professor of educational leadership at Loyola University Maryland where his research focuses on 1) gifted/high-achieving Black males' educational experiences PK-PhD; 2) diversifying the teacher and school leader workforce; 3) equity and access in gifted education for students of color; and 4) exploring the significance and contributions of historically Black colleges and universities. His work has been featured in *Adult Education Quarterly*, *The Urban Review*, *Journal of African American Males in Education*, *Journal for Multicultural Education*, and *Adult Learning*. Goings can be reached via email at rbgoings@loyola.edu.

Dari Green is a doctoral student in sociology at Louisiana State University. Green's work examines the nexus of race and gender through sociological lenses. Green can be reached at Dgree47@lsu.edu.

Irvin Guerrero teaches introductory level adult English as a Second Language classes through the Las Vegas Clark County Library District. He recently completed an M.Ed. in the Multicultural Education program in the Department of Teaching and Learning at the University of Nevada, Las Vegas. Guerrero can be reached at guerre49@unlv.nevada.edu.

Jesslyn Hollar is the teacher candidate assessment director in the School of Education at Edgewood College in Madison, Wisconsin, and a doctoral candidate at the University of Washington in educational policy and leadership analysis. Her interests focus on teacher education reform and teacher education policy. Hollar can be reached at jesslyn.hollar@gmail.com.

Jim Hollar is assistant professor in the School of Education at Alverno College in Milwaukee, Wisconsin. His interests range from teaching preservice educators the importance of culturally relevant pedagogy to encouraging practicing teachers to infuse Afrofuturism into English and language arts classrooms. Hollar can be reached at jimhollar1@gmail.com.

Melinda Jackson is a senior doctoral student at Louisiana State University. Jackson's work centers on intersectionality, criminology, crime and communities, critical race theory, and qualitative and quantitative research methods. Her publications include articles in the *Journal of Pan African Studies*, the *Journal of Democracy and Education*, and in *Taboo: The Journal of Culture and Education*, and books with Praeger Publishers and Rowman & Littlefield publishers. Jackson can be reached at mjack69@lsu.edu.

Gloria E. Jacobs is a research associate at Portland State University in the Literacy, Language, and Technology Research group, where she examines the digital literacy acquisition of adolescents and adults and the implications of digital technology use for engagement in society. Jacobs has published in the *Journal of Adolescent and Adult Literacy*, *Reading Research Quarterly*, *The Journal of Literacy Research*, the *Journal of Media Education*, and the *Journal of Research in Reading*. Jacobs can be reached at gljacobs@pdx.edu.

Michael E. Jennings is associate professor in the Department of Educational Leadership and Policy Studies (ELPS) and associate dean in the College of Education and Human Development (COEHD) at the University of Texas at San Antonio. In his capacity as an associate dean he oversees the Consortium for Social Transformation, an innovative administrative unit that seeks to promote social justice, diversity, and interdisciplinary scholarship in education and human development, and serves as the current editor of the *Journal* *of Educational Foundations.* Jennings can be reached at Michael.Jennings@utsa.edu.

Kelsey M. Jones is a postdoctoral fellow at the University of Pennsylvania where she focuses on racial literacy in schools, dis/ability studies in education, and the school-to-prison pipeline. She has co-authored a book chapter with Howard C. Stevenson entitled "What if My Trayvon Came Home? Teaching a Wretched Truth about Breathing While Black" with Rowman & Littlefield publishers. Jones can be reached at keljones@gse.upenn.edu.

Runell J. King is a doctoral candidate in the educational leadership and research program at Louisiana State University. His research centers on high-achieving Black male student athletes and exclusionary discipline practices in elementary and secondary schools. King can be reached rking26@lsu.edu.

Kerii Landry-Thomas is a doctoral student at Louisiana State University in Baton Rouge. She is a former assistant public defender, and her work seeks to combine legal analysis to issues of education. Landry-Thomas can be reached at kland84@lsu.edu.

Brian D. Lozenski is assistant professor of urban and multicultural education in the Educational Studies Department at Macalester College in St. Paul, Minnesota. His research explores the intersections of African American education, critical multicultural education, critical research methodologies, and heritage study as a literacy practice. Dr. Lozenski can be reached at blozensk@macalester.edu.

Kasim Ortiz is a doctoral student in the Department of Sociology at the University of New Mexico, as well as Health Policy Fellow in UNM's Center for Health Policy. Kasim's work broadly centers on social stratification and social inequality in terms of health equity and educational trajectories. Ortiz can be reached at kortiz5@unm.edu.

Tifanie W. Pulley is a doctoral candidate in the Sociology Department and women's and gender studies at Louisiana State University. Her primary research interest involves examining the intersectionality of race, class, and gender in the academy. Pulley can be reached at tpulle1@lsu.edu.

Tracey M. Pyscher is assistant professor of secondary education in the Woodring College of Education at Western Washington University in Bellingham, Washington. Her research interests include (re)framing the cultural practices of children and youth with histories of domestic violence (HDV youth) and critical literacy learning. Dr. Pyscher can be reached at tracey.pyscher@wwu.edu.

Janessa Schilmoller is the director of Camp Rising Sun: An International, Full-Scholarship Leadership Program of the Louis August Jonas Foundation. She recently completed an MS in the multicultural education program in the Department of Teaching and Learning at the University of Nevada, Las Vegas. Schilmoller can be reached at jschilmoeller@lajf.org.

Michael J. Seaberry is a doctoral student at Louisiana State University. Seaberry's work centers on Black male racial and masculine identity formation as well as activism and healing during times of racial unrest. Seaberry can be reached at mseabe2@lsu.edu.

George Sirrakos is an assistant professor in the Department of Secondary Education at Kutztown University of Pennsylvania. His research interests include fostering equity in education, creating opportunities for students to inform the teaching and learning process, and cross-national studies of learning environments. Sirrakos can be reached at sirrakos@kutztown.edu.

Russell J. Skiba is professor in the school psychology program at Indiana University and director of the Equity Project at Indiana University. His work focuses on the causes of and interventions for racial and ethnic disparities in school discipline and special education with publications in the *American Educational Research Journal, Teachers' College Record, Educational Researcher, Exceptional Children, Urban Review, New York Law School Law Review*, and *Theory into Practice*, and books with Palgrave/Macmillan and Jossey-Bass, including *Inequality in School Discipline*, summarizing the work of the Discipline Disparities Research-to-Practice Collaborative. Skiba can be reached at skiba@indiana.edu.

Devon Wade is a doctoral student, Paul F. Lazarsfeld Doctoral Fellow, and National Science Foundation (NSF) and Ford Foundation Predoctoral Fellow in the Department of Sociology at Columbia University. Devon's research areas include race and ethnicity, social inequality, social psychology, education, and urban space. Wade can be reached at dtw2114@columbia.edu.

Tonya Walls is assistant professor in the School of Education in the College of Health and Human Services at Touro University Nevada. She is a PhD student in the Cultural Studies, International Education, and Cultural Studies program in the Department of Teaching and Learning at the University of Nevada, Las Vegas. She can be reached at Tonya.Walls@tun.touro.edu.

Ahmad Washington is assistant professor in the Department of Counseling and Human Development at The University of Louisville. He researches social justice counseling and hip-hop therapy. Ahmad is also the co-editor of the recent book, *Black Male Student Success in 21st Century Urban Schools: School Counseling for Equity, Access and Achievement.* Washington can be reached at arwash04@louisville.edu.

Gilman W. Whiting is associate professor of African American and diaspora studies, founding chair of the Achievement Gap Institute for the George W. Peabody College of Education, and director of graduate studies at Vanderbilt University. His areas of research include race, sports, and American culture; educational disparity; welfare reform and fatherhood initiatives; and special and gifted education. Whiting can be reached at g.whiting@vanderbilt.edu.

Natasha Williams is a doctoral graduate student at Indiana University and practicing school psychologist in the District of Columbia Public School System. Williams's work focuses on racial disparities in school discipline, particularly for female students, and she has worked with the Superior Court of the District of Columbia assisting with research to further examine racial disparities in the juvenile justice system. Williams can be reached at ntw@indiana.edu.

Elizabeth Withers is a doctoral candidate in sociology at Portland State University. Withers's areas of interest are in social determinants of health, digital literacy, and racial- and class-based inequality. She can be reached at elizabew@pdx.edu.

Lightning Source UK Ltd.
Milton Keynes UK
UKOW05n1347220617

303872UK00008B/294/P